Praise for *Voices of Harmony and*

Simply wringing your hands over the state of the world is not going to change anything. It's real action that changes the world, and this book gives the reader advice from people who wake up every day and do the hard work of building peace. Bravo!
—Jody Williams, Nobel Peace Prize Laureate

These stories and essays intimately and powerfully convey two fundamental truths. The first is that history changes only through the actions of people who decide it has to change. They refuse to accept what is and willingly step forward to do the difficult work of advocacy and change, refusing to give up. The second truth is that the human spirit is worth struggling for, day after day, year after year, no matter whether we are successful or not. In this work, which joins us at the heart, we will always find joy, even in the harshest of external circumstances.
—Margaret J. Wheatley, author of many books including *Perseverance, So Far From Home,* and *Leadership and the New Science.*

This volume teaches again and again one vital insight: peacebuilding in deeply divided communities requires a special combination of radical thinking, creative imagination and engaged action.
—Mairead Maguire, Nobel Peace Prize Laureate

The literature on peacebuilding has expanded significantly in the past ten years. This book stands out because it reflects and charts the creativity, energy and relevance of the field for global peacemaking. Containing a range of innovative case studies, a good blend of theory and practice and an exciting exploration covering the arts, humanities, politics, philosophy, and theology, it is an indispensable resource for educators, researchers and activist.
—Tom Woodhouse, author of *Contemporary Conflict Resolution* (University of Bradford, UK)

Voices of Harmony and Dissent holds the heart of how social change happens—people who believe deeply, develop significant relationships, and have the courage to engage together. Each and every chapter provides lessons and inspiration and, most importantly, has a deep resonance that rises from these voices of hard-won experience and reflective practice, an authenticity that touches the reader and points us toward the kind of learning that really makes a difference in our world.
—John Paul Lederach, author of *The Moral Imagination* (University of Notre Dame)

This book is an empowering patchwork of rich voices of harmony and dissent. There are lessons of humility about the greater importance of the inside than the outside mediator. There are lessons of diversity and lessons of the spirit, of the inner peace that enables a contribution to transformative justice. It is a book you can dip into here and there on a plane or before bed. This is because it is a compilation that lets the journey be your own in connecting up the many strands of wisdom it contains. All of us can be much better peacebuilders if we take that journey of the connections with this sumptuous volume.

> —John Braithwaite, author of *Crime, Shame and Reintegration* (Australian National University)

Voices of Harmony and Dissent offers readers a practical roadmap for peace: how peace really works from long-time practitioners of peace. I am proud to be a student of several voices in this book, and would recommend it to anyone interested in a just, sustainable and equitable future.

> —Liz Berstein, Nobel Womens' Peace Initiative, Executive Director

This is a book of wisdom. Themes of practical peacemaking through non-violent action flow through these pages. "Small" stories mingle with "grand" themes to inform and inspire our journeys toward peace. Even the experience of reading these essays can prompt a greater peace.

> —John Borrows, Canada Research Chair in Indigenous Law at the University of Victoria Law School

When given this book, I was prepared to wade through another assortment of scholarly articles of varying interest. Instead, I was immediately sucked in by the first chapter and, to my surprise, the quality and readability held true throughout the book. The chapters weave together practical theory and application with stories, many of them personal. The authors are clearly grounded in the real world, often drawing upon personal experience. This is a diverse mosaic of voices and subjects that is remarkably accessible and cohesive. It will be of interest to a wide range of peacebuilders.

> —Howard Zehr, author of *Changing Lenses* (Eastern Mennonite University)

In my travel—both continental and international—I've had the opportunity to meet many peace practitioners. Some of them were participants of the Canadian School of Peacebuilding (CSOP). This book affords us a rich opportunity to meet some of the instructors of CSOP in a fascinating collection of essays. Their range of ideas on peacebuilding is as expansive as the geographical and ideological terrain from which they come. What do cats, choirs, and driftwood have to do with peacebuilding? Read the book! Like the student participants of CSOP, you may not agree with everything you learn, but you will be engaged, challenged, provoked and encouraged.

—Donald G. Peters, Mennonite Central Committee Canada, Executive Director

In a time when our world is being shaken by relentless and seemingly insurmountable forces of climate change, war, fundamentalisms and terrorism, resource extraction, and endless consumerism, this book is a gift. The writers share not just their passions, but smart, practical tools drawn from direct experience in global struggles of food sustainability, health, violence, racism, classism, and colonialism. The book does not retreat into abstractions; rather it unflinchingly faces the worst of humanity to find the best of humanity, and only there is hope possible. Critical questions are raised about civility and civil society, gender and feminism, human cruelty and vulnerabilities, class and power, beauty and art—and through these discussions one finds humanity across difference. These are not stories of lament and resignation but an invitation to ways of working and thinking to change what we can, where we can.

—Val Napoleon co-editor, *First Nations Cultural Heritage and Law* (University of Victoria), Law Foundation Professor of Aboriginal Justice and Governance, and Director of the Indigenous Law Research Unit, Faculty of Law, University of Victoria

I highly commend this admirable effort. We should not only transform ourselves from within but also should share with others our experience in transforming the outsider world.

—A.T. Ariyaratne, President of Sarvodaya Movement, Sri Lanka

This ambitious volume is remarkable in its impressive scope and simple humanism alike. *Voices of Harmony and Dissent* delivers as advertised, highlighting the personal narratives of scholars and advocates for peace as they work to transform their— and our—world. The chapters offered are eminently engaging, the issues covered are perpetually timely, and the lessons delivered are truly profound.

—Randall Amster, Executive Director Peace and Justice Studies Association (Georgetown University) and author of *Peace Ecology*

In my own peacemaking work, I've often been confused by my own sense of admiration for the uniqueness of every human being and the wonderful sense of oneness we aspire to. How can both be admired and rejoiced? As I read the papers in this book, they showed the same pattern, celebrating both uniqueness and oneness, but in reading them my confusion fell away. I could see that while we may begin our individual journeys from unique positions in the universe, our struggle involves moving ourselves toward a common centre. Honouring the differences honours the movement and celebrates the goal. This is a wonderful book, highlighting why it is that so many of us, beginning from such different places, can celebrate our coming together toward a common, vibrant, peaceful sense of the fullness of life. It's not just about peacemaking; it's about who we are and who we can become, individually and together. I recommend it to anyone.

    —**Rupert Ross, author of** *Indigenous Healing*

These inspiring, thought-provoking, and profoundly moving stories from across the globe call us to embrace dissent and invite harmony. They remind us that everyday acts of peacebuilding and reconciliation in the midst of conflict can sometimes transform minds, hearts, and spirits. The practitioners in this book speak to the ethics and pedagogy of peacebuilding in cross-cultural contexts, the power of life stories, the value of humility, and the importance of deep listening. Courageously sharing their own struggles to walk uncharted pathways of peace, they encourage all of us to speak our truths and look for peace in the most unexpected places.

    —**Paulette Regan, author of** *Unsettling the Settler Within,* **Senior Researcher, Truth and Reconciliation of Canada**

This thoughtful collection unfolds whole worlds of vital understanding for all who seek justice and peace. In the Foreword, respected Indigenous leader Ovide Mercredi emphasizes that poverty in the aftermath of colonialism is psychological and emotional, not only economic. Thus, the tone is set for a multi-dimensional, international exploration of peacebuilding across boundaries of time, territory and tumult. The authors—seasoned peacebuilders themselves—offer particulars of their creative, transformative work with clarity and humility, opening doors to applications beyond their contexts. I recommend this book to anyone who yearns for the tools to cultivate sustainable peace and a hope that roots itself in the hearts, minds and bodies of those who walk it, step by step, into being.

    —**Michelle LeBaron, author of** *Bridging Cultural Conflicts* **(University of British Columbia)**

The essays in this wide-ranging collection have several things in common, the two most important being the profound commitment they exhibit on the part of their authors to active peacebuilding in situations of conflict and complexity, and a wisdom born of the marriage of deep personal experience with solid scholarship. There is much to learn from these pages and much to be inspired by.

    —**Chris Marshall, author of** *Compassionate Justice* **(Victoria University of Wellington, New Zealand)**

There are institutes around the world researching and advocating peace-building, but none is quite like the Canadian School of Peacebuilding where cross-cultural, inter-generational, and global peacebuilding efforts are both critically explored and gently nurtured. As a peace/non-violence researcher working in Asia, I have learned much about conflict trans-formation and peacebuilding from this unique school. Raising questions such as, How can peace workers work with someone labelled a terrorist? Or what can cats teach people about identity and peace theology? *Voices of Harmony and Dissent: How Peacebuilders are Transforming Their Worlds,* reads like an adventure into a fantastic world of conflict engage-ment informed by both theoretical and experiential challenges by some of the best peace/non-violence workers/engaged academics in the field.

> —Chaiwat Satha-Anand, co-editor of *Protecting the Sacred, Creating Peace in Asia-Pacific* and *Three Prophets: Nonviolence, Murder, Forgiveness* (Thammasat University, Thailand)

Voices of Harmony and Dissent offers an inspiring account of peacebuild-ing applications in a wide range of contexts through storytelling and scholarship that raises awareness and inspires action in the pursuit of social justice and peace. Narrated by instructors who taught courses at the Canadian School of Peacebuilding, some chapters are academically thoughtful, while others engage the reader through personal descriptions of peacebuilding. Taken as a whole, the topics and cases presented tran-scend the usual disciplinary divisions, instill a sense of agency, and offer a compelling roadmap for personal and social transformation.

> —Daniel J. Christie Editor, *Encyclopedia of Peace Psychology* (Ohio State University)

Some say peace is a dream; some say peace can never be. Yes, peace can never be if we lose the dream or only dream without passionate peace work. This book tells the stories of those who dream of peace and pas-sionately invest in peace. These stories beckon us to dream of peace and see so many different ways that peace work is within our reach. We are all connected. These stories call on us to see in small every day ways how we can bring peace to all our connections, to all our relations. Read, dream, and make your dream of peace happen in your unique way.

> —Barry Stuart, Chief Judge, Yukon (retired), author of *Peacemaking Circles*

In Fiji, our islands are joined together by the largest ocean in the world, the Pacific Ocean. This is how the rest of the world is connected to us. We like to say we are the liquid continent.

My earliest connection to the peacebuilding field began in 2001, and Jarem Sawatsky was one of the first peacebuilders that I had met, which led to our first connection to the Eastern Mennonite University. Thank you, Jarem, for this. This book shares experiences and critical reflections to strengthen the voyage of peacebuilders as we navigate this journey of transformation in open seas and open skies that have many obstacles and many new insights to what we are yet to uncover and discover. If our canoes are to survive these long voyages ahead, these gifts of experience by the authors will strengthen our ability to not only survive but to reach our destination with others joining us along the way. *Vinaka saravakalevu* for this gift, *Voices of Harmony and Dissent*, to assist us all in sustaining our long journey ahead.

> —Koila Costello-Olsson, Executive Director, Pacific Centre for Peacebuilding (Fiji)

Peacebuilding is a complex process in a complex environment of systemic injustices and deep hurts and resentments. This book brings to life the subtle interactions between deliberately planned processes and unpredictable "surprises of the Spirit" resulting in emergent creativity of transformation. It stimulates the imagination and inspires hope, while keeping the reader grounded in the overwhelming human and structural challenges present in each context—from dealing with a Palestinian "terrorist" to changing food policies at the national and international levels.

> —Vern Neufeld Redekop, author of *Introduction to Conflict Studies* (Saint Paul University)

Voices of Harmony and Dissent presents articles by committed CSOP peace practitioners that combine theory and practice through their own peacebuilding stories that inspire the reader "to become a justice seeker and peace builder." This book illustrates the importance of building relationships and seeking root causes of conflict and violence as a way toward building a just peace for all humanity.

> —Christine Vertucci, Director, Mindanao Peacebuilding Institute Foundation, Inc. (MPI) (Philippines)

Peacebuilding cannot happen without courage. *Voices of Harmony and Dissent* helps us to see that the sacrifice of often entrenched individual or collective perspectives in order to resolve conflict may not be the supreme sacrifice, but it is often supremely difficult, and always supremely important.

> —Bill Blakie, Director of Knowles-Woodsworth Centre for Theology and Public Policy (University of Winnipeg)

Until now, to my knowledge, there have been no readily available practical materials that capture the realities and the paradoxes in peacebuilding so well as what is presented in the *Voices of Harmony and Dissent*. This book will touch your heart deeply and will inspire you to develop self-confidence and strong resilience by the powerful and passionate stories and illustrations from these catalysts of peace practitioners. This is a "must read" book for anyone working for peace and service of humanity.

—**Gopar Tapkida, MCC Representative in Zimbabwe and former MCC Regional Peace Advisor for West and Central Africa**

Voices of Harmony and Dissent

How Peacebuilders Are Transforming Their Worlds

Edited by

Richard McCutcheon, Jarem Sawatsky, and Valerie Smith

CMU Press

Winnipeg, Manitoba 2015

Voices of Harmony and Dissent: How Peacebuilders Are Transforming Their Worlds, edited by Richard McCutcheon, Jarem Sawatsky, and Valerie Smith

ISBN: 978-0-9207182-6-1 (softcover)
ISBN: 978-0-9207189-6-4 (e-book)

Published by CMU Press
http://www.cmu.ca/cmupress.php

10 9 8 7 6 5 4 3 2 1

Printed and bound in Canada

Book Design by Jill Ronsley, suneditwrite.com

Library and Archives Canada Cataloguing in Publication

Voices of harmony and dissent : how peacebuilders are transforming their worlds / edited by Richard McCutcheon, Jarem Sawatsky, Valerie Smith.

Includes bibliographical references and index.
ISBN 978-0-920718-26-1 (paperback)

1. Peace-building, Canadian--Case studies. I. McCutcheon, Richard, 1959-, editor II. Sawatsky, Jarem, editor III. Smith, Valerie, 1974-, editor

JZ5584.C3V64 2015   303.6'9   C2015-903092-7

For my son Declan Thomas, whose bright three-year-old Light reminds me of all that is good in the world.

—Richard McCutcheon

To all seekers of peace, wherever they may be. To all who have ever wondered if peace and love can be built through peace and love. This book is for you. May it help you to become better love-makers and peacebuilders.

—Jarem Sawatsky

For my dad, who taught me the importance of both imagination and discipline. And to my mom, for her enduring care.

—Valerie Smith

Contents

Foreword

SEEKERS OF JUSTICE AND PEACE

—Ovide Mercredi

PEOPLE WHO SEEK PEACE AND UNDERSTANDING are special people. Their worldview is not restricted or constrained by the culture or society of their birth. Their common denominator is humanity: that core idea that we are one people and that we are all connected.

The Canadian School of Peacebuilding, under the kind leadership of my friend Jarem Sawatsky, is a place where the peacebuilding of all traditions is nurtured, Indigenous traditions are respected, and Elders and youth of all traditions can learn from each other. Peaceful coexistence is one idea that recognizes the diversity of humanity. It is an important Indigenous idea that recognizes our shared responsibility: that as individuals and as collectivities we all have a human right to be different.

The "human condition" is one expression used to explain the present-day situation affecting Indigenous people. While it can describe a lot, it pales in contrast and comparison to the standard of life enjoyed by the majority of Canadians. It says nothing about the impact of colonialism and the oppression inherent in that kind of a governance system. Trying to explain contemporary Indigenous life and challenges using societal measurements of quality of life fails to disclose the real human condition at its very core, namely, the human soul.

To Indigenous people, poverty is not purely economic. It is emotional and psychological. It is feelings and the emptiness of feelings. It is discrimination and isolation. It is the lack of freedom of choice. It is loss of governance, culture, authority, land, and resources. It does not predate contact, but it begins shortly after the entrenchment of European settlers. It is history as much as it is politics, courts, and police. And by far the greatest loss has been the loss of power one derives from a peaceful and quiet soul, a soul devoid of shame, anger, fear, sorrow, and pain.

For Canadians who do not understand the true human condition of Indigenous people or choose not to, it is always easier to blame the original people as the authors of their contemporary situation. Fortunately, this virus of disdain does not affect all Canadians. Nowadays, with the emergence of Indigenous authors and literary figures, there is a growing wealth of literature available for the general public to become better informed and engaged in seeking solutions to a broken and divisive relationship between Canada and Indigenous Peoples.

There is more than hope! We live at a time when thousands of Indigenous youth are striking out on a new discourse and narrative engaging Canadian people. Their voice is neither hostile nor docile. They speak with confidence and authority. They seek to rebuild their fractured nations while being equally committed to perfecting this country. In their world of the future, there is more than hope. For them there is more than just recovery and healing; there is also the spirituality that comes when our common humanity is acknowledged and nurtured. Our emerging leaders will not only lift up their people to their rightful place on Earth, they will also help to lead a more peaceful world.

But in the meantime, listen to the voice of my generation one more time. It is the voice of grievance. A voice that became necessary when this country needed a reminder of the nation-to-nation relationship and when Canada needed to be told softly and not so softly that it is far from being whole and perfect.

Take It All, But

Take it all ... you say, even my dreams don't belong to me
What right have I to insist on my destiny and my lands?
Here, keep all the land, you say I do not use it anyway!
Rule the animals, the fishes, the waters, even the majestic Mountains
What need have I to tell the land how to divide itself for sale?
I have no desire to scrape the face of the Mountains or dam the rapids
Neither do I have the interest to erect skyscrapers and high rise banks
You say many different peoples will come to occupy and own this land
That I am obsolete! That my way is disappearing, that new ways are
      appearing
That life will be better. That you will change my children, even how
      they think
Take it all ... but when you do be very careful not to destroy my life
      and land
For the Earth knows no bosses, all rulers are pretenders as you will see
In fact if I listen to the Earth speak to me, as it did to my ancestors
It will become second nature to me to question your brand of prosperity
I think it is best that I hang on to what my people have been taught
You can believe what you will but I too will keep my ways, mind and soul
For in the end, one will never know who the Earth will honour and
      sustain
I will keep my ways, my language and culture, just in case the Earth
      favours me
In the meantime I will pray for life to carry on as before, for my
      people to prevail!
Just as my ancestors did, I pray to the Creator for my Colonizer to
      accept this truth,
So that you will finally understand
That you cannot rule my people, my land nor my heart.[1]

---

1. Poem written on August 3, 2009.

Peace is about justice in the present and in the future, creating harmony in our world. Where there is injustice, it must be resolved, otherwise conflict and distrust will prevail. The Canadian School of Peacebuilding strives to instill knowledge and understanding in its students, which is a pre-condition to finding lasting peace. My hope is that the ideas in this book will inspire the reader to become a justice seeker and peace builder.

—Ovide Mercredi

November 2014

Introduction

—Richard McCutcheon,
Jarem Sawatsky,
and Valerie Smith

IMAGINE INVITING WISE ELDERS OF PEACE from different traditions around the world to a sharing circle focused on inspiring and sustaining peacebuilders. What if these elders were asked to share first-hand stories about their experiences of working for peace over a lifetime? What if they were asked to reflect on what they have found profoundly moving in their work, and what they have learned over the years about how peace can be fostered? What if they were asked to speak from the heart about the wisdom they have gleaned as they have lived as peacebuilders in the midst of violence?

We have been turning that "what if" into reality over the past six years at the Canadian School of Peacebuilding, held annually at Canadian Mennonite University. Each year we invite peacebuilders from around the world to come to Winnipeg to teach intensive five-day courses. They are invited to teach what they are most passionate about and what they are currently learning about. Each June participants from around the world and across Canada gather into a community of dissimilar peacebuilders. Some are students, some are doctors, some are frontline peace practitioners, and some are farmers. Some of these peace workers are rooted in particular faith traditions, while some come from other passions and perspectives not rooted in any particular faith tradition. All of these people—instructors and learners—respectfully gather to learn about the myriad ways to engage in the work of building and sustaining peace.

Until now, peacebuilders needed to come to Winnipeg each June to benefit from this learning community of engaged peacebuilders. Through this book we hope to offer more broadly the kind of wisdom and learning found in the CSOP community. Each chapter has a different author (or two), all of whom are peacebuilders who taught at the Canadian School of Peacebuilding during the first five years of the school. Not all of these authors are "technically" elders but they certainly all are wise teachers with experience living peace in the midst of violence and seeking a deep transformation of the space around them. Each of them begins from their own experience and knowledge, and through stories, reflection and analysis, draws the reader into the work and wisdom of peacebuilding in its many forms.

Each chapter stands on its own—each is a self-contained piece that offers knowledge, tools, skills, and inspiration to assist the readers in the work of peacebuilding and in their growth as peacebuilders.

As you read this book, you may notice the diversity between the chapters. The differences in topic, style, and perspective stand out at first. This is not surprising, given that the authors come from such diverse backgrounds, cultures, and worldviews. They are men and women, Mennonite, Quaker, Indigenous, Catholic, and Buddhist. They are Thai, Canadian, Bosnian, and South African. And their writing styles are very different. The topics themselves range from food to Mennonite theology to civil society advocacy. There is technique mixed with reflection, and story juxtaposed with academic analysis. Three of the pieces (by Mubarak Awad, George Lakey, and Stan McKay) began as speeches at CSOP Peacebuilder banquets. The result is that at first blush a person might think this is not a uniform collection. Yet we believe that each chapter builds on the voice and identity of the author in an exciting and helpful way. We realize that there is enough difference among the chapters in this book that it may not be obvious what holds these pieces together.

We are convinced, however, that these pieces do indeed belong together. Put together, what emerges through all of the chapters is a tapestry of peace. There are common threads that run through the book. Ideas and patterns are repeated. With deeper reflection, readers will see that there are affinities among the authors and commonalities that bind the chapters together. Most importantly, the commonality is found in the essence of who these authors are. They are not just academics and teachers. They are all practitioners who, in a remarkable variety of ways, practice the peacebuilding that they teach and write about. Karen Ridd writes about "teaching who we are." And Harry Huebner talks about Mennonite understandings of peace and justice being rooted in "who and whose we are." This same idea surfaces in other chapters as well because these writers do not just write and teach about peacebuilding—they are convinced of the importance of living, embodying, and being peace. And should you spend any amount of time with these incredible peacebuilders you will sense the power and wisdom that comes from decades of these practices and understandings. Though these writers are humble and consistently modest about their work and experiences, when invited to share of themselves, they have astounding stories and experiences to share. This looks different in every chapter, in the life of each author, but in all its different forms, if you take time to look closely, you will see the common threads of wisdom, passion, persistence, humour, openness, and compassion that run through the lives of these remarkable peacebuilders.

Common threads are also found in the little and big connections that hold these pieces together. George Lakey was a mentor to Karen Ridd, who tells a story about Stan McKay. Maxine Matilpi and Ouyporn Khuankaew both refer to Thich Nhat Hanh in explaining their own thinking and practice. Stu Clark and Sophia Murphy and Piet Meiring mention ways in which the work of their CSOP courses spilled over into peacebuilding actions to address current issues of injustice in Canadian society. The connections, the common threads, are present. As editors who have had the remarkable and moving experience of working with each of these authors both in their writing for this book and facilitating their time at CSOP, we invite you to look for the connections and common threads as you move between the pieces.

One of the central threads in this tapestry is a common centre in the way peacebuilding is approached. Each chapter offers stories and reflections that have radically different starting points and yet, for us at least, what stands out is not so much the differences of identity, culture, and context. What emerges in these pages is a relationship approach to change, which is rooted in identity, compassion, and loving-kindness. Different traditions have different ways of naming this loving approach. Some of our Canadian Aboriginal brothers and sisters call it a way of peace that is rooted in seven sacred teachings: love, respect, courage, honesty, wisdom, humility, and truth.

Another thread of the tapestry is a hope rooted in the awareness that the impossible is possible. This is not a hope rooted in escape or distraction but rather in the awareness that some people are living the future now. It is a hope not of abstract ideas but a hope rooted in first-hand glimpses. It is rooted in the real life stories of those who are confronted by violence of all kinds but choose to respond with a healing form of justice. As the great Buddhist peacebuilder, Thich Nhat Hanh wrote, it is a hope rooted in "a compassion that can make flowers bloom all over the earth."

Yet another thread of the tapestry woven by these authors is a sense of agency rooted in amazement and awe. Hidden between the stories and tools for engaged peacebuilding is a call to action. This call to action is not rooted in guilt or fear but instead is rooted in the empowerment of other people's stories. We hope that you will be provoked and inspired by the stories of those who face deep suffering and yet are living peace and compassion in the here and now. These stories of those who passionately pursue peace dare us to imagine, not how to replicate their actions but rather to envision what kind of peace action may be possible for each one of us.

The pieces in this book share many common threads even while they contrast with one another in style, perspective, and theme. As the title suggests, there is both harmony and dissent. We have encouraged this juxtaposition because we feel it fits well with the work of peacebuilding. Peacebuilders work hard to create harmony, to transform conflict, to seek resolution. But more often than not, peacebuilders are also troublemakers. To get to a real and lasting peace there often needs to be discussion of difficult issues, histories, and emotions. To get to deep peace, there needs to be justice, and that often means disrupting the status quo, speaking or shouting out, and ignoring the rules that maintain injustice. And so, perhaps paradoxically, on the way to harmony, to the deep and lasting peace we seek, there is also real difference and much dissent.

The pieces in this book, then, like peacebuilding more generally, contain both harmony and dissent, and we believe this is as it should be. To create beautiful tapestries, you must use threads of more than one colour and designs that incorporate multiple shapes and patterns. The trick is to put the different threads and patterns together in a way that is beautiful, that is richer and deeper and stronger than any one thread by itself.

And so we offer you this collection of writings that transcends the usual divisions and structures and forced narratives that academia sometimes imposes on collections like this. Rather than grouping the chapters in a way that emphasizes one thread over another, we have chosen to list the pieces alphabetically by author to allow you to find your own connections. We invite you to travel your own journey through this book. Read the chapters in the order given or find your own, but as you dive into them look for common threads, be open to points of connection. Observe repeated patterns in the tapestry. And, yes, we encourage you to look for difference, even dissent, too.

In the end, it is our deep hope that the following chapters will inspire you, equip you, and sustain you in whatever kind of peace work you are doing, wherever in the world you are doing it. We hope that the stories of engaged peacebuilding included in this book empower you as you weave your own thread of peace into the tapestry of peace that Martin Luther King Jr. referred to when he wrote, "We are tied together in the single garment of destiny, caught in an inescapable network of mutuality." This, we believe, is the beauty of harmony and dissent.

Peace, Justice, and Non-Violence in the Middle East

—Mubarak Awad

I HAVE BEEN VERY INVOLVED WITH young children, youth, and families, working with the idea of non-violence for several decades. For Middle Easterners generally, and Palestinians particularly, the issues of violence and non-violence affect many lives locally and globally. At the present time there are a lot of challenges facing people in the Middle East.

Many outsiders think that they "know" the Middle East but, generally speaking, I find that they do not really understand the region. The region has been experiencing rapid change and there is very little understanding by outsiders of what is really going on in the region.

There are many actors who have become part of the Middle East narrative that were not on the scene before. Turkey is one example. Turkey occupied the Arab world for 400 years. Generally speaking, Palestinians have not tended to appreciate Turkey as a country. Suddenly, or so it seems, the Turkish government has been so good to the Palestinians that now, if you visit Palestine, you may well see Turkish flags in refugee camps. A recent prime minister from Turkey suggested the Turkish people are for the Palestinians; it is as if the four-hundred-year history is forgotten.

In the Middle East, another important factor might be Iran (even with the revolution), which tends to affect the region a great deal. Iran is primarily Shia Muslim, which because of the size of the country, contributes to the way people in the Middle East are increasingly dividing themselves along lines of Shia and Sunni. The power of that apparent division has the potential to devastate in the Middle East. If you look at conflicts in many areas in the region (other good examples are Lebanon and Bahrain), the conflict is deeply affected by the Sunni-Shia divide. It's helpful to note that Iranians are not Arabs; neither is the country of Turkey an Arabic nation. Generally speaking, neither Iran nor Turkey are typically seen as part of the Middle East.

Another challenge to understanding on a broader level is the Arab Spring. I don't believe that anyone thought the Arab Spring would happen so fast. In Egypt, in Libya, in Tunisia, in the Gulf, as well as in Palestine, people are saying dictatorships need to end. In some parts of the region, citizens have been very successful in getting rid of dictatorships. In Egypt they successfully removed Mubarak from power, and in one year they also wanted to get rid of the current president. Will the current president listen to the popular demands or will he, too, use guns and violence? We don't know. All of these external realities are affecting Palestinian people.

The principal way these factors are affecting the Palestinian situation is through the constant reinforcement of divisions between people, divisions that get reflected in the Palestinian cause. We are divided, for example, between Hamas and the Palestine Liberation Organization (PLO)—or, if you want, call it Fatah—and it is hard to resist the division. It is difficult to resist on many fronts if the community does not have unity. For Palestinians, if one part of the community resists, the other may not; so it does not work well for the larger resistance to occupation and to the statehood agenda. The issue of violence or non-violence is not clear. Even more precarious is the situation of Gaza.

There has often been silence about Gaza and a tendency to think that things are all right because Israeli soldiers are not inside Gaza; but they surround Gaza. Indeed, they surround it so much that they are choking it to death. No boats are allowed into Gaza, and none are allowed to leave. It is extremely difficult for people to enter and exit Gaza. In the end, it has become a big prison. It is alarming that the international community is so very silent about it. Even the United

Nations (UN) is mostly silent about it. Sometimes the UN wants to please both the Israelis and the Palestinian leadership in Ramallah, which is not fully supported by the Palestinian community. The challenges are overwhelming. There are both the external challenges and the internal challenges, all of which are significant and complex.

As a person who has devoted his life to the idea of non-violence and has worked extensively in the area of non-violent strategy and social movements, I have to ask, What can be done? and How we can do it? The challenges are many, not only in changing the government, but how to do it in a non-violent way. For those who seek peace in the Middle East, the question of how to deal with fundamentalists and other extremists is pressing; there are extremists who are Christian, who are Jewish, and who are Muslim. Do we, as peace scholars and practitioners, have the tools to reach extremists, to work with them, and ultimately to help them to find a way back to their own senses and to recognize that they are part of a common humanity, rather than continuing to focus upon hatred and destruction?

Perhaps an even greater challenge is to ask, Do we as peace groups and academic groups have the tools to deal with terrorists? Or have we gotten so far away from those committed to performing acts of terrorism that we can no longer talk to them because we do not see them as human beings? How do we deal with terrorists? Do we ignore them or keep our distance far away from them? To do so will have the result of letting them decide to do whatever they want to do, believing that it is okay with us because we have already determined that "they" are terrorists. They do not call themselves terrorists. We call them terrorists; and when we call them terrorists, we expect from them terrorist acts. In that equation, we have a significant and pressing problem.

I would like to tell you story. I went to see Yasser Arafat in Tunis. I was sitting quietly when suddenly he got up from his chair, came across the room, and kissed my head saying, "I have to ask a favour of you. There is a Palestinian named Halid. I don't know his last name. We don't know where he's at. He was our ambassador in Cypress. He disappeared and I think that the United States or Israel has detained him. Will you help us find him?"

I replied, "You want me to do that, but I will then ask you also for a favour."

He asked, "What favour?" to which I replied,

"I practice non-violence, and I would like to bring a group of non-violent people to train you, and to train all the Abus, here in Tunis."

He agreed by saying, "Okay, I accept that."

I returned to the United States (USA) and wrote to all the prisons in the USA. After three months I got a letter back: "I am Halid. What are you doing?"

I said, "Are you the Halid that said you wanted to kill Golda Meir?" for that was the charge against him.

He said, "Yes."

I said, "Okay, I'm coming to see you in prison." I put on a nice tie, with good shoes and socks—it was that important—and went to prison to see Halid.

Halid had been in one room for twenty-two years. They had cameras on him, metal on his feet, hands, and neck but I said I would not see him that way and asked them to remove the metal restraints, because I wanted to sit with him like a human being. The prison officials replied, "No, he might kill you," to which I replied, "That is my problem, not your problem."

After a half hour of intense discussion they said, "He was interested in killing Golda Meir."

And I said, "It doesn't matter to me what he was interested in. I just want to talk to him unfettered." Eventually they let me sign a document that said if anything happened to me it was my fault. So I finally got in to talk to him.

My first question to him was, "What is this? Why did you want to kill Golda Meir?"

He said, "I was planning to do it. I was part of the PLO planning—in case this happens, we'll do this. In case this other scenario happens, we'll do this. And part of my strategy was to look into how to kill the prime minister. I actually wrote about how to kill a lot of people, but it's only in books. None of it ever happened." In the middle of his work with the PLO, as Halid was travelling from Cypress to France through Italy, the United States picked him up and he stayed in jail for twenty-two years. I became very well acquainted with him once I met him.

Later I said to Arafat, "I met Halid. He's in that prison." Now Arafat had to give me five days of his life for non-violence. I asked Gene Sharpe to accompany me to Tunis to speak to Arafat and all the Abus. I also took several other people: a Quaker and a Mennonite, a professor from American University named Abdul Said, and a priest named Father Dennis Maddon. I asked my cousin Jonathan Kuttab as well, but he refused to come because it was illegal to meet Arafat. We had an excellent five days to communicate with people who know nothing about non-violence, people who commit themselves to an armed struggle. In the end it was a bit like talking to a wall, but we did it.

Halid's story, however, was not done. I received a phone call from a fellow in the United States by the name of Hank who said, "Mr. Awad, you met Halid and he is supposed to leave after he finishes his sentence, but if he leaves the prison, immigration will deport him because he is illegal in this country."

I said, "What do you mean? You brought him here."

He said, "No, it wasn't immigration who brought him here, it was another part of the government. He's illegal here, so we want you to find a place for him."

How do you find a place for someone who has been labelled a terrorist? If he is sent to Palestine, it is possible he would be put in jail, or even shot or killed by any number of people. Which Arab country would be willing to accept him? The underlying question is, Can you work with a person who has been labelled a terrorist? Is it possible to see him as a human being after twenty-three years in prison and to know that he changed in that period? Some people may say, "You're crazy. You know, he's a terrorist, he stays a terrorist."

If you think that way, and you identify as a Christian, then I think maybe you are not a Christian. Surely we teach that a sinner can repent and then he has the kingdom of God. It doesn't matter what a person has done. Christ didn't say, "If you are not a terrorist, you can have the kingdom of God." He did say, "Believe in me and you'll have the kingdom of God, whether or not you are a terrorist." Some people might say, "Heavens, your Jesus is a weird one, then!" to which I reply, "Yes."

Here's how I worked with a person labelled as a terrorist. First, we had to find him a passport, but where? Second, we had to find him a job. Third, we had to find his family and his children. This last thing is not so easy. Once he called me (he had the right to call me once a month) to find his wife and his children. I found his wife and children and, in one call, I put them on the phone on a third line. Later, I was called by the prison officials who said, "You are not allowed to come and see Halid because you let him talk to his wife and his children."

Sudanese officials eventually said they would provide him with a passport. I had to arrange for the Sudanese embassy to go to the prison so that when he was released he would not step on the ground outside the prison, only straight into the car, because the Sudanese have an embassy giving them diplomatic immunity. It's sort of funny, but it's real. When we got him in the car we said, "Okay, we are going to Sudan." But the American immigration officials said no, because they had to have two people from the immigration along. They have a sheriff concept, which means they have to accompany the former prisoner to confirm that he is being taken to Sudan. I was okay with the arrangement, but then when we arrived in Sudan with the two American officials who—perhaps because they have this idea that they own the whole world—came to Sudan without a visa! Now I had Halid with me and the Sudanese detained the two Americans. The officials called the American State Department and the American State Department called me.

Hank, the immigration guy I mentioned previously, called me to say, "Please, those guys have been in the airport for three days without showers. Can you help them?" I agreed to help them and I told Halid to help the American officials after we got the permit from the Sudanese to get them out of the airport hotel. Ironically, I had to explain to Halid that he needed to go tell them, "Come with me. I'll help you."

Halid is now in Syria with his wife and kids. In the end, I encouraged a friend to provide Halid and his family with some money to help him make his life in a decent way, especially so that he does not put into practice whatever he put on paper so many years earlier.

I am recounting this story because truly we have thousands of Halids around the world. Do any Canadians know how many so-called terrorists there are in Canada who may need their help? Several important questions follow: Are you able to help them in any way? Or is your response to stay at arm's length by saying, "No, we can't." Many of these people have spent numerous years in prison. Maybe the Canadian government is so secretive that you don't actually know how many political prisoners there are who have served their time and have no place to go.

Halid's story is an example of non-violence in action. When we talk about non-violent peacemaking, this is what we mean. It's important because there are few who can do this difficult work. Once a person studies peacemaking and knows what it means, then it will also give the person a conscience that says, "Hey, I can help." But, believe me, it does mean you have to live with your conscience.

Now, after helping Halid, any time I enter or leave an airport a security officer says, "Oh, you work with terrorists." Sometimes it takes me three hours or more to go through security, and I am not even talking about the Israeli airport. I'm talking about crossing from Canada back to the United States. Officials pick me up from the plane and they say, "You work with terrorists." I say, "I work with terrorists because you don't have a place for them." After all the shenanigans, they still call me, for example, to ask, "Can you help us with these Cuban detainees?" I usually say, "Why should I help you?" And then I follow up by saying, "If I do, we have to get them back to their home." They often say, "No, just help them. Find them other places, but don't send them back home." I insist that, if they aren't allowed to go home, then I cannot help them because they have to be with their families. It's crazy-making and crazy work, but we do our best to work things out.

Strategy is important to non-violent movements. Palestinians have been developing several layers of strategy. To mention just one of those layers, one aspect of the Palestinian strategy is to have a lot of boats full of refugees. When the time comes we will arrive on the shores of Israel … thousands upon thousands of refugees. We will say we are tired; we want to go back home. Refugees from Jordan, Lebanon, and Syria want to go home. But we need a common Arab understanding. And we need the Palestinian Authority to say, "Yes, we can do that in a non-violent way." We need to fill the streets on a daily basis saying we are tired of having occupation.

Clearly, eventually, the Palestinian situation is going to be resolved. The histories of modern nation states suggest that no country can be oppressed forever; thus, at some time, in some way, there will be a solution to the Palestinian situation. We want the Palestinian situation to be resolved soon so that we don't experience more unnecessary death and destruction. There are many examples of other conflicts that were seen to be intractable that have been resolved: Northern Ireland, South Africa, the black civil rights movement in the

USA. Look at the demise of the Soviet Union; it was resolved without resorting to civil war.

The Palestinian and Israeli problem also will be resolved. Sixty-five years under occupation is too much. We need leadership, among the Israelis and the Palestinians, to resolve the problem. We need a popular people's movement on both sides to resolve the problem. It's a worry that, if we do not create that movement, then we will have the fundamentalists taking leadership roles, people who think that God tells them that we should not resolve that problem.

Are we ready to talk to extremists in the religious groups? People have difficulty talking to extremists partly because the extremists say that their ideas come from God; if you don't agree with them it means you don't agree with God. How can you agree to talk with extremists, who say that they talked to God? If we as peacemakers cannot talk to these people, then how can we get upset because a fellow puts bombs around himself and kills hundreds of people? He says, "God told me to do that. Who are you to tell me 'no'?" We have to intervene between those extremists and their God, and convince them that God is a God of love, not a God of hate, not a God of killing. In that way, maybe, we can touch a few of the extremists and help them to see that there are better ways.

Here is an interesting action that we have been doing as a part of a Palestinian freedom movement. We bought an old boat, and we are putting produce from Gaza on it to send to Europe with the hope that we will have the Israelis wondering what to do: Stop it? Sink it? Let it go? It is part of an effort to try to break the siege of Gaza. Perhaps after one boat, then we could build another boat and another boat and help the people in Gaza to have some fresh produce to deal with the Europeans and also to help open a sea passage.

Can we say that things are getting better? If you read the works of Israeli writers over the past five years, they are telling us their stories. If you compare them, Palestinians have been telling the same stories as Israelis are now telling, but nobody believed us. An Israeli writer says, "Hey, I was there in 1948 and this is what I did. I was pushing the Palestinians out of their villages. I was burning many villages. I did this, I did that." Most of the books that we see now are Israeli confessions, telling us and telling the world that Israelis did wrong toward the Palestinians. This is a new sign and it is a hopeful sign for us as Palestinians, helping us to say, "My God, there is going to be peace," because people are saying exactly the right thing and it is exactly what happened.

It seems that, on the whole, Canadians, unfortunately, believe a lot of the things that have been said from the Israeli side of the story; statements that do not reflect accurately the situation in Palestine and are not accurate reflections of the Israeli treatment of Palestinians. There are pockets of people who do not accept all of the reports from the Israeli perspective as accurate. Those of us who participate in the work of the Canadian School of Peacebuilding, in general, seek to hear voices from all sides and to test those voices against on-the-ground peace workers in the region.

I have frequently heard Europeans and North Americans play on the concept of God. However, some Jewish people in Israel hardly believe in God. When European and North American visitors to Israel ask the Israeli settlers, "Why are you in this country? Why you are in settlements?" Israelis casually note, "God gave us this." We Palestinians challenge this response by asking, "How come God gave you this land, and yet you do not believe in his existence?" Usually at that moment the Israelis choose to be religious, soberly claiming, "God gave us this land." This claim by the Israelis is a repetition of the "land without people and people without land" narrative that was adopted by so many Europeans and North Americans, language that has been long used to reinforce European and North American support for Israel.

In the end I do not want some peacebuilders to support the Palestinians while other peacebuilders to continue to support Israel. Really what I want is for all peacebuilders to support justice, which is far more important than supporting a particular group. I encourage you to tell people in your area that Israelis and Palestinians deserve peace, but we cannot wait another sixty-five years.

With your help, with your support for both sides, working with non-violent peaceful means, we can achieve our goal.

Speaking Out ... and Being Heard: Peacebuilding through Citizen Advocacy

—Stuart Clark and
Sophia Murphy

Introduction

P UBLIC POLICY ADVOCACY IS A PARTICULAR type of peacebuilding. Advocacy is a way to give non-violent voice to messages
from citizens to their government about the rules that affect
people's lives. Public policy advocacy encourages a democratic and
participatory conversation that diffuses frustration and discourages
more violent expression, whether in riots, crime or, at worst, civil
war. Democracy is about so much more than periodic elections; and
even elections are more representative when an active and engaged
citizenry supports them.

This chapter comes out of a one-week course held at the Canadian
School of Peacebuilding in June 2012, titled *Speaking Out ... And Being
Heard—Citizen Advocacy.*[2] The course was co-taught by the authors.
We sought to equip the participants with a conceptual framework and
with the practical tools for public policy advocacy in democratic jurisdictions. Although our Canadian and international experiences have
occurred in jurisdictions that uphold democratic norms, the essential

2. The authors are grateful to the directors of the Canadian School of
Peacebuilding, Jarem Sawatsky, Valerie Smith, and Wendy Kroeker for their
support in presenting this course.

elements of the course are applicable to situations in which freedom of speech and association are more restricted than they are in Canada.

We have more than fifteen years of experience working together on international policy issues related to food and agriculture. We draw on the successes and failures of this work to illustrate the elements of citizen advocacy. The results of this course were immediately and successfully applied to Canadian refugee policy with the creation of the 59 Cents Campaign, which is the story that concludes the chapter.

The chapter begins with an introduction from each author that explains what motivates us to engage in this form of peacebuilding. Following this we review definitions of the "territory" described, particularly advocacy and civil society. We then describe how to go about a public policy campaign, first looking at the steps involved and then at some of the tools a practitioner would need to use, before offering a few words in conclusion. Several cases are used to illustrate our ideas, with examples drawn from our work and experience.

Introducing Stuart Clark

In the face of so many seemingly insoluble problems (for example, climate change or the resource/consumption/population balance) and the strong forces maintaining the status quo, sometimes I am tempted with despair or—worse—with resignation. The things that always draw me back are the stories of successful attempts to change policies, particularly those that seemed impossible until just before the change took place (for example, the collapse of the Iron Curtain or the end of apartheid).

Certain elements of these stories hold particular power to restore hope. First, there is so much in the story of humanity that is simply unpredictable. Sometimes unrelated events can completely change the outlook, as was the case of the Indian Ocean tsunami's impact on the Canadian Food Aid Untying Campaign, a story told later in the chapter. Second, money and power determine many things, but they do not control everything and are themselves subject to unexpected events. Third, the power of the human imagination is immeasurable. A good idea, like that of the 59 Cent Campaign conceived one evening over a beer, can change the dynamic surrounding an issue. And, finally, as a Christian I believe that there is a tide in the affairs of humanity that constantly tugs at the events of history, a tide called love that can be resisted but not extinguished.

The only attempt at policy change that will always fail is the attempt that is never made.

My personal experience of advocacy comes from establishing the public policy program at the Canadian Foodgrains Bank, a consortium of most of the Canadian church-related international development non-governmental organizations (NGOs). But the roots of my engagement go back over forty years of working to ensure that people have more to eat in Bangladesh, Nepal, Vietnam, Ethiopia, and Sudan.

Introducing Sophia Murphy

I am passionate about my work, and have the great good fortune to love what I do. I am committed to being an active and thoughtful contributor to the community of people who seek to make food systems fairer and more respectful of our planet. It is a big and diverse community—food, like the search for peace and justice, draws people together across many boundaries, whether of class, caste, gender, age, or language. Finding our shared humanity through common goals (and a shared meal) that cut across our differences is one of the most joyful and rewarding aspects of a life of civic engagement.

People's right to a political voice and to informed consent is not a given. Our world is full of unacceptable injustice and inequality. Some fights take hundreds of years, as Adam Hothschild's account of the abolition of slavery, *Bury the Chains*, reminds us.[3] Reading Hothschild's book suggests a few simple rules to keep us going: do not give up even if it takes a lifetime (and more); give women the chance to lead; and be brave, because wresting the power from the powerful is not easy. Engaging as civil society is the chance to build and demonstrate our courage together. Remember that the ability to accept compromise is vital, but so is the ability to dream.

From teenage activism on peace issues in the UK (including an unforgettable visit to Greenham Common) to attending, fresh out

3. Adam Hothschild, *Bury the Chains: Prophets and Rebels in the Fight to Free an Empire's Slaves* (Boston: Houghton Mifflin Company, 2005).

of high school, the Concluding Conference on the UN Decade for Women in Nairobi in 1985, through two decades of policy and advocacy work with the Canadian Council for International Cooperation (CCIC), the UN Non-Governmental Liaison Service, and the Institute for Agriculture and Trade Policy (IATP) in Minneapolis, I have had the chance to work on public policy advocacy in many and varied contexts, with many civil society organizations and in interaction with many government officials as well. I am a member of the High Level Panel of Experts of the Committee on World Food Security (CFS), a creation that is itself the outcome of a hard fought and successful civil society intervention to shape governance of food issues that we mention again below.

What is Civil Society? What is Advocacy?

Civil society is a fluid concept. Much like the term "sustainability," civil society has different connotations in different contexts. A BBC World Service series from 2001 offered a definition that we find helpful: "A civil society is a public space between the state, the market and the ordinary household, in which people can debate and tackle action."[4] The crucial elements in this definition include, first, the notion of public space. This is not private space, as exists in a company boardroom or in the kitchen of a household. Nor is it a formal political space, in which organized political parties dominate. Civil society occupies non-governmental public space: space where people act collectively, as communities, with a shared set of objectives and often (if not always) a common set of ideals or values. Second, the definition uses the words "debate" and "action." That is, civil society is a place where ideas are discussed, argued over, framed, created, adopted, or rejected. It is a place where people mobilize and engage—where people are encouraged to act on the basis of their ideas, so as to effect immediate change or alter decisions that have created, or will create, undesirable situations. CSOs encourage people to get informed, to sign letters, and to make phone calls; to come together in protest or

---

4. BBC World Service Online, "What is Civil Society?" July 5, 2001. (Accessed April 30, 2014.) http://www.bbc.co.uk/worldservice/people/highlights/010705_civil.shtml.

support, to march or dance or blockade; to design T-shirts and posters; to write stories and to tell them widely, whether in the neighbour's living room, a town hall or on national radio. Civil society is organized; it is people engaged in collective action to affect outcomes.[5]

An advocate is someone who presents an argument. The Latin root combines *ad*, meaning "to" or "toward" with *voca*, meaning voice. Advocacy should not be conflated with lobbying. Lobbying is the activity of those making arguments in favour of a position from which they stand to benefit. Advocacy implies more distance; an argument is made on the merits of the situation. Public policy advocates argue for policies they think will improve outcomes in the public interest, and many CSOs dedicate resources to this work.

CSOs play other important roles, for example in service provision. Examples are Meals on Wheels for people who are no longer able to prepare food for themselves, hospices to care for people who are dying, and soup kitchens to provide food for the destitute. These are examples of organizations created as not-for-profit service providers. They typically depend upon a large number of volunteer staff, which, in part, reflects an effort to keep financial costs to a minimum. This in turn reflects the value of helping one another that, for most people active in civil society, provides a powerful motivation to engage. There are a number of international organizations, such as the International Federation of Red Cross and Red Crescent Societies (IFRC), whose work is, in large part, about service provision.

Ethnic organizations are forms of CSO that are important in immigrant countries such as Canada. Religious institutions (when they are not formally a part of the state) are also important actors in civil society. In many cases CSOs fulfill two or more roles. For example, the International Committee of the Red Cross was founded to serve the wounded and the dead in battle, but has also come to have a very highly respected place in policymaking linked to humanitarian intervention in situations of armed conflict.

---

5. Michael Edwards, "The Rise and Rise of Civil Society," (Accessed April 30, 2014.) http://www.futurepositive.org/docs/RISE.doc.

Tyranny's Foe and Democracy's Watchdog

Civil society is not always benign. Commentators such as Neera Chandhoke, professor at the University of Delhi, discuss the violence and intolerance that civil society can exhibit. Humanity will organize collectively not only in support of human rights, but also to deprive other groups of their rights.[6] There is nothing inherently "progressive" or even moral about civil society organizing and advocacy.

While acknowledging the potential for civil society to act "uncivilly" (Chandhoke's example is that of India's Shiv Sena, a group that militantly—and sometimes with violence—promotes the rights of Hindus and creates fear and hatred of non-Hindu minorities), it is possible to argue that CSOs per se make a vital contribution to democracy. It is good for democracy that people organize and mobilize and speak out. In the wake of the murder of twenty-six teachers and children in Newtown, Connecticut, in December 2012, National Rifle Association (NRA) President Wayne LaPierre proposed that schools should hire armed guards rather than tightening gun control laws. His remarks proved inflammatory. While the NRA represents the views of many Americans, others organized and publicly challenged the NRA's resistance to any form of gun control. Part of the role of civil society is to encourage debate.

At its best, civil society is a force against tyranny, against government that allows no dissent. In a totalitarian state, civil society does not exist. There may be trade unions and women's groups, youth organizations and church choirs, but they operate under the control of government. Tibor Fisher's novel, *Under the Frog*, describes how even basketball was politicized in Communist Hungary.[7] Modern use of the term "civil society" dates back to the largely peaceful dissent that ended the totalitarian rule of the Union of Soviet Socialist Republics. Tahir Square in Egypt is a more recent echo of popular gatherings that have enabled profound political change without civil war. We explore this kind of resistance later in the chapter.

---

6. Neera Chandhoke, "What the Hell is Civil Society?" March 17, 2005. (Accessed November 6, 2014.) http://www.opendemocracy.net/democracy-open_politics/article_2375.jsp.
7. Tibor Fisher, *Under the Frog* (New York: Picador USA, 1992).

Professional and Voluntary Non-governmental Organizations

Each of the authors has professional experience with the specific subsection of civil society that is composed of formally organized and constituted organizations. These organizations have hired staff members who are dedicated to a public policy objective such as reducing poverty, realizing women's rights, ending hunger, or vaccinating children. The organizations are often called NGOs (non-governmental organizations). In the United States they are more often called nonprofits or private voluntary organizations. Some have a voluntary base, sometimes quite large, while others have only professional staff. Typically, NGOs are exempt from certain taxes (because of their non-profit designation), but their freedom to engage in political speech of various kinds is constrained. The laws governing NGO political activities in Canada have been tightened significantly in recent years. Many Canadian NGOs benefit in their fundraising by a tax ruling that allows contributors to deduct their contributions from their income before paying income tax. However, this provision requires that these NGOs devote no more than 10 percent of their budget to "political advocacy." In recent years the definition of political advocacy has been tightened and the penalties for exceeding this limit increased.

NGOs are a subset of the broader world of CSOs. It is now common to distinguish social movements from NGOs. Social movements are inherently more political than NGOs. They are organizations built by people who are fighting to improve their situation, as trade unions or farmers' organizations or women's groups do. NGOs tend to have paid professional staff (if also often a large volunteer base) and to be acting on behalf of others. Social movements can be highly organized and well funded (as some trade unions are) but are membership organizations whose members have a direct stake in the issues the social movement seeks to address. All are part of civil society as described above.

We believe that, while service provision is important, CSOs should be committed to solving the problems that create the demand for their services. It is important to correct the structural causes of injustice. This is a powerful motivation for civil society's engagement in advocacy work. In the case of NGOs such as the Canadian Foodgrains Bank, playing the role of service provider and the advocate strengthens both roles.

Civil Society in Action: Trade Rules for Agriculture

The story that follows is an illustration of advocacy as it unfolds in practice. The experience of engaging with multilateral trade rules on agriculture proved fertile ground for a wide range of issues, from the political fight for food sovereignty to the more technical matter of food safety standards. A wide range of actors, from government diplomats and trade ministers to trade unionists, African pastoralists, and environmental activists, got involved in the debates. Both of us were active in the creation of, and disagreements over, multilateral agricultural trade policy between 1999 and 2005. Much of what follows is based on our personal experience of these events.

Agriculture and International Trade Rules: the Uruguay Round Agreement

In April 1994 in Marrakech, Morocco, the governments that were signatories to the General Agreement on Tariffs and Trade (GATT) signed the Uruguay Round of trade agreements, thereby establishing the World Trade Organization (WTO) and significantly expanding the reach of multilateral trade rules. The Uruguay Round brought agriculture into the fold of multilateral trade rules, ending forty years of exemptions from trade treaties.

Between 1986 and 1994, during the negotiations on what became the WTO Agreement on Agriculture (AoA), civil society engagement was limited. NGOs had long engaged with the UN on social policies such as health and education. Trade unions had been integrated into the governance structure of the International Labor Organization from its inception in 1919. Human rights and disarmament talks also had seen their share of CSOs actively participate. But trade and finance were historically closed arenas, with some engagement from the private sector but almost none from citizens' organizations. Some farmers' organizations certainly engaged in the GATT talks on agriculture, especially those in exporting countries such as Australia, Canada, and the United States, and those with more defensive interests, such as the European Union (then the European Community) and Japan. But it was primarily the private sector, not civil society, that engaged with governments on trade issues. There were exceptions—one of the most active being the Third World Network, which is headquartered in Malaysia. But overall participation by civil society was tiny. Development NGOs that worked on economic issues at the time were preoccupied with the debt crisis and structural adjustment programs (SAPs), not trade.

This started to change as the Uruguay Round agreements came into effect. NGOs began to analyze the text of the agreements and to write their critiques. By 1998, several of them had published analyses of what the rules said and what they might imply for developing countries and for food security.[8] CSOs, including La Via Campesina (a global network of peasant organizations), IATP, and a number of church-based organizations, organized meetings for CSOs to learn what the WTO agriculture rules were and how they worked, and to discuss possible strategies for action. NGO advocates began to request meetings with trade officials, to organize seminars with economists and other experts to air their concerns in front of delegates, and to propose possible changes to the trade rules for agriculture. The WTO rules called for a process, termed the Analysis and Information Exchange, that was intended to allow governments time to prepare a further round of reforms to the rules, in negotiations that were expected to start in 2000.

Much of the WTO membership was initially hostile to NGO participation in trade talks, especially to participation by the developing countries. But over the first five years of the organization's existence this changed, in part due to the support of the South Centre, an intergovernmental forum for developing countries, as well as to the establishment of several new NGOs in Geneva that were dedicated to trade issues. When these organizations began to interact with

---

8. For a general discussion, see Sophia Murphy, *Trade and Food Security: An Assessment of the Uruguay Round Agreement on Agriculture* (London: Catholic Institute for International Relations, 1999).

government officials on a regular basis, diplomats had the chance for the first time to exchange views with civil society. Over time a high level of trust emerged. To a lesser extent, something similar occurred with developed country missions as well.

NGOs began to develop focused proposals for reforms to the AoA, working with a few developing country governments and the South Centre. The proposals addressed such issues as how to protect the agriculture of developing countries from dumping by exporters, how to protect the livelihoods of small-scale producers, how to protect the humanitarian purpose of food aid from commercial interests, and how to help poor net food importing countries cope when food prices in international markets spiked upwards. This led to joint government and NGO work on what became known as the "development box"—measures to create a non-commercial space for food and agriculture policies that could be protected from the pressures of globalized markets.

During those five years, as NGO and government relationships over trade and agriculture drew closer, tensions between NGOs and some social movements grew. La Via Campesina rejected the role given to the WTO to adjudicate over domestic agriculture. The organization articulated a concept they called food sovereignty, expressed at the time as the right of all countries to decide democratically their own food policies and to protect access to local food markets by domestic producers. They campaigned with the slogan: "WTO out of Agriculture!" They firmly rejected all WTO rules. La Via Campesina engaged in direct action and protest to express their opposition, refusing to negotiate with an institution whose authority they did not recognize.

The Battle in Seattle

In some respects, the different paths chosen by social movements and NGOs crystalized at the third WTO Ministerial Conference, held in Seattle late in 1999. A this point, just five years after Marrakech, a broad swath of international civil society was engaged in trade issues, and tens of thousands of people came to Seattle to be present at the conference. The governments were expected to launch a new round of talks. (It was quickly dubbed the Millennium Round.) Most

CSOs—social movements and NGOs alike—were there to stop the round from launching, though there were important differences within civil society on both tactics and even the objectives of rejecting a new trade round.

Some CSOs were gathered in Seattle to blockade the streets and deny government delegates access to the convention centre. Others came to join a peaceful march planned by the trade union movement. On the first day of the conference, these actions were combined and chaos resulted. What started as peaceful demonstrations ended in riots, in part because provocateurs in the crowd wanted to raise the pitch of the protest and in part because the Seattle police and other civic authorities were wholly unprepared for the scale of the crowd and the choice of some to engage in civil disobedience. Batons, tear gas, and mass arrests ensued, followed by a curfew. For most of the first day of the conference, many delegates were trapped in their hotel rooms, unable to get through the streets to the convention centre where the meetings were taking place.

For those who were in Seattle, it was impossible to forget the masked demonstrators, the smashed shop windows, and the clouds of tear gas. Yet this drama hid from view some powerful and non-violent CSO organizing. For example, the march brought together thousands of trade unionists and environmentalists in a "Blue Green Alliance," an historic uniting of two disparate political and institutional cultures that had a long history of disagreement and mistrust. CSOs also organized teach-ins with renowned NGO activists and writers, who gave speeches on the wrongs of globalization. Activists organized training camps to teach protesters the art of civil disobedience from passive resistance in the face of arrest to basic first aid to cope with tear gas.

The NGOs who chose to get an accreditation to enter the convention centre worked with government delegates and the media, putting forward their arguments against the proposed new round. NGOs were able to track what was going on behind closed doors because of the relationships they had built over the previous several years in Geneva.

Governments did not launch a trade round in Seattle. Angered by a process that excluded them during the negotiations, a number of developing countries announced they would not co-operate without full consultation. NGOs supported this message. The demonstrators outside heralded the collapse of the talks as a victory.

Another period of strategizing and analyzing began, with CSOs building on the work they had begun. Some NGOs produced more analysis and continued to document the negative effects of the WTO trade liberalization agenda, while others worked with social movements to disrupt government meetings that focused on globalization, including trade, whether held in Davos with the World Economic Forum or with the annual meetings of the G-8 or the World Bank.

The Doha Development Agenda

Two years later, at the fourth WTO Ministerial Conference, held in Doha, Qatar, WTO member states launched a new trade round. Many CSOs were bitterly disappointed. Yet during the Doha Ministerial, Pakistan chaired a meeting for governments and NGOs called "friends of the development box." The ideas to protect food security that had started to take shape in the years immediately after the WTO was created were now taking root.

By the time of the fifth ministerial conference, in Cancun, Mexico, in September 2003, a new informal group, called the Group of 33, or G-33, had emerged to work on agriculture. The group included a number of small developing countries. Members had a clear focus on food import concerns. Informally, the Philippines and Indonesia assumed a leadership role. From 2000 through 2005 NGOs, working with the Food and Agriculture Organization of the United Nations and other experts, compiled case studies to document the effects of import surges and dumped food in domestic markets to underline the need for stronger trade rules to protect food security. NGOs in Geneva continued to meet with government delegates and to provide regular information on developments in the trade negotiations for the wider world of CSOs.

Twelve years later, the Doha Agenda has proved to be stillborn. After very nearly coming to agreement in 2008, but failing, the WTO membership was barely able to cobble together a small collection of agreements at the Ninth WTO Ministerial Conference, in Bali in 2013. Perhaps the CSOs could have claimed victory in Doha back in 2001 after all, as the seeds of the trade agenda's undoing were already planted. These seeds were planted, not only, and not least, in the preoccupation of a number of net food importing countries to secure better protection for domestic food production and food stock management. Civil society, in the meantime, has established a lasting and reasonably well-functioning relationship with trade officials. Closed doors remain all too common, yet there is more access to negotiating texts, and there is a continuing informal sharing of information and ideas that, arguably, have transformed the trade negotiating process.

At the same time, La Via Campesina, and others who refused to co-operate with the WTO, have built strong and institutionalized relationships elsewhere in the multilateral system, in particular with the UN Committee on World Food Security (CFS). Trade negotiations are about as opaque an area of government policy as a CSO might expect to encounter. We argue that the achievements over the past fifteen years are a testament to what concerted civil society action can achieve.

We have suggested that, among the complexities of citizen advocacy, social change is usually a protracted process. To be successful, advocates must be able to exhibit long-term patience and be able to resist fatigue; and they must be alert to, and accepting of, the unpredictable mix of converging responses from all parties to a social issue. And, in this state of acceptance, advocates' alertness must lead to appropriate action (shifts in strategy) when evidence of shifts in government policy offer new opportunities for advocacy. Moreover, advocates must be creative and flexible in recognizing and analyzing social dynamics so that—while accepting interim success or failure—they can be active in pursuing a logical next step toward effective social change. The history of the Canadian Foodgrains Bank expresses each of these aspects of social advocacy, including the importance of looking beyond a dramatic success with the government of one country (Canada) to the possibilities of extending change around the globe.

Civil Society in Action: Untying Canadian Food Aid

Food aid, like other kinds of foreign aid, has had a history of combining the altruism of helping poor countries and their people with the self-interest of the donor country. This balance has shifted over time, in recent years emphasizing the altruistic side with a primary focus on the reduction of poverty and hunger. Food aid has been one of the last areas of foreign aid to be influenced by this trend. The United States, which provides almost half the global food aid, continues to tie its food aid program largely to food commodities produced in the USA and shipped on American-registered cargo vessels. Canada, while not requiring the use of Canadian cargo vessels, until recently, required at least 90 percent of Canadian food aid to originate in Canada.

This policy seriously reduced the effectiveness of Canadian food aid programs. Most notably, the requirement to use Canadian food commodities resulted in lengthy delays in providing food to hungry people. It took about three months to deliver food from Canada, which, in the context of emergencies, was a serious disadvantage. In addition, with the changes in global shipping and the rise in fuel costs, the shipping costs took an increasingly large part of the food aid budget. Finally, there were some strong advantages of locally procured food commodities. They were often cheaper, much faster to deliver, more suited to local diets, and, potentially, they offered a way to stimulate local agriculture.

The Canadian Foodgrains Bank Food Aid Untying Campaign

As the largest Canadian non-governmental food aid delivery organization, the Canadian Foodgrains Bank was very concerned with ensuring that food reached people in emergencies as quickly and cheaply as possible. Local purchase of food was often the preferred way to provide food, but because the organization used Canadian government funds to support its work it was obliged to send food from Canada for most of its activities.

In the late 1990s, the Foodgrains Bank began to focus some of its efforts to change public policies, notably the promotion of the human right to adequate food as a norm to reduce hunger everywhere. At the same time, the leaders of the Foodgrains Bank began efforts to persuade the Canadian government to allow more Canadian aid money to be used to purchase food aid commodities locally.

The Foodgrains Bank's early efforts were focused on documenting, through reviews of existing literature and through their limited local purchase experiences, the increases in aid effectiveness associated with locally procured food aid commodities. This information was then turned into short briefs written for different audiences. Presentations were made to the Parliamentary Standing Committees on Agriculture and Foreign Affairs/International Development and at meetings held with key Members of Parliament. Approaches were also made to the Canadian Wheat Board, which benefited from the existing policy by obtaining premium prices for supplying Canadian food aid wheat, and to other Canadian farm commodity organizations. The responses were mixed. The government aid bureaucracy, however, had long been in favour of food aid untying and proved a helpful ally in spreading the message of the Foodgrains Bank.

By 2002 it appeared that the time was right for the government to untie Canadian food aid. Canada was to attend the UN World Food Summit Plus Five and was looking for announcements to make at this global event. However, it was rumoured that when this change was proposed in the Canadian cabinet, Canada's highest policy making body, it was rejected out of concern for a backlash from Prairie wheat farmers. A concern for the possibility of a negative reaction by domestic interests trumped a major step forward in Canadian aid effectiveness.

Revising the Strategy. Following the failure to acquire the desired change in Canadian government policy, the Foodgrains Bank carried out a thorough review of their strategy for change. Several new directions were identified:

- It was vital to persuade the government politicians that there was support for the change from Prairie wheat farmers. This had to go beyond the many farmer supporters of the Foodgrains Bank, but they could play an important role in voicing their support.
- It was important to get farm organizations to support this change, particularly the Canadian Federation of Agriculture (CFA), which represented the provincial farm and commodity organizations.
- Other important stakeholders and government bodies should be enlisted as well.

In the years that followed, farmer supporters of the Foodgrains Bank met with the minister responsible for Canadian International Development Agency (CIDA), the Canadian government aid department, as well as key government Members of Parliament. Foodgrains

Bank staff presented the arguments for food aid untying to annual meetings of the CFA, where the Foodgrains Bank was recognized as an organization supported by many of its members.

Perhaps most importantly, at the World Trade Organization agricultural negotiations in Doha, the link was made between Canadian negotiating goals and food aid untying. Canada was one of several countries that attacked the United States food aid for its unfair effects on international agricultural trade. By untying its own food aid, Canada would strengthen its negotiating stance at the Doha Agricultural negotiations.

The Decisive Factor. At Christmas 2004, a huge undersea earthquake off the coast of Indonesia set off a tsunami that devastated the coastlines of Indonesia, Thailand, and Sri Lanka. The media gave twenty-four hour coverage of the damage and of the plight of the coastal people affected. The coastal people had lost everything, including their ability to obtain food. They needed food and they needed it right away. Yet only a few kilometres away crops were ripening in the sun. It made no sense to send food from Canada. The national media in Canada came across one of the Foodgrains Bank briefs about food aid untying and made this a national story to accompany the tsunami coverage.

This coverage had two important effects. First, it provided a high-profile challenge to government policy in terms that the general public understood. Second, it put pressure on the CFA at their annual meeting one month later to come out in support of the Foodgrains Bank campaign.

Three months later Canada untied 50 percent of its food aid program and followed that three years later, at the time of a global food price crisis, with 100 percent untying of this program.

Elements for Successful Advocacy

It seems obvious to say that it is essential to know what you want to change by your advocacy work, but what is obvious is not always easy to achieve. Public policies are rarely isolated. Typically a particular policy has been developed on top of a web of pre-existing policies, and these interconnections anchor particular policies. Understanding these interconnections is an essential first step in undertaking any public policy advocacy. Failure to take these interconnections into account can mean months of fruitless effort and frustration.

Strategic Inquiry as the First Step

Assuming that you have a clear idea of the immediate problem you want to address, the first stop in understanding the context of the problem is to speak with the people who are responsible for implementing the problematic policy.[9] At this point you are not trying to change anything, so it is important to resist the urge to start advocating right away. Officials are often much more relaxed if they know you have come to listen rather than to speak. Instead of advocating, you should explain the problem as you see it and ask why it is that way. At this point, in addition to collecting information, you are trying to establish relationships. Government officials are citizens too, and may even be personally sympathetic to the problem about which you are asking. A positive relationship with them may be helpful in your subsequent work. This stage offers a chance to learn whether others see a problem where you do. If so, find out what they think the problem is and how it might be solved. And if not, evaluate whether you need to review your opinion or determine what might be helpful to make the problem more evident.

If you agree there is a problem, examples of the type of questions to pose to government officials include the following:

- What policy or policies are creating the problem?
- Where do these policies come from? How long have they been in effect?
- Which department or level of government is responsible for the policies?
- Have there been other reports of difficulties with the policies?
- How important is the issue to the government?
- Are there any changes planned for the existing policies?

---

9. Approaching officials will reveal your interest, which, in some situations, carries some risks. In more sensitive situations, talking to former or retired officials may be a better alternative.

Other sources of information for your strategic inquiry include government speeches (often available on the Internet), other CSOs working on the same or similar issues, media reports, access to information requests and even those who may be opposed to the changes you are seeking. Understanding the opposition is crucial.

The results of the strategic inquiry should include the following:

- A list of the policies causing the problem, including their history
- Levels and departments of government involved
- The key government personnel involved
- Any obvious roadblocks to change
- Any timelines for changes that are already planned

The ultimate outcome of your strategic inquiry should be a clear statement of what policy changes you are seeking. Getting this first step right is essential for success.

It might be helpful to work with three broad categories—the three "I's."

1. Ideas: What was the failed policy trying to achieve? Do the goals need to be changed?
2. Institutions: Who is responsible for the policy? Do others need to be involved?
3. Interests: Who gains from the status quo? Who would gain from a change to the policy you want?

Research

Once the policy change you want to achieve—the destination—is clear, it is time to do some serious research. Passion and commitment are important elements of advocacy work, but it is essential to get to know the issue inside and out. Advocates should aim to know at least as much about the issue as the government officials involved. If you are not informed about the issue you wish to discuss, you cannot be persuasive. Credibility with bureaucrats often rests on their respect for your knowledge of the issue. The cornerstones of effective advocacy are careful research and good organization of the information obtained so that you can find it later. You should be bringing new information, or a new perspective, while respecting the fact that the officials will know things you cannot know (and need to learn) to bring about lasting change.

Level of Contention

As you develop your advocacy strategy it is important to consider the level of contention surrounding your chosen issue. This is often a question of power and/or money: Who stands to lose if you are successful in your advocacy? The answer is a critical point in forming an advocacy strategy.

- Low Level of Contention—an example of this would be the advocacy to untie Canadian food aid. (See below.) Very few individuals or groups had much to lose from the purchase of food aid in Canada. Such cases require mostly awareness-raising and careful background research.
- High Level of Contention—an example of this would be the advocacy to monitor and publicize the use of foreign aid funds in a developing country where corruption misdirects a substantial part of that aid. In such cases, there are powerful interest holders who have a lot at stake, so the advocacy group must have a high degree of independence and be able to mobilize strong public support to resist pressure or intimidation.

The level of contention can change during an advocacy activity. What appears to be relatively uncontentious initially can change, obliging advocates to change their strategy if they are to succeed.

Awareness-Raising Versus Policy Change

Another consideration concerns the advocacy objective. Is it to raise awareness of an issue or to change a policy? These may be two stages of the same advocacy campaign, but they call for different approaches.

The basic objective of awareness-raising is to change the way the public sees a particular issue. There is no need to compromise, and those with militant approaches can be important actors. Successful examples of this are the Occupy Movement and their slogan "We are the 99 percent" and the first stage of the 59 Cent Campaign on Refugee Health Care, discussed below.

The media play a key role in raising awareness with the general public. Using press releases is a good way to start a campaign but it can be difficult to get noticed in the blizzard of press releases received regularly by media outlets. When starting out as a new group, it may make sense to look for a well-known organization to co-author the first releases. Alternatively, to get the attention of the media, groups sometimes use stunts such as the colourful puppets of the G-8 leaders that Oxfam pioneered and the banners that Greenpeace and other environmental activists unfurl during intergovernmental meetings such as the negotiations on climate change. In addition, giving the public something to do (letter writing campaigns, or coming out for a public meeting or demonstration) is often important to help change people's thinking and to build understanding of the issue.

In addition to media and public engagement, it may be appropriate to use political engagement to raise awareness. This starts with having a meeting with a sympathetic elected official, whether from the governing party or the opposition. Such a meeting requires careful preparation—you are unlikely to get a second chance if things do not go well, and may not get a second meeting even if it does go well. A clear well-reasoned argument, backed up by a request for a clear action by the official (for example, requesting that an MP ask a question during Question Period in Parliament), is essential. Taking a group of recognized constituents from the official's riding can improve the potential for success in gaining the official's support and commitment to action.

If you already have substantial public support for your issue, a petition to Parliament or elected assembly is also an option. In Canada, if you have more than twenty-five signatures and an appropriate format, any MP has the right to read the petition out in Parliament. Even if the government ignores it, the parliamentary press gallery may pick it up.

The overarching objective of raising awareness is to get noticed. It is also a good opportunity to find allies as your public profile on the issue increases. As is often the case, a combination of strategies is the most likely to meet with success. For example, if you can time an op-ed to come out in the days before a meeting with an elected official, the press coverage can help bring your issue to the fore.

Changing policy is not the same thing as raising awareness. Raising awareness gives a problem greater profile; changing policy seeks to solve that problem. In many ways, policy advocacy is like a poker game where you seek to improve the value of your cards and choose the critical moments to play each of them. If your objective is to change policy, some of the cards you can play might include the following:

- A carefully written analysis of the issue with a rationale for change
- Personal anecdotes of those who are victims of the current policy
- An account of the financial cost of the current policy and the savings the recommended changes could realize
- Opportune media events (for example, raising the need to buy food for disaster victims locally—untying Canadian food aid—in the aftermath of the Indian Ocean tsunami)
- Collaboration with other political actors—perhaps governments of other countries or other levels of domestic government—to put pressure on the officials who have the power to decide on the issue. (This might mean arranging an opposition question during Question Period in Parliament, proposing an informal and off the record meeting among unofficial or potential allies, or seeking to raise the profile of the issue within a province or in several provinces to create more national pressure.)

For each of these actions, timing matters. For example, there is little point in pushing for a certain policy change if the government has already made the decision. Similarly, advocacy action before a policy is under review may be a waste of effort unless that advocacy can create the policy review. Advocacy actions must come while the policy decisions are being considered, which underlines the importance of knowing the government timetable for making decisions related to the policy of interest.

The art of compromise is also vital. Policy advocates rarely get all they ask for, and it is important to have a clear idea of one or more acceptable "second best" outcomes. It is never simple to judge when and how much to compromise, and the room to manoeuvre is dependent on how much political will you have been able to generate before the decision is taken. This is one of the hardest parts of coalition politics, and one of the most important.

Political Will

Getting the policy change you are seeking right, and knowing the issues involved as deeply as possible, are major parts of successful advocacy. But there is a third component without which no change will happen: political will. This is particularly so if the change you are seeking is at all contentious.

Gaventa and McGee have proposed a useful framework for understanding how to create political will.[10] They set out three key elements:

- Political Opportunities refers to external events that occur unexpectedly and that open the possibility for change. Such events can destabilize the status quo or block the possibility for change. They must be exploited with care, but they offer significant opportunities.
- Mobilizing Structures refers to those institutions or organizations that care about the issue, including those that are directly affected and will offer support. Coalitions, which can include allies in government as well as technical resources in professional associations, are examples of "thickening" these mobilizing structures.
- Framing refers to the set of values that you appeal to in promoting the change you seek. Appropriate framing is important to ensure that the call to action is understood by a wide cross section of society. Wherever possible, expressing the issue in simple language that is linked to culturally important values should be used. Framing is particularly important if the change sought involves a redistribution of power and if it will therefore generate significant opposition.

---

10. John Gaventa and Rosemary McGee, *Citizen Action and National Policy Reform* (London: Zed Books, 2010), 11.

This last point about framing is central. Knowing all about the issue you want to address and being clear about what changes you are seeking are important first steps, but finding the right frame for your issue is critically important. In the context of a polarized national political debate, you might need more than one frame.

In Canada today, this poses a particular challenge for those seeking social reforms that have been traditionally framed in liberal terms (for example, for the common good or taking care of the most needy) but must now be framed in newly dominant conservative terms (for example, freedom, individual choice, loyalty, security, or free markets). Increasingly the battle for policy change is determined by the advocate who frames the issue in the most compelling way, whatever the merits of the change being proposed. Classic examples of this are the debates about abortion policy (pro-choice versus pro-life) and tax policy (public investment versus tax relief). Effective advocacy relies upon being able to frame the changes you seek in terms that resonate with the values of your audience.

Joseph Overton, the former director of the Mackinac Centre for Public Policy, pointed to an additional aspect of framing: the range of politically acceptable options. His concept, called the Overton Window,[11] says that at any point in time there is a range of politically acceptable policy options and that some options represent too great a political risk to be considered. When your advocacy is directed to options outside the Overton Window, the task is to expand or to move the window. For example, an advocate might propose much more radical changes to pull the window in a particular direction, knowing the radical changes being articulated could never (or not soon) be realized. Greenpeace boats that defy whaling ships are an example of radical action that helps pull the window toward Greenpeace's view. Otherwise the wider public might be tolerant of whaling, which largely takes place well out of sight. This time-consuming process of pulling political discourse toward the Overton Window has been used very effectively by conservative think tanks in recent decades to move popular political discourse toward freedom and security rather than compassion and tolerance.

Framing played a key role in the campaign to untie Canadian food aid. The original framing for the Canadian food aid program

---

11. Wikipedia, "Overton Window," http://en.wikipedia.org/wiki/Overton_window.

was to do good for others while helping Canadian farmers. Advocates gradually shifted the focus to cost effectiveness and to rapid delivery of food after an emergency. This shift has still not happened in the USA, where groups benefiting from the procurement of food aid at home have maintained the focus on domestic benefits.

When Asking Nicely is not Enough—Opening Closed Doors

Sometimes reasoned discourse with government produces nothing because there is no willingness to engage in dialogue or consider changes. At times like this other tactics are necessary. The CSOs involved in civil society work on agriculture and trade fought hard among themselves over their own role in relation to the role that the WTO should have in regulating agricultural trade. La Via Campesina denied that the WTO should play any role, and refused to engage with trade officials because they did not want to lend legitimacy to the organization. Most of the development NGOs involved in the issues believed it was important to engage with trade officials so as to influence their decisions. Many people understood both sides of the argument and saw the advantages of a combined strategy, a strategy in which the protests and demonstrations in the street lent strength and credibility to the arguments of the policy analysis presented in the corridors and seminar rooms. We agree that both the "outside" and "inside" strategies (as they were known) were necessary and in-strumental in bringing governments to the point of listening to civil society voices. Of course, knowing you need both strategies does not make them easy to achieve!

In some instances, the non-violent witness of CSOs has con-fronted the violence of the state to demand respect for human rights. One such organization was started by fourteen women who met at the historic May Square in Buenos Aries in 1977 to demand to know from the military government what had happened to their children, all of whom had been imprisoned by the military junta or had "dis-appeared." Most of the "disappeared" were murdered, and their bodies were dropped out at sea or buried without trace. No information was ever provided to the families of the missing. The movement grew and became known as The Mothers of May Square, women who met every week, wearing white headscarves embroidered with the names of their missing children. The women risked imprisonment and death (three of the original fourteen organizers were murdered by the regime) and became a powerful voice for human rights in the face of brutal political oppression.

A number of governments have used public fear of terrorist attacks to curtail their citizens' freedom of speech and action. For example, the organization Article 19 has documented the effects of several legal changes in Britain, justified by government as necessary to fight terrorism but deeply worrying from the perspective of protecting civil liberties.[12] In our Speaking Out class, we heard about the Ethiopian government's clamp down on the use of the Internet, which people were using for low-cost, long-distance telephoning. The clamp down effectively cut off the sizable Ethiopian diaspora population from contact with family and friends who still live in Ethiopia. It is a constant struggle for civil society to resist this kind of oppression.

While celebrating the examples of CSOs that organize to fight oppression peacefully, we note that there are groups that fit the definition of civil society but that do not respect basic norms of tolerance and non-violence. Throughout history, civil society has turned to violence, or condoned violence, when its members see no other avenue. The fight against apartheid in South Africa was long and bloody. Many groups eschewed all violence, even in the face of violent oppression. Others did not. The African National Congress saw violent struggle as necessary in the 1960s but when Nelson Mandela came out of prison in 1990, he led a peaceful transition to multiparty democracy, against very significant odds. The People's Power Revolution that overthrew the Marcos regime in the Philippines in 1986, and the Czechoslovakian Velvet Revolution in 1989, are other powerful examples of civil societies bringing about lasting political change in the face of repressive states without surrendering to violence themselves.

History teaches us that a simple polite request to those in power, even with well-marshalled arguments, is seldom enough to make

---

12. Article 19, Global Campaign for Free Expression, "The Impact of UK Anti-terror Laws on Freedom of Expression," (Accessed April 9, 2014.) http://www.article19.org/data/files/pdfs/analysis/terrorism-submission-to-icj-panel.pdf.

change. We also need to stand strong and stand together, to bear witness to injustice by talking about it, documenting it, and broadcasting it. Many professional NGOs are too quick to dismiss the contribution that resistors make, choosing instead to speak quietly (or worse, not at all) for fear of compromising their access to those in power. It is important to remember that the door one walks through may be opening only because others, more outspoken, are keeping up real pressure for change. Knowing when to be silent, when to talk, and when to walk out is not easy. The drama, with all its tensions, can be illustrated by the meeting in Canada in early 2013 between the Assembly of First Nations and Prime Minister Stephen Harper that Chief Theresa Spence of Attawapiskat refused to attend. She insisted that, without a representative of the Queen present, the talks would not meet her minimum sense of legal formality. These are not situations for a manual or a checklist, but for debate and discussion and, in all likelihood, disagreement. Striving for mutual respect in the face of disagreement has to be the starting point.

Evaluating, Adjusting, and Measuring Progress

Very often advocacy campaigners are so busy with the work of "the next step" that they do not take the time to stop and consider what has changed since the campaign started and what those changes mean for "next steps." There is an important balance to be struck between getting on with the work and taking stock of what has changed so as to keep the advocacy strategy relevant. Not only can such reflection lead to changes in the strategy but it may even lead to a review and restatement of the advocacy goals of the campaign.

The process of evaluating advocacy efforts and measuring progress is something policy advocates need to consider when they determine their advocacy goal and strategies at the outset. A key characteristic of a well-stated goal is its measurability: that is, how will you know whether you have succeeded or not? Some goals are readily measured; for example, increasing girls' participation in elementary school or increasing the number of infants receiving vaccinations. Others are harder to discern because so many influences are at work simultaneously and in interaction with each other. Tools do exist to help with the task. See Michael Patton's book, *Developmental Evaluation* for some exciting examples.[13]

Evaluation is not useful just for measuring progress toward meeting a specific goal. It is also useful to examine the assumptions upon which the advocacy program is based. Sometimes it is these assumptions that are the problem. One of the ways of making these assumptions more obvious is by the use of a tool called "the theory of change" with which you construct a model of how you think the change you are seeking will take place. The Canadian food aid untying campaign is an example of the initial failure to achieve the goal being due to the assumption that developing a solid economic and development case would be sufficient to cause the change. The model was flawed and it was only when the politics of other stakeholders were included that the change we sought was achieved.

Beyond simply measuring the achievement of a specific policy goal, evaluation should also consider progress on broader outcomes that underlie civil society advocacy more generally, including the following:

- Strengthening the practice of citizenship and participation
- Strengthening the responsiveness and accountability of governments
- Developing an inclusive and cohesive society

As noted by Gaventa and McGee,

> "Success" can be understood in many different ways, especially among the different actors in a broad based campaign or social movement. In general, robust and sustainable changes require campaigns which link the national to the local and which pay attention to the processes of empowering citizens and deepening democratic governance as well as to effecting policy change itself.[14]

---

13. Michael Quinn Patton, *Developmental Evaluation: Applying Complexity Concepts to Enhance Innovation and Use* (New York: Guilford Press, 2011).
14. Gaventa, *Citizen Action*, 35.

Assessing where we are and where we have come from can be tough but also inspiring. CSOs often work on the margins, in relative powerlessness, persuaded by their commitment to justice but facing an opposition that is better funded and better connected to political power. It can be disheartening if we look at only a single measure. Seeing the impact of our work on a range of outcomes can help avoid burnout.

Tools for Civil Society Advocacy

Principles of Persuasion

Another way of looking at the task of advocacy is in terms of persuasion. Persuasion is more effective if it is grounded in some simple principles:

- Reciprocity: In relating to those you are seeking to persuade, be mindful of the potential for each side to gain some benefit from the change you seek. This is often a feature of successful advocacy.
- Consistency with Commitments: Look for ways that the change you seek is consistent with commitments already made by those you need to persuade.
- Authority of the Source: Marshal your arguments using highly credible sources right from the start. This is particularly important for your credibility, which, once lost, is very difficult to regain.
- Validation: Look for successful examples where others have made the change that you want to make. Policy makers will want to know whether the change you propose has ever been tried and whether it works. If you can demonstrate it has, you have a more powerful case.
- Scarcity: Particularly in politics, timing is critical. If you can show that the opportunity to make a successful policy change is limited to a particular time period, there is added impetus to make that change.

- Friendship: Friendly relationships make communications more effective but must never be allowed to become manipulative. If manipulation is even suspected, the doors to effective communication can close quickly. Looking for common ground and even mutual advantage can be important, but it depends upon honesty and trust. Like credibility, once trust is lost, it is very difficult to re-establish.

The Elevator Speech

Whether for awareness-raising or for policy change, gaining the support of a large number of people requires that an advocate be able to express succinctly what he or she wants. This is sometimes referred to as the "elevator speech": the ability to explain what you want to change, why it needs to be changed, how the change you propose will solve the problem and, possibly, what the listener can do about it—all in less than the time of an elevator journey and for a person who is a total stranger to you and your cause. Creating an effective three-to-five minute narrative is an important test of whether you have really understood and refined the essence of the change you seek. This speech will be essential for communications with the media and important in public meetings. It should bear repeating, perhaps many times, and should also be worked into longer interventions and statements.

Developing an elevator speech necessarily involves reducing the complexity of the issue. Simpler must not become oversimplification, however, or the argument will be vulnerable to dismissal by those who oppose you. Be careful to test the "elevator speech" with your supporters—and, ideally, even with some friendly opposition—before using it more widely. Nonetheless, and especially when looking for the attention of government officials, an advocate's ability to say succinctly what should change and how it should be changed is vital to success.

The Policy Brief

Particularly when relating to elected officials, it is also important to have a concise written document that makes the case for the change you want to promote. The written version must have the elements of an "elevator speech" but should also address the complexities of the political process. Consideration of the Overton Window and the principles of persuasion are important. The keys to an effective policy brief are brevity and quality. Though the length is to some extent dependent on the nature of the issue, the rule of thumb is not more than two pages (and some issues can be dealt with in one page) of carefully and clearly written text. Avoid creating an advertisement! The outline provided by Amanda Sussman is useful.[15]

- A simple brief title followed by the name of your organization.
- A one-line summary of the topic of the brief: what the issue is, what the solution is.
- Some background on the issue and the reason for your interest. (This is key to transparency and to avoiding any perception of manipulation.)
- The rationale for the proposed solution including, if possible, where this solution has been used successfully.
- The immediate action requested of the official (the "ask").
- Your contact information.

Communication Strategy

Communication refers primarily to work with mass media (for example, newspapers, radio, and television) and increasingly with newer media such as blogs, Facebook, and Twitter. It is important to have a deliberate and carefully thought-out strategy for these activities because putting out public messages is not only highly political but is also a very quick way to destroy your credibility if the messages are not carefully thought through. Communication via the media is both powerful and risky.

An effective communication strategy should be closely linked to your advocacy plans. The strategy should be calibrated, whether to a lower or higher profile. A low-profile communication strategy seeks to build public awareness of an issue through such actions as providing human interest stories showing the consequences of a policy

---

15. Amanda Sussman, *The Art of the Possible: A Handbook for Political Activism* (Toronto: McClelland & Stewart, 2007), 221.

that you are seeking to change. A high-profile strategy seeks to exert political pressure on the government and might include large advertisements in a national newspaper, interviews on major radio or television stations, or publicity stunts that attract media attention. A high-profile strategy can be costly, both in financial and reputational terms, but can also be highly effective. Particularly if you are working with government officials while producing and engaging in a high-profile campaign, it is wise to alert them to your action before the high-profile campaign is launched. Embarrassing public officials is a sure way to make future collaboration with them much more difficult.

Submitting a letter to the editor of a newspaper, a common low-profile communication strategy early in an advocacy campaign, can be an easy way to get your issue noticed. There are often many competing demands for this kind of space, however, so it is important to make your letter as "newsworthy" as possible. Some of the ways of doing this follow:

- Use clear language adjusted to the educational level of the likely readers.
- Make sure the issue you are raising is easy to understand, even if simplification is necessary. Include no more than one or two central ideas.
- If possible, relate the issue to a real person. Human interest is part of newsworthiness.
- Keep it short. A five-hundred-word limit is common.

Test your letter with others to check it very carefully for any errors. If you can get a letter to the editor published it will make it easier to generate future media interest. A follow-up might include a request to meet with the editorial board, to see if the newspaper would consider an editorial on the question. Particularly for local issues and local media, this can be very effective. National media are far less accessible for most NGO campaigners.

With the advent of online publishing, blogs have also become a tool for advocacy work. A blog can be a way to build a sustained audience for issues that are poorly understood or that will take time to change, issues such as more accountable use of overseas aid budgets. A successful advocacy blog becomes a repertoire of successful examples of change, offering clear explanations of difficult issues and a "go-to" place for the latest analysis or debate on a topic. An example from the world of development is the "From Poverty to Power" blog authored by Duncan Green at Oxfam GB.[16]

Use of New Media

New media such as Facebook and Twitter rose to sudden prominence during the "Arab Spring" in 2011 and have continued to be import-ant tools of communication for protesters everywhere the Internet is available. But such tools can also be used in more modest ways. Facebook is a powerful way to spread an idea if your audience is likely to use this social networking tool. Humour, and even ridicule, can be important to ensure that your message gets passed on widely. As the case study on the 59 Cent Campaign below illustrates, having an easy, fun activity linked to your message can also increase the reach of your message.

Twitter, in addition to being a way to communicate quickly with many people as an issue begins to pick up, can also increase your pol-itical influence. If Twitter "traffic" picks up on a particular issue, this is likely to be noticed by pollsters and political parties, who then feel the pressure to act quickly to be seen to respond. Some commentators credit Twitter with playing an important role in creating a meeting be-tween the Canadian prime minister and First Nations leaders during the Idle No More campaign. It is also a good way to quickly identify potential allies in the advocacy you are pursuing.

One of the common critiques of the new media is the difficulty of sustaining interest in an issue for any length of time. Groups such as Avaaz command many millions of signatories on their petitions, but there is no easy way to turn those signatures into a sustained cam-paign. While these are fair insights, it is also clear that the new media have provided tools that campaigners have used with great effective-ness to shift public opinion on issues and also to raise awareness of human rights injustices and environmental disasters. These media are

---

16. Duncan Green, "Missing in Action, Why NGOs Shy away from Geopolitics," Oxfam: From Poverty to Power, http://oxfamblogs.org/fp2p/missing-in-action-why-do-ngos-shy-away-from-geopolitics/.

very new and still in evolution. Most NGOs and many social movements have embraced the technologies as cheap and effective in a world in which the ownership of major media outlets (newspapers, radio, and television) is highly concentrated and to some extent discredited by scandal.

Students in Action—The 59 Cent Campaign

Appropriate to our life work, and to the work of the Canadian School of Peacebuilding, we conclude this chapter by relating an incident of social advocacy undertaken by novices who were guided by the above principles, the 59 Cent Campaign. These advocates were CSOP students in our 2012 course, *Speaking Out ... And Being Heard—Citizen Advocacy.*

The students were asked to work in teams to construct an advocacy plan. One group of students chose to work on the issue of government-funded health care to refugees in Canada. The federal government had announced it was going to end all health care for refugees who did not suffer from a contagious disease. The policy was to take effect within weeks of the time of the course. This student group had calculated that the cost of providing health care to all refugees was equivalent to fifty-nine cents per Canadian per year, and so the students' key strategy was to encourage the public to mail fifty-nine cents to the Prime Minister's Office. The money was sent with a message urging the Prime Minister to restore funding. The campaigners' message and the accompanying video were so compelling that the entire class encouraged them to actually undertake the campaign. After some hasty contact with other groups working on this issue, including refugee advocacy groups and associations of health workers and doctors, they posted their video to YouTube, created a Facebook page and a Twitter account, and began spreading the word. They reached out to news media and got coverage in local papers.

After the initial burst of enthusiasm and evidence of widespread participation in this action, the resources to continue the work were limited. The Canadian government did respond positively to the demand of the campaign but only partially: it restored health care funding to just twenty percent of the refugees. However, several unplanned outcomes of the campaign were also significant:

- The students involved realized that creative ideas can become the source of unexpected power.
- The students learned the importance of establishing links with other groups pursuing similar interests (Canadian Doctors for Refugee Care, Mennonite Central Committee).
- The importance of building a sustainable resource base for advocacy campaigns (in this case, mostly time and energy) was made very clear.
- The issue of refugee health care was brought to the attention of hundreds of young adults.

The students involved remained engaged on the issue and encouraged their supporters to take part in a Christmas card campaign to remind the government of the unfinished work of restoring funding for refugee health care. The issue is still in the news and in the public eye.

Conclusion

We both took great pleasure in teaching a short course on advocacy experiences for CSOP. Though the course was not overtly about peace-building, both of us understand citizen advocacy to be a cornerstone of democracy. Democracies are founded on the principle of civic and political engagement by the *demos*—the people. That engagement is a responsibility, too. Too few societies in the world today allow civil society its voice. Those of us who enjoy democratic government must accept civic engagement as one of the necessary, if informal, institutions that make our governments work.

Our experiences are a reflection of the times in which we live and work. Democratic institutions change over time, and the relative importance of tools such as testimony before parliamentary committees or opinion pieces in newspapers will ebb and flow. Yet the basic methodology of change as set out in this chapter will persist.

If you want political change, you need to find out who is in charge and what they think, find out who else is affected by the problem and why they might welcome (or fear) change, and consider why others in your society who are not so directly involved might care. Speaking up and being heard will give you the satisfaction of contributing to

problem-solving by peaceful means while allowing you the opportunity to meet and work with a wonderful community of similarly
engaged citizens. We can assure you there is much joy to be had in
the struggle!

Bibliography

Article 19, Global Campaign for Free Expression. "The Impact of
     UK Anti-terror Laws on Freedom of Expression." (Accessed
     April 9, 2014.) http://www.article19.org/data/files/pdfs/analysis/
     terrorism-submission-to-icj-panel.pdf.
BBC World Service Online. "What is Civil Society?" July 5, 2001.
     (Accessed April 30, 2014.) http://www.bbc.co.uk/worldservice/
     people/highlights/010705_civil.shtml.
Chandhoke, Neera. "What the Hell is Civil Society?" March 17, 2005.
     (Accessed November 6, 2014.) http://www.opendemocracy.net/
     democracy-open_politics/article_2375.jsp.
Edwards, Michael. *The Rise and Rise of Civil Society.* (Accessed April
     30, 2014.) *www.futurepositive.org/docs/**RISE**.doc.*
Fisher, Tibor. *Under the Frog,* New York: Picador USA, 1992.
Gaventa, John, and Rosemary McGee. *Citizen Action and National
     Policy Reform.* London: Zed Books, 2010.
Green, Duncan. "Missing in Action, Why NGOs Shy away from
     Geopolitics." Oxfam: From Poverty to Power. (Accessed April
     30, 2014.) http://oxfamblogs.org/fp2p/missing-in-action-why-
     do-ngos-shy-away-from-geopolitics/.
Hothschild, Adam. *Bury the Chains: Prophets and Rebels in the Fight
     to Free an Empire's Slaves,* Boston: Houghton Mifflin Company,
     2005.
Murphy, Sophia. *Trade and Food Security: An Assessment of the
     Uruguay Round Agreement on Agriculture,* London: Catholic
     Institute for International Relations, 1999.
Patton, Michael Quinn. *Developmental Evaluation: Applying
     Complexity Concepts to Enhance Innovation and Use.* New York:
     Guildford Press, 2011.

Sussman, Amanda. *The Art of the Possible: A Handbook for Political Activism.* Toronto: McClelland & Stewart, 2007.
Wikipedia. "Overton Window." (Accessed April 30, 2014.) http:// en.wikipedia.org/wiki/Overton_window.

Additional Resources

Edwards, Michael, and John Gaventa, eds. *Global Citizen Action: Perspectives and Challenges.* USA: Lynne Rienner and Europe: Earthscan, 2001.
Green, Duncan and Phil Bloomer. "NGOs in Economic Decision Diplomacy." In *The New Economic Diplomacy: Decision-Making and Negotiation in International Economic Relations*, edited by Nicholas Bayne and Stephen Woolcock. Surrey, England: Ashgate Publishing Limited, 2011.
John Howard Yoder. *The Christian Witness to the State.* 2nd ed. Waterloo, Ontario: Herald Press, 2002.
Jordan, Lisa, and Peter van Tuijl. "Political Responsibility in Transnational NGO Advocacy." *World Development* 28 (2000): 2051–65.
Pimbert, Michel. "Putting Citizens at the Heart of Food System Governance." Briefing. London: International Institute for Environment and Development. (Accessed April 30, 2014.) http://pubs.iied.org/pdfs/17125IIED.pdf.

Combining the Strengths of the Insider and Outsider in the Peacebuilding Process

—Dave Dyck

Case Study Introduction

THE CALL WAS LIKE SO MANY others we have received over the years. A highly placed regional administrator within the Canadian health care system was phoning from northern Ontario, a neighbouring province. A particular nursing unit within the hospital in a small town had been experiencing some tensions within the team.

The administrator explained that, although she had tried to provide informal assistance to the hospital's chief administrative officer, this was proving challenging, in part because she herself was based several hundred kilometres away in a larger town, where most of the provincial government's regional offices were located. It was also difficult because she had limited patience for what she considered "high-maintenance people and trivial complaints." "But don't get me wrong," she quickly added, "my door is always open. I mean, I mediate every day. There's always something to work out between people, especially in health care, right? In a situation like this, though—just between you and me—I really think some people just need to grow up and do their jobs."

Things had recently escalated to the point at which she had sought advice from a colleague in Manitoba, the province in which our conflict-resolution firm is based. Her colleague had recommended our group of mediators on the basis of having used our services on numerous occasions in the past at a major hospital in Winnipeg, the largest city in Manitoba.

The Ontario-based leader, pleased at the prospect of using a service provider from another province—and therefore presumably less likely to have biases or other political entanglements—called us the very next day. A face-to-face meeting soon took place, and she contracted with us to complete a workplace assessment.

We were to interview twenty-seven staff members and then report to her as to possible next steps to remedy the situation via group mediation. Beyond the hospital's chief administrative officer, the group of interviewees was to include fourteen nurses (one of whom was the head nurse and several of whom held senior positions), four nurse practitioners, four nurse's aides, and four administrative support staff. There were "power and ego issues," she informed us that were related to the varying degrees of professional status and salary associated with these roles. Twenty-four of the twenty-seven people we would interview were women.

As we stood to exit the room at the conclusion of our meeting, the administrator suddenly paused with her hand on the door and, as an apparent afterthought, added,

> Oh, there is one other thing. As you know, the town in which the hospital is located has a significant Aboriginal population, and our nursing staff is no different. About twenty-five to thirty percent are Aboriginal[17] and most of them are members of the local First Nation.

---

17. In Canada, various terms are used to refer to the peoples who are Indigenous to North America. The terminology set is complex and is not used consistently. Three websites are listed at the end of this footnote to provide access to some details regarding this terminology set.

For the purposes of this chapter, I will use the terms First Nations, Aboriginal, and/or Indigenous interchangeably. When so doing, I am referring to the various nations (each with distinctive language, culture, customs, traditions, and territory) who were living in North America for an estimated 10,000–30,000 years prior to the arrival of European settlers in the sixteenth century.

Although treaties were eventually signed between the European powers and many of the First Nations, the history of relations between European and Indigenous peoples in the country, now called Canada —like peoples

Besides the nurses' union, then, you might want to place a quick call to the local executive director at the band office. Some of our staff have made him aware of the tensions in the unit and—although we certainly won't involve him and the band directly—it probably can't hurt to keep him informed in a general way. He'll be very supportive.

Upon making the phone call the administrator had suggested, we discovered a different reality. The executive director, along with the chief and three band councillors, actually had grave concerns about the proposed process. Feeling that they had been ignored repeatedly in the past when attempting to raise awareness of the concerns of their people— whether they were people employed by or seeking the services of the local health care system—they now had very little faith in the administrator, in anything she might initiate, or in anyone she might enlist.

By proxy, then, they distrusted us. After all, no one had even consulted them about our involvement. No, they concluded, they felt

---

in many other nations around the world—is largely one of pain, exploitation, and trauma. Beyond negotiation of treaties, a process many consider to have been duplicitous and exploitative in and of itself, European nations and the government of Canada used various forms of coercion, including armed force, to seize lands, to outlaw Indigenous customs and languages, to remove children from the care of their parents and communities, and generally to attempt to impose assimilation on Indigenous peoples.

Despite some efforts now underway to face this legacy of abuse, so as to engender trauma recovery and reconciliation (please see the Canadian Truth & Reconciliation Commission reports), Aboriginal people in Canada continue to suffer under much higher-than-average rates of poverty and incarceration. They also remain under-represented in positions of societal status and influence. Put simply, racism against First Nation peoples, and distrust and disconnection between Canadians of European and Indigenous descent, remain significant challenges in Canadian society.

Three websites that offer insights into the terminology sets used to indicate or to describe Indigenous peoples in Canada follow: Aboriginal Affairs and Northern Development Canada, *Terminology.* (Accessed July 5, 2014.) http://www.aadnc-aandc.gc.ca/eng/1100100014642/1100100014643. The University of British Columbia, *First Nations Studies Program*, (Accessed July 5, 2014.) http://indigenousfoundations.arts.ubc.ca/home/identity/terminology.html. National Aboriginal Health Organization, Publications, (Accessed July 5, 2014.) http://www.naho.ca/publications/topics/terminology/.

that they had no choice but to counsel their members, the Aboriginal people on staff in the nursing unit at the hospital, to avoid cooperating with, or engaging, the process we were proposing. In other words, we were starting from a deep deficit.

When we eventually proceeded to the workplace assessment—with the blessing of the Aboriginal leadership, which came about only after many hours of listening and intentional inclusion in process design—our twenty-seven interviews revealed more than just a few team tensions or "trivial complaints." We discovered a deeply divided and wounded staff.

Many of the Indigenous employees shared painful and traumatic stories of discrimination. Many non-Indigenous staff shared their beliefs that racist statements and attitudes against First Nations people were indeed commonplace, and they reported feeling deeply disturbed. Other non-Indigenous staff members denied the presence of racism on the nursing unit or at the hospital. This group accused some of the Aboriginal staff members of isolating themselves and operating in a "work to rule" mindset. In some cases they went further, contending that it was they, as non-Aboriginal people, who were being mistreated by their Aboriginal peers on the basis of their ethnicity. In other words, they alleged that it was in fact they—as Caucasian people—who were the victims of "reverse discrimination."

Beyond the issue of racism, numerous staff members of Aboriginal and non-Aboriginal background also spoke of grossly hierarchical relations in which those with less professional status were ridiculed by some of those with more status. Leadership was almost universally viewed as entirely ineffectual at addressing any of these concerns. Some leaders were viewed as culpable because they had permitted the destructive behaviours to continue unchecked. In one case, a unit leader was viewed as having actually engaged in or having promoted the discriminatory and abusive behaviour.

We were told that a toxic, disrespectful, elitist, and—at times—openly racist atmosphere had been allowed to develop, to fester, and to proliferate. Even the regional administrator who had contracted with our firm to do the workplace assessment was viewed with suspicion by some of the nursing staff because she had taken too long to act. Many reported feeling hopeless, cynical, angry, and/or isolated.

Dilemmas and Challenges

There were many dilemmas and challenges raised by such a case. For example, we were immediately conscious of our limits as a mediation firm comprising mostly Canadians of European descent. Closely related was the question of how to build trust and to work inclusively and effectively with local First Nation leaders and hospital staff who exhibited a deep distrust of leaders in the health care system and who, by proxy, distrusted us. On the other hand, how might we accomplish the above without—at the same time—alienating the people and entities who hired us and without alienating the numerous nursing staff who believed there was no reason to include First Nations band leadership in matters they considered internal to the hospital?

These attitudes of distrust, in turn, were reflective of a health care system, of a hospital, and of nursing department leadership and staff—non-Indigenous and Indigenous—who had little to no consciousness of white privilege or of racism at the individual, institutional, or historical level. In addition, like most institutional settings in Canada, hospital leaders had little, if any, conflict resolution or interpersonal communication training. On the contrary, in many cases, leaders had developed counterproductive habits in these areas.

Entering a situation that clearly included the presence of long-standing injustices and agitation (mental, emotional, physical, and spiritual) we also needed to consider carefully how we might cultivate a listening and non-anxious presence, while also making room for truth telling and strong emotions. As professional mediators earning a living doing this work, how could we ensure that we were not unduly beholden—and did not appear to be unduly beholden—to only one stakeholder in the process, in this case leaders in the health care system who were paying our wage? Finally, and most critically, from the perspective of the purpose of this chapter, how might we, as *outsiders,* give effective leadership to a mediation process that simultaneously would grow the justice and peacebuilding capacity of those *insiders* who would remain in the situation long after we have departed?

Purpose of this Chapter

The focus of this chapter has been foreshadowed in the preceding narrative. The focus is upon an expression of disharmony within the local health care system, involving *insiders*, and between the local people and those of us who were brought in to assist the local people, involving *outsiders*. Bound within these relationships were questions of *neutrality* and *partiality*: Who was able to provide a *balanced* perspective on the issues and on the actions of the people involved in the state of disharmony? "Insiders, outsiders, neutrality, partiality," and "balance" constitute a terminology set that is integral to the work of peacebuilding, terminology that will be the focus of the chapter. These terms will be used to describe the complexities that attend the work of peacebuilders.

Based on my experience as a peacebuilding practitioner over the past two decades, including my experiences as an instructor at the Canadian School of Peacebuilding, it is my belief that the dynamics and dilemmas described above are common to many parts of the world. Wherever one finds people gathered together—working, playing, living, worshipping—one finds conflict. And likewise, where one finds conflict, one also frequently encounters relationships steeped in generational trauma involving clashes and/or abuse between different identity groups.

Yet the core questions remain the same: How then shall we live together? How shall we work together? How can we begin to recover? How might we as peacebuilding practitioners respond to the individual, interpersonal, and small group wounds within our everyday, immediate reality—that is, within our current schools, hospitals, factories, homes, and places of worship—in such a way as to recognize the roots of those wounds in a larger past, and their place in a much longer journey of large scale, societal truth telling and healing? How can we respond to the micro-reality of a particular situation in which we find ourselves, while not neglecting to attend to its connection to a larger systemic reality? And how might we sow the seeds for future well-being by recognizing and investing in the internal resources found in any given situation? Language permits us to think well about the questions; it also permits us to reflect upon possible answers.

Paul Wehr and John Paul Lederach introduced the terms "insider-partial "and "outsider-neutral" to the discipline of peacebuilding.[18] They set out the tension between *insiders* who are partial to one position or another and *outsiders* who are neutral, noting that the *insider-partial* participant is particularly important in resolving disputes, and that the insider-outsider tension is culturally nuanced. Ultimately I will challenge the notion of "neutrality" as an appropriate description for either the outsider or insider. In my experience, all effective forms of mediation are grounded in the cultivation of an authentic relationship and rapport (versus distance) and all third-party helpers are partial to something.

It is because of the commonplace nature of these dynamics and the degree to which many of the accompanying dilemmas and questions can begin to be addressed through recognizing the role of the *insider-partial* mediator, that I led a course at the Canadian School of Peacebuilding on this topic in the summer of 2011. The course was designed for those who have strong stakes, or partialities, in the conflicts in which they are attempting to mediate; that is, they are not impartial. Likewise, rather than being geared to those who seek to provide assistance through their status as an *outsider-neutral,* which most North American mediation training focuses on, this course was intended to equip those who need to mediate between people they know well and with whom they share much history, some of it not so good.

In this chapter I will offer a description of the insider role, discussing how it continues to surface as a valuable asset in my work, in the context of an urbanized Canadian setting. I will review the more frequently catalogued role of the outsider, and will explore how it has achieved its current place of ascendancy in Western settings, as well as some of the unique advantages it brings. Of particular interest for my purposes, however, will be the exploration of the nexus of these two forms of mediation: that is, how, in many escalated and complex situations, outsiders and insiders can be brought together to function

---

18. Paul Wehr and John Paul Lederach, "Mediating Conflict in Central America," in *Resolving International Conflicts: The Theory and Practice of Mediation,* ed. Jacob Bercovitch. (Boulder, CO: Lynne Rienner Publishers, 1996), 56. http://books.google.com/books?id=rT0xjgkexCcC.

much more powerfully and effectively as a team than either could hope to do on their own.

Thus, the goals of this chapter are threefold. First is to inspire and equip mediators like me—who primarily occupy the role of outsider—to recognize and embrace the wisdom of working more closely with insiders. Second is to inspire and equip insiders to embrace the possibility of a more active conciliatory role in those very situations in which they may have thought themselves to be ineligible due to their strong stakes and close relationships. Third, in both cases, I will seek to illustrate how these things can be accomplished through the lens of our hospital case study.

Hallmarks of the Insider

The insider as mediator is a much older role than that of the outsider.[19] In any situation—throughout history and continuing today—in which the parties in conflict know one another and participate in the same larger web of relationships (such as a hospital nursing unit) they often naturally seek out third parties known to both to address their problems. However, emphases of the third-party insider in responding to situations of conflict or harm differ from those of the outsider. These differences include the presence of connection and relationship (versus distance) as the key to gaining access to the dispute, the role of community status or institutional standing (versus training) in legitimizing the mediator's function, the expectation of wise evenhandedness[20] (versus neutrality) in the facilitation of the process, and

---

19. See, for example, John Paul Lederach, *Preparing for Peace* (Syracuse, NY: Syracuse University Press, 1995).

20. C. H. Mike Yarrow, *Quaker Experiences in International Conciliation* (London: Yale University Press Ltd, 1978), 165. Another way to describe what is meant by "wise evenhandedness" can be found by turning to the work of Quaker conciliator Mike Yarrow, who coined the term "balanced partiality." The term—as Yarrow employs it—suggests that the oft-assumed goal of pure impartiality on the part of the third-party helper is neither realistic nor desirable from a descriptive or prescriptive standpoint. While it is true that insiders will inevitably have more significant emotional and substantive connection to the parties and issues, all mediators—whether insider or outsider—have partialities, and all eventually develop relationships with the

the place for advice-giving, influence, and "say" (versus no voice) in ultimately deciding/resolving the matters in dispute. As defined above, workplace leaders (for example, supervisors, union representatives, human resource consultants) are often well positioned to play the role of the insider mediator when it comes to workplace conflict.

Hallmarks of the Outsider

In a highly urbanized, more individualistic social context, like that of twenty-first century Canadian society in which people are no longer as connected to a web of relationships, the role of the outsider mediator has emerged. Emphases include the importance of equidistance and lack of relationship (versus relationship) for gaining access to the dispute, the need for specialized training and professional status (versus community or organizational standing) to legitimize the mediator's function, the expectation of impartiality (versus balanced partiality) in the facilitation of the process, and the expectation that the mediator will facilitate disputant choice and self-determination (versus giving advice and influencing the outcome of the dispute). As defined above, people with specialized training, education (for example, mediation certificates or conflict-resolution degrees), and experience in leading group processes as a non-stakeholder are thus often best positioned to take up the role of outsider mediator in the workplace.

Current Ascendancy of the Outsider Role

Insider forms of mediation as described above have virtually no profile in current mainstream, Canadian consciousness.[21] By contrast,

---

principals in conflict. Rather than deny or hide from these realities the goal should be to exhibit transparency and balance. All mediators should know what their biases are and should be prepared to share them, as necessary and appropriate, with the people in conflict with whom they are working. Likewise, all mediators must acknowledge and attend to the state of their own relationships with the disputants and with the clients. Ultimately, mediators—both insiders *and* outsiders—must acknowledge that their partialities and relationships will influence their own behaviour, the parties themselves, and the outcomes of the disputes in which they provide assistance.

21. Exceptions to this general mainstream trend are important to acknowledge. In my professional experience, people who retain a strong sense of

outsider forms of mediation have been on the rise for the past forty years, and particularly since the 1980s. Simply put, when people in Canada hear the word "mediation," they generally think of suits and ties and a formal, professional role not unlike that of therapist, doctor, or lawyer. They do not generally picture informal, insider, forms of the practice.

But does this matter? And what might it mean for responding to peacebuilding challenges like the one presented by our hospital case study?

It matters because, when a situation like the one involving trouble at the nursing department surfaces and people begin considering the option of a third-party helper, they generally picture an outsider and often give little consideration to the question of either turning to or developing insider resources. This, in turn, may seem like good news to the outsider mediator. From the standpoint of our having the opportunity to make use of our specialized training to provide assistance in a place of acute need, and our making a living, it is good news.

On the other hand, if the unilateral focus on our outsider expertise leads us and those we are assisting to neglect the insider aspects of the situation, it is also likely to result in—at least some—unintended negative consequences. For example, it makes it more likely that whatever peace we may succeed in building rests on a "false homeostasis"[22] —that is, a new level of apparent health that is not sustainable because it is too dependent on outsider involvement and therefore prone to disintegration upon our departure.

Beyond this, sometimes people in conflict situations instinctively distrust an over-reliance on outside resources, and they see a need to

---

connection to their traditional identity group(s)—be they ethnic, religious, geographic, socio-economic or all of the above—are more likely to continue to practice various forms of insider mediation (though they are perhaps unlikely to call it "mediation"). First- and even second-generation Canadian immigrants, for example, are likely to continue to be linked to an extended network of community and kin. These people are likely to turn to someone from within that network for third-party help with conflict and correspondingly less inclined to rely on outsiders.

22. I first heard this very helpful metaphor for the dangers of creating outsider dependency in dialogue with Kristine Paranica and Sarah Prom. At the time of this writing, both work for the Center for Conflict Resolution at the University of North Dakota.

find complementary insiders to integrate into a more holistic team approach. For example, in our case study it was some of the First Nations staff members, in particular, who distrusted an outsider of management's choosing and therefore felt the need to see one of their own (that is, insiders from among their staffing ranks, or from the First Nation band leadership, whom they knew and generally trusted more) working closely with the situation. Some of the management team at the regional level also saw the need to identify internal resource people from within the health care system to work closely with us so as to grow future capacity to address these situations more proactively and effectively.

Elements Common to Both Insider and Outsider Mediation

In order to gain a greater appreciation of the way in which the outsider and insider roles differ, but can function in a mutually complementary fashion, it is useful to consider the aspects that they share in common. Author John Paul Lederach has described five universal elements in the mediation process.[23] They are entry, gather perspectives, locate, arrange, and a way out. He elaborates as follows:

- **Entry**—The mediators need to gain access to the situation, in order to …
- **Gather perspectives**—get people talking and sharing, so that they can …
- **Locate**—what this is all about, in order to …
- **Arrange**—those necessary adjustments that will allow ……
- **A way out**—of the destructive patterns and/or stalemate.

To illustrate, let us contrast the ways in which each of these universal mediation elements was expressed—but in potentially complementary and mutually enhancing fashions—by the outsiders and insiders working on the nursing department conflict.

---

23. Lederach, *Preparing for Peace*, 94. I have adapted terms and concepts from Lederach's work. Helpful literature on insider-outsider dynamics can be found in Additional Resources at the end of this chapter.

Entry. Whereas our firm was invited in by a high-level, regional health care system administrator to do a workplace assessment as a function of our professional, outsider reputation, several First Nations members of the nursing staff chose to approach two band councillors from within their community for help with the same problem. Others chose to approach a particular doctor in the hospital who had earned their trust in the past. Still others approached a peer from an adjacent department over coffee, a peer who was well-regarded by most people on all sides and also happened to be the shop steward.

Gather perspectives. Outsiders generally approach the task of gathering perspectives in a highly structured way. It occurs at a specific place and time generally via the direction of one or two people hired for this purpose. In the hospital case study, our firm sent a team of four people (two female, two male; one Aboriginal person, three Euro-Canadians) to interview all twenty-seven staff members in one-hour blocks of time over a two-day period. At the same time, insiders were already engaged in the task of gathering perspectives but at multiple times and in a much more loosely structured way. The band councillors, the doctor, and the shop steward all began listening more carefully to the perspectives of the people with whom they had relationships within the nursing department. Some also looked for informal opportunities to connect with those they had not yet heard from, including venturing into conversations with other "side." This happened as a part of formal meetings in one or two instances, but also unfolded informally via "the grapevine", that is, over the punch bowl at a seasonal town gathering and in the stands at the local hockey game. They acted primarily in a sounding board capacity (that is, they listened to a lot of emotional venting) but, in some cases, began to also engage more actively in a coaching and/or advocacy capacity.

Locate. With an outsider, the emphasis tends to be primarily on the issues in the conflict, the content, and the decisions. For example, a typical outsider mediation firm tends to focus analysis and recommendations on those topics that have been identified as particularly divisive (for example, the abuse of sick time, the presence of racist humour, the lack of regular unit staff meetings) rather than on troubled relationships or communication patterns (for example, the widespread distrust, fear, and unhappiness, patterns or of not listening/ignoring in various interpersonal and group meeting contexts).[24] Insiders, in contrast, are often better positioned—especially initially—to understand the people and relationship dynamics involved. For example, the insiders in the hospital case concentrated their efforts less on naming divisive issues and more on trying to figure out who was not "getting along" with whom and why, including assessing (sometimes very quickly) who they thought was behaving inappropriately. Some insiders actively challenged the regional administrators—people more removed and with more authority—to get more involved. They wanted these higher-level leaders to acknowledge and investigate (rather than "look the other way") the events and people they kept hearing about.

Arrange. When it comes to the challenge of making arrangements and adjustments that may ultimately allow for resolution, outside mediators tend to place greater emphasis on individual self-determination by the parties who are directly involved in the conflict. With the hospital case study, this entailed bringing the staff and leaders from the nursing unit together to discuss the "hot" issues so as to take responsibility for past problems and for future solutions. The assumption is that if you can get those who actually have to interact on a daily basis to come together and engage one another about what each of them may need to each do differently going forward, the conflict will eventually be addressed.

Insider helpers, in contrast, tend to place more emphasis on their own solutions or advice or, alternatively, on the right and the responsibility of certain others (as opposed to the disputants themselves) to influence or decide who needs to do what differently. In our case study, the insider third parties took a more wide-ranging and varied approach to arranging solutions than our firm did. Some worked with a similar focus to us as outsiders; that is, they encouraged people in the unit to come together to "talk it out" and decide themselves. Others—especially those who came to believe that the problems were rooted exclusively in the inappropriate conduct of one side or one

---

24. In the case study, our mediation firm produced a written report of some twelve pages that included a bullet-point list of issues that needed attention, a description of the troubled relational dynamics, and a list of process-focused (versus solution-focused) options for attempting to address the concerns.

person—shifted into a stronger advocacy or advice-giving role. These people were not shy about promoting specific outcomes and/or advocating that management simply punish or terminate certain members of the unit. It must be said that some insiders became frustrated with us as outsiders for our reluctance to promote specific outcomes. In a few cases, insiders appeared to have a fundamental misunderstanding of our role, believing that we had both the responsibility and the capacity to enforce certain outcomes. This sense of impatience, this urgency to "get to the end," can probably be explained, at least in part, by insiders' proximity to the people and to the emotions involved.

A way out. With respect to ultimately finding ways out of the stalemates and dilemmas, outside mediators are often ultimately hoping to bring some sort of clarity or closure to those outstanding issues that were identified earlier in the process. In the nursing scenario, outsiders would typically strive for the creation of clear agreements and detailed, specific, future-oriented behavioural commitments on work-related issues such as the use of sick time, the use of electronic forms of communication, and the frequency and structure of unit staff meetings. Their hope in creating such agreements was that "flare ups" would occur much less frequently and overall organizational health and productivity would increase.

In contrast, insiders tend to be more focused on the overall feeling or morale of the group in question rather than on the specific elements mentioned above. In the nursing conflict, insiders consistently talked about the goals of reducing overall stress and drama. Above all, the insiders wanted everyone to be able to get along, do their job, and be happy.

Another difference between outsider and insider forms of mediation is the degree to which the processes involved are experienced as linear versus circular, clean versus messy, formulaic versus natural. Outsiders, initially foreign as they are to the relationships and context, tend to describe and to enact their processes in the step-by-step fashion depicted in Figure 1a, below. For example, because they are not normally at the hospital in which the conflict drama is playing out, outsiders must actually schedule, as a discreet, concrete, formal step, the acts of entering and exiting the workplace and gathering perspectives.

Insiders, on the other hand, by virtue of their constant presence and participation within the flow of daily routines and relations, are free to enter and exit the arena of conflict more subtly. They are also able to gather perspectives and influence the players informally and nearly constantly. While it may be possible to discern when they first became more involved as third-party helpers and when some of the subsequent shifts toward improved relations occurred, exactly what they did along the way between these two points is usually more difficult to pin down (Figure 1b) than with their outsider counterparts.

a. The Outside-Mediator's Process

b. The Inside-Mediator's Process

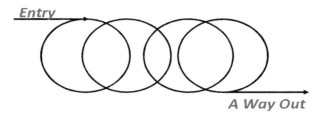

Figure 1: The Outsider-Mediator Process
versus the Inside-Mediator Process

a. The outside-mediator process is relatively rectilinear and discontinuous. As one would expect, the path is not absolutely rectilinear, but it usually follows an established sequence of events. The outside mediator works intermittently, coming and going from the workplace, interacting in separate steps with the parties involved in conflict. The outside mediator brings the benefits of 1) formal preparation for the work and 2) greater objectivity than does the inside mediator. Finally, the outside mediator exits the community after a period of service, whereas the inside mediator continues as part of the community.

b. The insider-mediator process is relatively curvilinear and continuous. As one would expect, the path is not absolutely curvilinear, nor is it absolutely continuous, but it usually consists of a sequence of ad hoc events. The inside mediator works continually, remaining in the workplace, interacting *pro re nata* (prn) with the parties involved in conflict. The inside mediator brings the benefits of 1) relatively equal status with the parties involved in conflict, 2) continuous on-site availability to the conflicted parties, 3) advice, guidance and wisdom that is free of the stigma of professional diagnosis, and 4)ongoing presence that continues after a particular crisis of conflict has subsided. The inside mediator continues as part of the community.

In sum, mediation takes the forms of the informal insider and the more formal outsider. The two forms share certain universal elements, yet usually give expression to these elements in different, yet potentially complementary, ways.

In reality, it must also be pointed out, neither is pure in expression. That is, the outsider is not solely focused on issues and the insider is not solely focused on relationships. The effective outsider develops relational rapport, becomes less dependent on structured approaches to gathering perspectives, exerts influence and wisdom, and attends to people and process as much as bringing specialized expertise to bear on substantive issues. Likewise, the most effective insider, despite possessing an intimate knowledge of the players and being subject to stronger biases, does not fall into blind one-sided advocacy for any party. Rather, the insider consciously strives to empower those most directly involved to play a principal role in the process and the outcome, attends to those outstanding substantive issues that need clarity and resolution (as opposed to maintaining a sole focus on restoring a sense of harmony), and is open to the value of formal training to enhance one's conflict management skill set.

Both/And Rather Than Either/Or

It is helpful to begin to conceive of the characteristics of the insider and outsider less in terms of opposites and more in terms of a series of polarities. Rather than either/or, the task for all mediators—whether practising as insider or outsider—becomes both/and. The mediator maintains a delicate balance in the tension that always exists between two apparently "opposite," but actually complementary, values and functions. For example, the dynamic tension that exists between building a relationship with the parties in conflict, on the one hand, and maintaining a balanced, even-handed perspective, on the other, can be depicted as follows:

Connection/Rapport AND **Balance/Perspective**

The remaining sets of characteristics introduced earlier can like-wise be understood as complementary pairs rather than as either/or opposites:

Insider Status/Knowledge AND **Outsider Specialized Knowledge**

Stakeholder/Have-an-Interest AND **Non-Stakeholder/Not-My-Business**

Direct/Influence AND **Empower/Self-Determination**

Acknowledge/Express Partialities AND **Acknowledge/Limit Partialities**

While the insider's practice will naturally be more driven and ex-pressive of the left side and the outsider's practice will be expressive of the right side, insider and outsider will be wise to recognize the value and reach for a practice that is reflective of both sides. That is, present-day conflicts require insiders who bring elements of the outsider and vice versa. Contemporary conflicts require all third-party helpers to be adept at knowing when to bring one side of the polarity to the fore while letting the other one recede momentarily to the background. Elements of both sets of characteristics are necessary in the holistic ex-pression of either role.

Another example is in order. One of the students in the class I taught on mediation at the Canadian School of Peacebuilding was a church pastor from Edmonton, Alberta, Canada. Comprising a near-even split between Canadian-born church members and newcomers of African descent, his congregation had differing expectations of him when it came to addressing church conflict. Most of his Canadian-born parishioners expected him to help resolve tensions but to lean heavily toward the outsider/facilitative end of the continuum—that is, primarily to *elicit their say in the development of their own solutions.* These congregants generally called him "James," his first name, and interacted with him in a manner that presumed their equality of status.

In the same way, most of the church members who were born in Africa also expected their pastor to deal with conflict. However, these members generally expected him to lean strongly to the insider/adviser end of the continuum—that is, to *take authority/responsibility for deciding the solutions himself before essentially telling them how the tensions were to be addressed.* These church goers generally called him "Pastor Brown" and behaved quite a bit more deferentially to him than did their Canadian-born counterparts.

Pastor Brown laughed as he told me that pastoring a multicultural church in a contemporary urban Canadian context thus requires a deft ability to shift between outsider and insider mode, depending on the person with whom one is working and on what issues. Even apart from the consideration of culture that the pastor identified so memorably, my experience as a mediator over the past twenty years tells me that everyone—regardless of cultural origins—ultimately requires a thoughtful blending of each "side" of the characteristics described above in order for there to be forward movement in "stuck" situations of conflict.

In Sum, Three Key Ideas Thus Far

So, what is news in all this? Given the current ascendancy of the outsider model in contexts like my Canadian one, I would argue, there are at least three ideas that I have discussed that are not yet commonly considered in the contemporary teaching and in the dominant practice of mediation in this country.

These are, firstly, the role for an insider mediator still exists, this role is critical to building a sustainable and just peace, it differs from, but overlaps with, that of an outsider mediator, it can be defined and taught, and it needs to be nurtured. Secondly, for these reasons, those of us practising as outsider mediators need to find our insider counterparts so as to intentionally work collaboratively wherever possible. And thirdly, there are aspects of the insider role that can and should inform and round out the practice of the outsider role. In particular, the common assumption that the outsider is neutral and does not, or should not, influence the parties and outcomes is false. Outsider mediators, like insiders, correctly build relationships with their clients and have biases. They consciously draw on these connections and partialities to influence both the people and the outcomes of their mediation sessions, hopefully for the better.

To the extent that outsiders begin to consciously recognize these realities, the gap between their rhetoric and practice also begins to close. As mediators, accept the fact that cleaving to a principle of pure impartiality is a misleading simplification that limits the work of mediation; and as it is replaced with the more realistic construct of balanced partiality, a blended, more holistic, and more effective practice begins to emerge. This is a good thing.

Before turning to a description of our own attempt to intentionally engage these differing, but overlapping and complementary, roles in the context of our nursing unit case study, I offer one more framework that I have found useful in teaching different forms of mediation. The Spheres of Application model (Figure 2, below) includes three spheres of mediation activity and therefore presents a somewhat more fulsome and possibly less binary picture of mediation practice.

Figure 2: Spheres of Mediation Application

Professionals: The sphere of activity represented by the small sphere includes people who make their living as mediators. They generally have specialized training and they practise primarily as outside mediators. When considered within the realm of all mediation practice—that is, all forms of third-party help—professional mediation constitutes by far the smallest percentage, hence it appears as the smallest sphere.

Para-professionals: The middle-sized sphere includes people who volunteer their time as third-party peacebuilders and/or who do mediation as one aspect of some other role, or "off the side of their desk." Examples—beyond the workplace examples cited earlier—include elders, religious leaders, sports coaches, community organizers, school guidance counsellors, community board chairs, social workers, doulas or midwives, and teachers. This form of mediation may involve some level of formal education in mediation but often does not. These people typically practise more toward the insider end of the insider-outsider continuum, but may bring outsider elements in as well.

Life-stylers: The largest sphere represents anyone who makes a conscious effort as a third party to build peace in their relational circles, including their personal life and/or their community as a whole. While this level may include practitioners who have formal training in mediation and conflict resolution, the vast majority do not. These practitioners are usually engaged as insiders. Anyone can choose to practise this form of mediation to some degree, hence it's representation as the largest sphere.

The Spheres of Application model increases our ability to see mediation taking place at multiple levels and in more subtle forms. It affirms the work of mediation in all its many varied manifestations; and it suggests that, regardless of the sphere in which a person engages as a mediator, that person be mindful to look for opportunities to join forces with those working for peace in other ways.

Application to Our Case Study—A Four-Phase Process Overview

So, what does this all mean at the level of application in our nursing case study? If, as I have argued above, many contemporary conflict situations require both insider and outsider mediators to function together as a cohesive team, what is the best—most practical—way to go about this?

What follows is one model for outsider-insider collaboration in situations of protracted, complex conflict at the everyday level of an institution. The model is laid out in four phases. Each phase is illustrated with examples from our nursing unit case study.

PHASE I—Contracting (typical time frame: two to seven days)

- The outside mediator receives intake call from person(s) requesting assistance with a conflict, for example from health care system regional administrator.
- The mediator[25] discusses services and mediation processes and typically introduces the four-phase approach at this juncture.
- The mediator typically discusses fees at this stage.
- The mediator typically submits a process and a fee proposal to the person making contact or to another body/person as appropriate; for example, the regional health administrator in our chapter case study, a board, an executive leadership team, or a pastoral leadership team.
- The group requesting assistance clarifies, and ultimately accepts, the proposal.

---

25. In this section, the term "mediator" will be used to connote the outside-mediator unless otherwise stipulated. I will also use the term to reference a team of conflict analysis and intervention professionals versus a single mediator working alone.

PHASE II—Assessment (typical time frame: one to two months)

1. **Preparing for Assessment**
   - The mediator generally negotiates access to a leader or administrator who is one level above/removed from any person perceived to be involved in the immediate conflict (for example, the mediator must have access to whomever the head of the nursing unit reports) human resources (HR), the union, and/or any other key bodies/stakeholders (for example the First Nation band chief and council)
   - The mediator makes arrangements for introductory meetings/conversations with each of the above parties.
   - The mediator makes arrangements for an introductory meeting with the members of the group that has been identified as being in or part of the conflict (for example, the leaders and staff members of the nursing unit at the hospital).
   - The mediator discusses the issues and reaches an agreement with the one-level-up leader/administrator, workplace leader(s), and other stakeholders with respect to what will be said during the introductory meeting by the mediator and by the various leaders and stakeholder representatives.
   - The mediator arranges to collect any other relevant documentation, for example a staff survey, a previous assessment, and letters on file.
   - The mediator may explore interactions to determine whether there have been any other recent events or situations that are, or may be, relevant (for example, recent grievances, harassment investigations, or other critical incidents in the hospital or community more broadly).

2. **Meeting with the Immediate Members of the Group in Conflict**
   - The mediator introduces the multi-phase process to the members of the conflicted group (for example, the staff and leaders of the nursing unit, along with other key stakeholders who might be First Nation chiefs and councillors, union representatives, regional representatives, or human resources

personnel in attendance as observers). This component is typically ten to fifteen minutes in duration.

- The mediator allows for and responds to questions of clarification about the multi-phase process. This component is typically five to fifteen minutes in duration.
- The mediator makes practical arrangements to conduct interviews and other agreed-upon methods of information gathering (for example, an employee survey).

3. Interviews and Report Preparation

- The mediator conducts interviews and engages in other agreed-upon information-gathering activities.
- The mediator prepares a draft report, either written or verbal, that reflects the themes—the strengths, concerns, and ideas to build on the strengths or address the concerns—heard in the interview and information-gathering process.
- The draft report also typically includes various process recommendations/options for
    a) ongoing stakeholder participation in mediation process design
    b) outsider-mediator–led intervention efforts (Phase III, #3 below)
    c) ongoing insider-mediator collaboration with the outsider mediator in carrying out intervention efforts

4. Delivery of Report

- The mediator shares a draft report with those who are providing leadership and/or who have a stake in the situation (for example, the leader/administrator to whom the nursing unit manager reports, the nursing unit manager herself, human resources, the union representative, and the chief and council of the First Nation band).
- The mediator collaborates with, and, if necessary, facilitates negotiation among, the above groups with respect to the wording, not content, of the draft report before it is presented to the conflicted group (for example, the nursing unit staff as a whole).

- If the interviews reveal particular members of the conflicted group who are seen to be of acute concern (for example, broadly seen by others to be a significant contributor to the conflict), the mediator often meets with these individuals separately, ahead of time, to inform them of this dynamic.
- The mediator delivers the report in person to the assembled conflicted group. Representatives of the various stakeholders groups identified above (see first bullet point under #4 above) are often also in attendance. This reporting to the conflicted group is typically fifteen to thirty minutes in duration.
- The mediator allows for, and responds to, questions of clarification about the contents of the report as necessary. Typically this question period is five to fifteen minutes in duration. The mediator does not engage the assembled group in substantive discussion of the issues in conflict at this stage.
- Attendees are encouraged to call the mediator, or other designated insiders, directly in the days or weeks to follow should they have further questions or concerns about the nature or content of the report. (For example, the staff of the nursing unit may call the mediator, a member of human resources, a First Nation band councillor, or the union representative under the shared assumption that one of these insiders will share the concerns with the mediator.)

PHASE III—Intervention (typical time frame: three to nine months)

1. **Negotiating the Terms of Engagement/Contract for Phase III**
   - The mediator negotiates the Phase III process, the fees, and the timeline with the person(s)/body who requested assistance. The mediator may include other stakeholders as appropriate in this activity.

2. **Engaging the Stakeholder/Employee Groups in Process Design**
   - The mediator provides, and may collaborate with stakeholders to generate, options for ongoing stakeholder involvement in the intervention/mediation process design. Some of the possible vehicles employed to this end include the following:

a) **Stakeholder Advisory Committee:** A Stakeholder Advisory Committee is composed of the various groups, beyond the employee group, that have an interest in successfully addressing the situation. Importantly, this body should include representatives of those groups whose collaboration will ultimately be required in order to create and grow sustainable peace. The purpose of this committee, which meets regularly—typically once every four to six weeks—is to provide high-level feedback and oversight to the outsider and insider mediators who are working on the conflict. In the nursing case study, this committee included the regional health administrator, other representatives of the hospital management and human resources, the union, the chief and council, and the executive director of the First Nation band office. At another level, the function of this body is to keep these various stakeholders talking with one another and engaged in relationship building since their ability to do so will have a direct effect on the long-term sustainability of any new patterns of interaction or agreements.

b) **Employee Steering Committee:** An Employee Steering Committee is composed of a representative sample of employees from the conflicted work group. Typically chosen by a combination of peer nomination and insider and outsider discretion, this group also meets regularly and provides more detailed feedback and collaboration on the development of the intervention/mediation efforts being undertaken "on the ground level" with the employee group. At another level, the function of this committee is to increase the chances of "buy-in" from all employees to the process. The committee also serves as a vehicle to increase conflict analysis and conciliatory capacity at the employee level.

3. **Engaging Intervention/Mediation Efforts with the Conflicted Group**
   - The mediator provides options and, with insiders, leads or co-leads the group in addressing the most immediate, distressing issues. Some of the typical options employed to this end include the following.

     a) **Coaching** involves one-to-one and two-to-one counsel for individuals with acute intrapersonal issues, communication issues, or performance gaps. For example, we provided coaching/training to the head of the nursing unit on her style of feedback and daily interaction, a style that the vast majority of her employees found too aggressive.

     b) **Mediation** involves engaging conflicted parties in facilitated conversation about the interpersonal tensions that are most affecting them and those around them. For example, we facilitated a conversation between the regional administrator and the executive director of the local band office about long-standing issues between them that had spilled over into other relationships and situations.

     c) **Facilitated Feedback Conversations** produce safe, respectful, and honest feedback to those who have contributed significantly to the troubled dynamics but who remain unaware of their contributions or who are resistant to change. In the nursing case study we facilitated feedback for one member of the nursing staff and two of her peers with respect to the nursing staff member's perceived lack of openness to feedback and collaboration on the hospital wards.

     d) **Group Processes** consist of leading the entire group, or sub-sections of the group, in activities such as the following:
        - *Sharing, discussion, or problem-solving* on a specific topic or event of concern: In the nursing study case we facilitated a conversation between three First Nation staff representatives and

three members of the management team from the immediate unit and from a higher level of authority. The group discussed the realities and effects of workplace discrimination. We also led a group discussion between the nurses and their leadership on the type of future they would like to build together.

□ *Critical incident debriefing:* In the nursing study case we led three nurses and two members of the management team in debriefing the effects and assumptions surrounding the suicide of a former member of the nursing staff.

□ *Training:* We led the entire nursing staff and management team in training related to interpersonal conflict-resolution skills and dismantling racism.

□ *Developing a conflict resolution protocol:* We led the same work team in a Building Respectful Workplace workshop in which they jointly developed and committed to a team charter/ protocol for responding to perceived moments of interpersonal disrespect or conflict.

4. **Engaging Insiders in the Mediation/Intervention Efforts**

• The mediator provides, and may collaborate with stakeholders and insiders to generate, options for engaging insiders in planning and/or carrying out the intervention efforts mentioned above. Some of the activities engaged to this end include the following:

a) **Identifying Insiders:** This work involves "keeping an eye out," and collaborating with higher-level stakeholders via the advisory committee, and with members of the conflicted group itself, via the employee committee, to identify insiders who are naturally positioned or endowed to assist in aspects of the group mediation process. In the nursing study case, a hospital human resources consultant identified a highly effective nursing leader from an adjacent unit whom the nursing unit leader in question respected. We then drew on the adjacent nursing leader's peer relationship with the latter nursing leader to ameliorate her aggressive interpersonal style.

b) **Co-Case Planning:** Such planning reaches beyond the advisory bodies mentioned above; it involves jointly discussing, and wrestling with, the many dilemmas that continuously surface in complex conflicts. For example, when planning for our Building Respectful Workplace workshop, we met several times with the hospital respectful workplace officer to ensure that we were not working at cross-purposes with his office.

c) **Co-leadership:** This element in the engagement of institutional leaders involves work with insiders, fostering jointly undertaken leadership in carrying out select aspects of the intervention process. Two examples are offered. While we as outsiders convened the first meetings of the stakeholder advisory committee, a member of the hospital human resources department and a band councillor eventually came to co-chair this body. In another instance, a member of the First Nation co-delivered, with an outsider-mediator, some of the workshop material related to dismantling racism.

d) **Increasing Capacity and Connection through Education:** This activity involves training conducted by outsiders designed to increase insiders' facility with conflict analysis and intervention tools, while simultaneously strengthening key relationships. For example, six hospital human resource professionals, the hospital respectful workplace officer, a band councillor, and two elders from the local First Nation jointly took part in a three-day *Mediation Skills for Insiders* course we conducted.

e) **Empowerment:** This involves the empowerment of insiders to lead select aspects of the work related to coaching, mediation, feedback, and training. For example, the chief of the First Nation played a pivotal role in encouraging/coaching three particular First Nation employees to serve as group representatives in talks with the management team.

Phase IV—Follow-Up (typical time frame: at six weeks, three months, and six months):

The mediator collaborates with stakeholders and insiders to generate an appropriate timeline for follow-up conversations with various parties in the months that follow the conclusion of active, outsider engagement. The purpose of these conversations is to check on the status of the situation and to determine whether further outsider engagement might be helpful.

Experience AND Outcomes of the Case Study

What fruit might be born of the efforts described above? What is to be gained by outsiders and insiders attempting to learn from and work closely with one another? In many ways, these remain live questions. At the time of this writing, the field of workplace intervention—and especially workplace intervention that includes an awareness of the need for insider engagement and capacity building—is still very young. Furthermore, the hospital case described in these pages is still unfolding, after we have spent more than ten months on the job. So, what can we say with confidence?

One thing we know for certain is that the process of working together is, like the conflict situation described, messy rather than clean; any forward movement has been in long, looping spirals rather than like anything approaching a straight line of progression. We have also come to see that many of the insiders we work with are, like us, broken and healing. They are far from perfect. Some of the "insider" parties among both the hospital system hierarchy and First Nation leadership have just as often escalated the dynamics on the unit as they have succeeded in defusing those dynamics. At times, some insiders have allowed their personal reactivity to cloud their judgment. If we are to be honest, it has sometimes felt like some participants are more interested in putting up roadblocks than truly joining us in good faith. As a team of outsiders we may be tempted, at times, to conclude that it is simply not worth it. It is easy to believe that they are only slowing us down, hindering more than helping.

Still, at these moments, we try to remember and remind one another that these insiders—these good folks who are giving of their time and passion to the process—are, in fact, the ones who will be on site in that northern Ontario community long after we, as outsiders, have departed. As such *they* are the people—*the only people*—it makes sense for us to team up with lest we simply feed another round of the false homeostasis noted earlier.

In the same way, we have also become more acutely aware of our own outsider imperfections. We have struggled to have the availability, energy, insight, and wisdom that such a complex, multi-layered conflict demands. Our limited roster of First Nation mediators remains both a practical and symbolic weakness. There have been several intervention moments led by a fully non-Indigenous team. Although we seem to have fared reasonably well on these occasions, we are aware that these moments make us vulnerable to cultivating further mistrust among our Indigenous brothers and sisters. Overall, it is fair to conclude that our work on this matter as a team of outsider-professional mediators has been an incredibly rich, rewarding, yet definitely humbling, affair.

In both cases then—as insiders and outsiders—we have weaknesses; but in both cases those weaknesses have been mitigated by our ongoing collaboration. As such, we must guard against letting the perfect become the enemy of the good. We have no choice but to continue to strive to "learn on the job" together; we are breaking new ground and, for all the challenges involved in attempting to go it together, the strengths born of doing so still outweigh the drawbacks. The only true progress in this matter is the type that insiders and outsiders can sew and grow together. For we know— based on experience—that progress based on anything less than the complex, hard-wrought kind born of the best of insider-outsider collaboration is highly likely to prove illusory over the long haul.

And there have been practical gains. To illustrate, let us return to the list of practical dilemmas and challenges listed out the outset of this chapter. Our limits as a mediation firm composed mostly of

Canadians of European descent have been mitigated by our partnerships with First Nation insiders who have provided counsel to us and invaluable coaching/support to First Nation members of the nursing department involved in the mediation process. Drawing on insider-outsider collaboration mechanisms, like the stakeholder advisory committee, has allowed us to build slowly a relationship of increasing trust and functionality over a ten-month period with local First Nation leaders and the non-Aboriginal leaders of the health care system, each who initially distrusted us, for differing reasons.

In the same way, the relationships we have built with non-First Nation insiders—some of the hospital staff and human resource consultants—who *do* see the need to build trust with First Nation stakeholders has allowed us to facilitate these parties taking the lead in advocating for a more inclusive process rather than attempting to do that solely on our own. Likewise, the rapport we developed with members of the hospital human resources department meant that they, rather than we, advocated strongly with upper administration to invest time and funds in the development and execution of the *Mediation Skills for Insiders* course. This was an important focus, better than focusing all attention on the immediately presenting crisis in the nursing department.

The impact of initiating a partnership approach from the outset—for example, a stakeholder advisory committee, an employee steering committee, and ad hoc co-case planning with insiders—has been that we have remained well positioned to both lead/influence and empower/be influenced throughout the process. These mechanisms also have enabled us, as outsiders, to give effective leadership to the mediation process in the midst of the immediate crisis while simultaneously growing the capacity of *insiders* to lead through future conflict and change.

By working closely with a range of insiders, including those who were more direct and forceful in nature, we have been witness to many necessary moments of confrontation, some of which we would probably have been tempted to avoid if we had worked alone. If we might have been tempted to mute honesty/truth telling in favour of a disproportionate focus on gentleness/conciliation, these partners have worked to keep us in appropriate balance.

As professional mediators who earn our living doing this work, we have continued to face the challenge of not becoming unduly beholden—and not appearing to be unduly beholden—to only one stakeholder in the process—in this case, to the hospital bureaucrats paying our wage. While this challenge admittedly remains difficult to address fully, our regular committee, co-planning sessions, and informal conversations with *all* stakeholders have meant that there have been *many* opportunities for parties on all sides to raise concerns about our even-handedness. And raise them they have, especially early in the process. We have noticed, however, as the months have unfolded, concerns of this nature have come up less frequently and with less intensity. We attribute this change—at least in part—to the hard-wrought but natural, incremental trust-building associated with our use of an insider-outsider partnership model.

Conclusion

While the process has not been perfect it has, perhaps, been good enough. More to the point of this chapter, it is my view—and the view of my colleagues and many of the insiders with whom we have worked—that the process has been significantly better, and more ef-fective, than had we approached the task without a keen awareness and ever-growing appreciation for the role of insiders and the insider mediator. We, outsiders and insiders, have listened to each other, challenged each other, taught each other, at times annoyed and trig-gered each other, and—ultimately and most critically—influenced one another as we have built relationships and learned together. And while the fruits of our labour remain a work in progress, we can also say with some confidence that both the harvest and the planning for another season have already begun.

Bibliography

Lederach, John Paul. *Preparing for Peace: Conflict Transformation Across Cultures.* Syracuse, NY: Syracuse University Press, 1995.

Wehr, Paul, and John Paul Lederach. "Mediating Conflict in Central America" in *Resolving International Conflicts: The Theory and Practice of Mediation.* Ed. Jacob Bercovitch. (Boulder, CO: Lynne Rienner Publishers, 1996), 56. (Accessed July 5, 1024.) http://books.google.com/books?id=rT0xjgkexCcC.

Yarrow, C. H. Mike. *Quaker Experiences in International Conciliation.* London: Yale University Press Ltd., 1978.

Additional Resources

Appleby, S. R. *The Ambivalence of the Sacred: Religion, Violence, and Reconciliation.* New York: Rowman & Littlefield Publishers, 1999.

Leatherman, J. *From Cold War to Democratic Peace: Third Parties, Peaceful Change, and the OSCE.* Syracuse, NY: Syracuse University Press, 2003.

Sherif, B. "The Ambiguity of Boundaries in the Fieldwork Experience: Establishing Rapport and Negotiating Insider/Outsider Status." *Qualitative Inquiry.* 2001. doi:10.1177/107780040100700403.

Teng, Chung-Chian. "Introduction: security, conflict management and resolution in East Asia" in Jacob Bercovitch, Kwei-Bo Huang, & Chung-Chian Teng, eds. *Conflict Management, Security and Intervention in East Asia: Third-Party Mediation and Intervention Between China and Taiwan.* New York, NY: Routledge, 2008.

Peacebuilding, Food Wars, and a Sustainable Future

—Martin H. Entz

The Arab spring was about food and water,
not Twitter and Google.
—P. Sainath[26]

The Front-Row Seat

A FRONT-ROW SEAT IS THE best place to watch the hometown team take on their opponents. It is from such a favoured vantage point that I have observed agriculture for more than five decades. My earliest farm memories are of warm sweet-smelling barns, kitchen gardens, manure piles, and fetching milk cows from the pasture. But then things changed. Animals were removed from pastures and placed into confinement. Manure piles became sewage lagoons. Kitchen gardens disappeared. The game changed, and it was difficult to know who to cheer for.

My family has been farming since 1717. I was a twenty-something-year-old graduate student before I took an interest in the history of our 1717 to 1945 German farm. When I opened the brown envelope and unfurled the sheets detailing crop rotation plans and field layouts, facts that my father had transferred from memory onto crisp white paper and placed in trust with Canada Post, I was fascinated. Our German farm had been well managed, using a progressive approach

---

26. Palagummi Sainath, *The Farm as the Last Frontier*. Prairie Festival lecture, The Land Institute, Salina, Kansas, September 29, 2012.

to production. Fertilizer use started soon after the Haber-Bosch process was discovered and industrial nitrogen production began in 1913. Between 1926 and 1945, the time when fertilizer use was intensified on our farm, traditional practices were not abandoned. My ancestors knew too well the value of Indigenous practices, like manuring fields, so they did not abandon them.

My family's Canadian farm started adopting green revolution technologies in the 1960s. After moving plastic bags full of clean, white pellets—my first look at synthetic nitrogen—my uncle looked over the line of bags and exclaimed "This pile of bags cost $3,000!" Later that decade, depressed wheat prices just about sank the farm. But fertilization was necessary.

During the first half of the 1900s, Canadian Prairie farms had relied on the natural capital of the land—the native organic matter of the soil—to feed their crops. Soil organic matter contains huge stores of nitrogen and phosphorous fertilizer, and this is what sustained the wheat crops from the time of European settlement to the 1960s.

How did those transplanted European farmers actually *feel* about green revolution technologies? Did their strong knowledge of sustainable practices lead to different behaviour than those of non-transplanted farmers? They knew, for example, that those white fertilizer pellets would work best if combined with high carbon animal manures, something that is now being purported as a progressive approach in Africa. Try as they might—economic forces, as well as government policies, were not friendly toward their ideas—like others, the new immigrants fell into line with the mainstream. Instead of feeding hay to their animals—hay that, rotated with grains, enriched the soil—they abandoned hay crops and resorted to feeding grains to their animals that now are raised in confinement.

By the end of the twentieth century, Canadian farming systems, for the most part, had been simplified to monoculture systems supported by inputs from agribusiness. The University of Manitoba, where I work as professor of Natural Systems Agriculture, consists of specialized departments where the whole agricultural system has been shattered into individual components. My European ancestors would not have known which department to visit or to study in. They knew that the connections, the ecology of the farm, were the key to a sustainable agriculture.

My father and I, and other members of my family, continue to love the land that many of us still work. My father has shared my front-row seat, allowing me to see further and to reflect more thoughtfully on the changing nature of the game.

The four-century history of the land that our family loves is a history of a subtle, creeping attack on the land, the people who inhabit it, and the people that the land was created to serve. Moreover, this history is a foreshadowing of the global food wars of the past century and their great cost to the land and to those of us who inhabit it.

This chapter provides a definition and a description of food wars, a discussion of the conflicts over the land, and an explanation of how we got here. The chapter describes challenges and threats to those who seek to effect change, focusing upon inequalities in empowerment and the global shift from particular locatedness to transnational placelessness. This work is brought to completion with the offering of some considerations for peacebuilding—including discussions of principle victims of the food wars—followed by suggestions for moving the peacebuilding process forward.

What Are the Food Wars?

There are people who see natural resources as there for the taking. These people promote smart natural resource management. Let's call them "miners." Others see nature not as a resource mine but as a model for sustainable societies. This group emphasizes natural processes and considers a fuller range of social processes. Let's call them "agroecologists." Many of us, me included, go back and forth, exhibiting both miner and agroecologist traits.

Before describing these protagonists and their typical actions in detail, it is helpful to offer a definition of food wars. Messer and Cohen defined food wars as follows:

> [Most] wars of the late twentieth century and early twenty-first century are "food wars," meaning that food is used as a weapon, food systems are destroyed in the course of conflict, and food insecurity persists as a legacy of conflict. We have shown that food insecurity, which as used here can denote

food shortage, lack of access to food, malnutrition, or some combination of the three, can also be a source of conflict. Our concern here is to demonstrate how globalization, including trade in primary agricultural commodities but also global norms and institutions promoting humanitarianism, human rights, and alternative development and trade, is connected to conflict and food insecurity.[27]

Messer and Cohen's definition is focused upon the relationship between food and military conflicts. This chapter, while including the abuses that attend military conflicts, seeks to address a broader understanding of the term "food wars." War between miners and agroecologists is a war of worldviews, a war of philosophies, a war of respect, or disrespect for that which is given to humans and the planet they inhabit. It is a war regarding the restraint, or the lack of restraint, of human greed. Food wars are fought with ideas, with money, with political and economic power, and with abstractions that permit the rhythms of nature and the planet's biota to be subsumed in the abstractions "development of natural resources" and "monetary profit." Bearing this understanding of "food wars" it is useful to return to the protagonists, beginning with the agroecologists.

Images of golden wheat fields waving in the wind, cattle grazing on natural meadows, and bumble bees pollinating apple blossoms depict the natural abundance of agriculture. University of Manitoba food scholar Vaclav Smil argues that there are "no insurmountable biophysical reasons we cannot feed humanity in the decades to come while easing the burden that modern agriculture puts on the biosphere."[28] He rejects the rush to technology for feeding the world. Agroecologists like this message.

Then there is beauty. Standing in a field of chest-height grain in August 2009, CBC morning show host Terry McLeod remarked on

---

27. Ellen Messer and Marc. J. Cohen, "Conflict, Food Insecurity, and Globalization," *International Food Policy Research Institute*, Food Consumption and Nutrition Divisions Discussion Paper 206. May 2006. (Accessed May 3, 2014.) http://www.ifpri.org/sites/default/files/publications/fcndp206.pdf.

28. Vaclav Smil, *Feeding the World: A Challenge for the Twenty-First Century* (Boston: MIT Press, 2001), 211–248.

the beauty of the place. "You are so lucky to work in these fields,"[29] he reminded our team of graduate students, many of whom were more intent on collecting utilitarian data than on appreciating the beauty of their surroundings. Perhaps not surprising, it is the more diverse, and hence more beautiful agricultural landscapes that host the most biodiversity. Several recent studies have confirmed that such *functional beauty* is indeed central to more productive and stable farming systems.

Long-time CBC Toronto farm reporter and founder of Farm Radio International George Atkins always ended his radio broadcast this way: "Serving agriculture, the basic industry, this is George Atkins."[30] Atkins was reminding listeners that modern civilization would not have been possible if we were still hunting and gathering. This is humbling: to learn that our sophistication is built on the backs of farmers engaged in this "basic industry." Perhaps this is why farmers are seen as among the most trustworthy members of society, and why many argue for the maintenance of family farming. Atkins' message is recognition that, for millennia, agriculture has provided sustenance, livelihood, and the foundation for modern societies.

Agroecologists argue that a sustainable agricultural system must pay attention to beauty, to a healthy society, and to the fact that the abundance of agriculture is based on natural processes. "Miners" see agriculture differently; they see agriculture as fuel for people and fuel for economic growth. Miner mentality runs the risk of gobbling up the planet.

When food is seen only as a commodity, as a source of economic power, many people suffer. When the British exported food from India in 1943, during the Bengal famine where at least three million people died of starvation, they clearly demonstrated that food can be a weapon.[31] Sadly, the Bengal disaster is just one in a long list of famines where people starved in a world of plenty. Desperate and starving people are the most likely to turn to violence, but in the case of the Bengal famine, who really fired the first shot? A more recent example comes from the horn of Africa. Are Somali pirates naturally

---

29. Personal conversation with the author, August 2009.
30. Farm Radio International. (Accessed March 31, 2014.) http://www.farm-radio.org/about-us/history/.
31. Madhusree Mukerjee, *Churchill's Secret War: The British Empire and the Ravaging of India during World War II* (New York: Basic Books, 2010), 131.

cruel or are they really just reacting to the loss of their fishery from first world trawlers scooping up the last of their catches?

When food is treated as an internationally traded commodity, economic forces demand lower costs for producing that food. Lower commodity prices mean that farmers make less profit per unit of land, and thus require more land to make the same income. Fair enough; so far the math is simple. But the reality of this math is that for some farmers to survive, others must cease to exist. This is the formula that has brought the food wars to communities all over Canada. Between 1991 and 2011, seventy-four thousand farms were lost in Canada, a decrease of 24 percent.[32] That is serious collateral damage.

The age-old struggle is about who gets food or who gets the land on which to grow the food. This struggle is easy to see and comprehend; the Irish potato and Bengal famines are examples. However, a major new point of conflict is less obvious. This is because deoxyribonucleic acid, or DNA, cannot be seen with the naked eye. DNA, the building block of life on earth, is now being patented, giving multinational companies and governments exclusive rights over nature's genetic code. In other words, creation is now being mined in new and dangerous ways. The most extreme and destructive version of this DNA mining, called biopiracy, is where extracts from native plants or animals already used by local populations, are patented. This is the work of "miners."

I witnessed a public skirmish between miners and agroecologists over lunch at the 2000 World Crop Science Congress in Hamburg. A yelling match broke out between supporters of the green revolution approach and some in attendance who had very much appreciated the words of Dr. John Vandermeer who had spoken the previous day about the important, and undervalued, contributions of agroecological approaches to food security. The Hamburg yelling match ended awkwardly. When boarding our tour buses for the trip back to the main conference venue, I noticed a segregation of miners and agroecologists, with each group boarding a different tour bus.

The level of hostility between miners and agroecologists has not abated in the intervening fourteen years. The disastrous tragedy of September 11, 2001 did not help; it focused attention onto

---

32. Statistics Canada. (Accessed May 7, 2014). http://www.statcan.gc.ca/daily-quotidien/120510/t120510a001-eng.htm.

heavy-handed solutions to a whole range of global issues, including food security. But it is time that we address our differences; the stakes are simply too high.

Into the Conflict

How did we get here? How is it that we can send people into outer space and onto the moon, but not provide humans with food security? Is it the lack of production capacity? Smil argues that it is not, and many scholars and development workers agree with his viewpoint.

I believe the problem has two parts. The first is that, for centuries, humans have ignored or subdued nature in the pursuit of food. This problem has become more apparent and dangerous as population pressure has increased. The second problem regards the commoditization of food and food workers in an effort to expand first world economies.

The contributions of World War I and World War II to the food wars cannot be overstated. World War I gave us fertilizer factories that ultimately set us on a path of ignoring global nutrient cycles. World War II brought us pesticides, again from retooled war factories looking for new markets and reasons to exist.

On the surface, fertilizers and pest killers seem like important tools to produce food for a growing population. At the Rothamsted plots, located fifty kilometres north of London, England, the beneficial effects of fertilizer, pesticides, and fertilizer-responsive crop seeds have been demonstrated since the establishment of this study in 1843. Wheat yields have increased from two tonnes to nine tonnes per hectare during this period.[33] The yield increases are attributed to the combined effects of fertilizer, better wheat varieties, and pesticides, especially disease-controlling fungicides. So impressive are these plots that they have become a sort of agronomists' mecca.

My pilgrimage took place in 2000. During my visit, I made two observations that were not part of the main tour. The first was that wheat yields in the farmyard manure-treated plots were every bit as good as the fertilized plots, perhaps even a bit better. Second, where

---

33. A.E. Johnson, "The Rothamsted Classical Experiments," in *Long-term Experiments in Agricultural and Ecological Science,* R.A. Leigh and A. E. Johnson, eds. (Wallingford: CAB International, 1993), 32.

no weed killers were sprayed, a low-growing, nitrogen-fixing weed had established itself, allowing these plots to function with less fertilizer. When fertilizer nitrogen is withheld, nature finds a way to fill that gap. This is an exciting example of the ecology of agricultural systems.

Rothamsted's lessons have encouraged farmers to ignore nature's principles of nutrient recycling and biological diversity, two critical pillars of agroecological farming systems. This fulfilled the dream of the founder of the Rothamsted plot, Sir John Lawes, an industrialist who built some of the first fertilizer factories in England. The lessons from Rothamsted have been exported around the world, mainly during the "green revolution" in the 1960s. In the dryer zones of the world, yields increased once irrigation was added to the mix. The green revolution technologies increased production of *certain* foods. Students of history will appreciate that the green revolution was more than just adoption of technology. Much of the motivation for the green revolution was as an antidote to the "red revolution;" in fact, that is how the term "green revolution" came about. Green revolution technologies were more palatable to Western interests than was land reform, which is distributing land to the poor. The green revolution was in many ways a cold war construct.

Opposition to the Lawes Rothamsted method started soon after the plots were initiated more than 160 years ago. Opponents expressed strong concern about the domination of nature and about the oversimplification of farming systems that made farmers dependent on industrial products. Ironically, the main opposition came from German-speaking countries, from people living in the society that invented most of the agrichemical poisons. Later, strong opposition was voiced by small-holder farmers in India and Central America, a story that is captured in Angus Wright's 1990 book, *The Death of Ramón González*.[34]

By the middle of the last century, the damaging effects of pesticide use were becoming impossible to ignore. The most striking example was destruction of bird populations from DDT, something that Rachel Carson brought to the attention of the public in her 1962 book, *Silent Spring*.[35] Some other examples of pesticide damage hit

34. Angus Wright, *The Death of Ramón González: The Modern Agricultural Dilemma* (Austin: University of Texas Press, 1990).
35. Rachel Carson, *Silent Spring* (Boston: Houghton Mifflin, 1962), 15–38.

"closer to home." The weed killer Atrazine is found in drinking water in many parts of North America. Frogs that live in ambient levels of Atrazine, that is, in water contaminated with Atrazine at a level found in many water bodies today, undergo a sex change. Atrazine-exposed male frogs become egg-laying males. If that is not frightening enough, University of Berkley researchers have observed that the male offspring of these egg-laying males are themselves egg-laying males, an example of epigenetics.[36]

Fertilizer use increased dramatically in the 1970s with promotion of green revolution technologies for wheat, corn, and rice production. Promotion of fertilizer nitrogen by national governments continues, especially in developing countries, despite earlier warnings of its negative side effects. It turns out that an important observation from the Rothamsted plots was that fertilizer nitrogen is not used very efficiently in annual crop production. In fact, just over half of the fertilizer that is spread on lands actually makes it into the food it is meant to enrich. The remaining portion is lost in one of two ways, as a gas, some as the potent greenhouse gas, nitrous oxide, or by leaching into water. More recently, scientists have learned that phosphorous fertilizer is a particularly problematic polluter once it enters waterways. By the 1990s water pollution from fertilizer losses were resulting in large "dead zones" in coastal waterways of industrialized countries. "Dead zones" are bodies of water that contain too little oxygen to support life; the oxygen is used up by algae whose growth is super charged by the fertilizer runoff.

Damage from fertilizer and pesticide use is not accounted for in most nations' economic models even though states like Iowa now spend millions of dollars filtering nitrogen from drinking water. These costs are simply externalized. Environmental problems from fertilizer and pesticide use have drawn environmentalists into the food wars. This has the unfortunate effect of pitting urban and rural people against each other.

The modern food system has recently come under a whole new set of criticisms. These include 1) high reliance on fossil fuel energy

---

36. Tyrone B. Hayes, Vicky Khoury, Anne Narayan, Mariam Nazir, Andrew Park, Travis Brown, Lillian Adame and others, "Atrazine Induces Complete Feminization and Chemical C in Male African Clawed Frogs (Xenopus laevis)," *PNAS* 107, no. 10 (2010), 4613.

use, owing to heavy reliance on energy-expensive nitrogen fertilizer, 2) low-caloric energy efficiency of the food system, owing to grain-feeding of ruminant animals and long transportation chains for crops and food products, 3) high obesity rates, owing partly to declining nutrition in new high-yield crop varieties, and 4) over promotion of genetically modified foods in the absence of any comprehensive testing.

Challenges and Threats to Change

Peacemaking is difficult when one side has all the power. This is the situation we find in agriculture. Power lies in the hands of governments and, especially, transnational agribusiness corporations. Consumers have some power, owing to their large numbers. Farmers have the least power. This situation sounds similar to previous struggles. It makes me reflect on one of the great peacebuilders of the world, a person who orchestrated peace under extremely difficult circumstances.

In 1915, when Gandhi returned to his home country after a twenty-year absence, he was curious and concerned. How were his people coping under unending British rule? At forty-six years of age, Gandhi set out on a one-year journey, crisscrossing India by train. Only after investing this much time did Gandhi truly understand the plight of his people. He saw poverty in the thousands of villages that made up India and witnessed the hard yoke placed upon Indian farmers by their British masters. Without such an investment of time, Gandhi may never have been motivated to action, nor would he have been able to understand the issues his brothers and sisters were facing.

If we were to take a "Gandhi journey" through our lands here in Canada, or in the less industrialized south, we would be equally moved by what we would see. Some things have changed little since Gandhi's time. For example, two-fifths of humanity still live on small-scale family farms. Rural people are increasingly vulnerable to outside economic forces and, incredibly, 75 percent of the food-insecure people in the world are small-scale farmers![37] Instead of these rural

---

37. Jacques Diouf, "Towards the World Food Summit and Millennium Development Goal Targets: Food Comes First," *The State of Food Insecurity in the World 2005*, Food and Agriculture Organization of the United Nations, 2005, 4–5.

people receiving help, they are being further victimized by the enthusiasm of those in agribusiness to replace peasant farms with larger farms, a trend not limited to developing countries. The movie *City of Joy* depicts an Indian farmer who lost his land and now must make a living in an urban slum; joy was mostly left in the village.[38] The United Nations predicts that by 2030, one-quarter of all of humanity will live in urban slums.[39] There are simply not enough city jobs to accommodate the new urbanites, and the jobs often bring new risks.

Another similarity with Gandhi's time is that small-scale farmers are still victims of unscrupulous money lenders. Farmers are encouraged to borrow money for new technologies like genetically modified (GM) seeds and fertilizers. When crops fail—and GM crops have failed often—farmers are left with debt which they cannot repay. Suicides, 250,000 in India alone in the past ten years, are often the result.[40]

What has changed since Gandhi's time is that weapons of the food war have become more insidious. Fifty years ago, for example, world trade consisted of real things like wheat and coal. Now the majority of the world trade is in financial instruments, instruments that play God with the price of food. When Canadians watch the evening news, they get a daily update on what the markets are doing. Instead of just seeing the effect of the market on our pension or investment earnings, we need to see the effect of the market on lives of the rural poor.

A journey through the agricultural landscape provides a fascinating picture of how transnational corporations are pushing people around. After their success with genetically modified canola in the mid-1990s, Monsanto Canada set its sights on genetically modified wheat. Senior executives from the pesticide lobby organization Crop Life visited universities to make sure people were toeing the line. Scientists who were sowing seeds of dissent, like our group at the University of Manitoba, were singled out for special treatment. It was the academic freedom offered by universities that saved us.

---

38. *City of Joy,* DVD, directed by Roland Joffe. (Culver City, CA: Columbia Tri-Star, 1992.)

39 UN-Habitat, 2003. *The Challenge of Slums—Global Report on Human Settlements,* 2003. (Accessed March 31, 2014). http://www.unhabitat.org/pmss/listItemDetails.aspx?publicationID=1156.

40. B. B. Mohanty, "'We are Like the Living Dead': Farmer Suicides in Maharashtra, Western India," *The Journal of Peasant Studies,* 32 no. 2 (2005), 253.

Governments were more collaborative with the corporations, sending directives to their scientists encouraging them to shut up. Only the bravest scientists, almost always senior people with strong reputations and little to lose, ever spoke up.

Farmers are much more vulnerable. Farmers have always faced peer pressure. A poorly managed field next to a highway will always get a reaction in the coffee shop or the church basement. This is part of healthy community life. However, the introduction of GM crops brought a level of intimidation never before seen in rural Canada. The pesticide companies hired ex-RCMP (in the USA, ex-military) personnel to police the use of the proprietary seeds.[41] Farmers showed me copies of letters from companies such as Syngenta and Monsanto; farmers who had done nothing illegal were being threatened. A new chill had begun. Once the altered DNA is patented, the variety is under the complete control of the company that developed it. In some cases, the genetically modified (GM) plants have contaminated non-GM seedlots, ending up on non-GM fields. The non-GM farmers have been sued or threatened by GM developers.

For those of us not able to take time to visit agricultural landscapes, it is possible to read about food issues. Verlyn Klinkenborg, a *New York Times* rural reporter, and Laura Rance, a journalist writing weekly columns in the *Winnipeg Free Press*, help us see and understand farm issues. Klinkenborg argues that "depopulated landscapes are de-democratised landscapes,"[42] and reminds us of what can happen when the rural landscape is owned by only a few. Raj Patel[43] and P. Sainath have both provided important insights into rural issues in developing countries.

One of the most impressive initiatives to bring stakeholders together on the future of the food system took place between 2002 and 2009. In an attempt to dialogue about the role of technology in development, the World Bank, the United Nations, and the World Health Organization, along with many different global NGOs, spent eight years working on the theme "International Assessment of

41. Anon., in conversation, January 2008.
42. Verlyn Klinkenborg, "Social and Biological Complexity." (Prairie Festival lecture, the Land Institute, Salina, KS, Sept. 26, 2009.)
43. Raj Patel, *Stuffed and Starved: Markets, Power and the Hidden Battle for the World's Food System.* (Toronto: Harper Collins, 2007), 2–45.

Agricultural Knowledge, Science and Technology for Development (IAASTD)."[44] More than four hundred scientists and NGO workers participated. Themes included biotechnology, biofuels, climate change, water, women in agriculture, and others. On the eve of the final document's release, two members of the group, both pesticide company representatives, went to the media and complained that the process was stacked in favour of small farmers and anti-technology NGOs. This act of sabotage had the desired effect; it clouded the credibility of the document so that no agriculture science student in industrialized countries has any clue that this comprehensive process ever took place.

The failure of the IAASTD report is an indication that agribusiness has won the food wars. "Feeding a hungry planet" has become an integral part of agribusiness speak, strongly supported by governments of the industrial powers. Who can argue with wanting to feed people, even though this particular message is attempting to "win hearts and minds"?

Considerations for Peacebulding

Respect Small-Holder Farmers

Sir Albert Howard, the imperial British mycologist, moved to India in 1908 to direct Indian plant disease research. Unlike many in his class, including those at Rothamsted, he actually believed that farmers had a great deal to teach to scientists. Howard discovered that Indian farmers had developed highly effective plant and animal disease management tools and so instead of teaching them, he considered these farmers as his professors. When he returned to England several decades later, he and Lady Eve Balfour started what has become the British organic farming movement.[45]

---

44. Beverly D. McIntyre and others, eds., "Agriculture at a Crossroads," *International Assessment of Agricultural Knowledge, Science and Technology for Development Synthesis Report.* (2009), 2. (Accessed April 15, 2014.) http://www.unep.org/dewa/agassessment/reports/IAASTD/EN/Agriculture%20at%20a%20Crossroads_Synthesis%20Report%20 (English).pdf.
45. Willy Lockertz, *Organic farming: An International History* (Wallingford Oxon, UK: Commonwealth Agricultural Bureau International, 2007), 187.

There are an estimated five hundred million small-holder farms on the planet, involving 2.5 billion people—producing over 80 percent of the food consumed in Asia and sub-Saharan Africa together.[46] We could add to this tally millions of gardeners, a group not typically included in food production statistics. Like Sir Albert Howard, many development workers and scientists argue that investing in small-holder farmers is job one for food security. French agronomists Mazoyer and Roudart[47] strongly support a chorus of international NGOs in the assertion that investments in appropriate technology for small-holder resource-poor farmers is the most important way to deal with dual problem of environmental degradation and food shortages. Let me share three examples.

Malawi is one of the most densely populated countries in the world, kind of a "ground zero" for food security challenges. Government fertilizer subsidies have been used for several years to boost production. However with recent inflation, the fertilizer vouchers do not buy as much fertilizer as they used to. This is a recurring theme in the developing world; the industrial model falls apart because it is not affordable for many farmers. In northern Malawi, a farmer-to-farmer education program is aimed at making farmers' food secure in the face of unaffordable fertilizer. The program trains local farmers in techniques such as crop rotation and intensive use of legume trees and shrubs. This program has successfully raised food production and improved livelihoods on thousands of farms.[48]

One of the really fascinating plant species in the Malawian agroecological system is *Faidherbia albida*, a nitrogen-fixing legume tree. The tree is ideally suited to enriching soils while buffering crops from rising temperatures, an increasing problem in southern Africa that appears linked to climate change. *Faidherbia* is referred to as a reverse phenology or reverse growth cycle tree. It drops its nitrogen rich leaves at the beginning of the rainy season, helping to enrich soils with nitrogen at the time of crop planting. Because there are no leaves to compete with the emerging crop for sunlight, a maize or bean crop

---

46. *Smallholders, Food Security and the Environment*, 2013. (Accessed April 1, 2014.) http://www.unep.org/pdf/Smallholder ReportWEB.pdf, 11.
47. Marcel Mazoyer and Laurence Roudart. *A history of World Agriculture: From the Neolithic Age to the Current Crisis* (London: Earthscan, 2006)
48. In conversation during field visits.

grows well under the skeleton of the leafless tree. At the beginning of the dry season, which coincides with crop ripening, the *Faidherbia* tree sprouts new leaves, providing shade and reducing high temperature stress on the ripening crops. This tree is almost too good to be true! It is a bit sad to learn that, while this tree is native to many areas of southern Africa, farmers have not been taught about its potential. In fact, many development projects dismiss the *Faidherbia* tree as a nuisance in the field.

The System of Rice Intensification (SRI) is a farmer-initiated rice production system that was pioneered not in the labs of the agribusiness companies from the first world but by a priest working with small-scale farmers in Madagascar. John Vidal of *The Observer*, quotes Cornell University scientist Dr. Norman Uphoff, who responded to criticisms.

> [SIR] is a set of ideas, the absolute opposite to the first green revolution [of the 60s] which said that you had to change the genes and the soil nutrients to improve yields. That came at a tremendous ecological cost, says Uphoff. Agriculture in the twenty-first century must be practised differently. Land and water resources are becoming scarcer, are of poorer quality, or are less reliable. Climatic conditions are in many places more adverse. SRI offers millions of disadvantaged households far better opportunities. Nobody is benefiting from this except the farmers; there are no patents, royalties or licensing fees.[49]

In January of 2013, former Nobel Prize winning World Bank economist Joseph Stiglitz visited Nalanda district in India and recognized the potential of SRI and organic farming. He told the villagers they were "better than scientists." "It was amazing to see their success in organic farming," said Stiglitz, who called for more research. "Agriculture scientists from across the world should visit and learn and be inspired by them."[50]

---

49. John Vidal, "India's Rice Revolution," *The Observer,* February 13, 2013. (Accessed April 1, 2014.) http:/e/www.theguardian.com/global-development/audioslideshow/2013/feb/15/india-rice-revolution-audio-slideshow.
50. Vidal, "India's Rice Revolution."

Ofilia and Litisia are Nicaraguans, farming seven hectares of productive land. They remarked that, before the Universidad Nacional Agraria in Managua started working with them in 2006, their only source of new knowledge was from agribusiness retailers whose information was unreliable. Interaction with the local university has transformed their lives. They have reshaped their farming system based, literally, "on a new set of ecological processes." They now employ vermicomposting, where worms are used to process manure from their twenty-six brahma cattle. They have also used botanical extracts as natural insecticides. During the recent drought, the improvements in their soils allowed them to harvest tomatoes when other farmers had none.

Women and Peacebuilding

Women are keys to peacebuilding in the food wars. One of Vandana Shiva's most popular quotes is, "We are either going to have a future where women lead the way to make peace with the Earth or we are not going to have a human future at all." The 2008 film, *Pray the Devil Back to Hell,* is the extraordinary story of a small band of Liberian women who came together in the midst of a bloody civil war, took on the violent warlords and the corrupt Charles Taylor regime. In 2003 these women won a long-awaited peace for their shattered country.[51] After peace talks failed, the women of Liberia, Christians and Muslims, formed an unshakable white line between the opposing forces, and successfully demanded an end to the fighting. The women of Liberia, like Gandhi, are living proof that moral courage and non-violent resistance can succeed.

But the role of women in the food wars goes beyond effective reasoning in times of conflict. In many places in the world, Africa for example, women do the farm work; they are the farmers. And they are good at it. Women are responsible for many innovations including adaptation of conservation agriculture to small-holder production. Tragically, women work the land but are often not allowed to own it. Globally, women and children represent a marginalized group,

---

51. *Pray the Devil Back to Hell*, DVD, directed by Gini Reticker (New York: Fork Films, 2008).

particularly in low- and middle-income countries. Less access to education, restricted decision-making power, lower wages, and fewer social and/or economic opportunities limit women's access to services and negatively affect their health outcomes.

Based on experience empowering resource-poor farmers through microloans and the like, the UN organization International Fund for Agricultural Development (IFAD) has learned that women are 30 percent more efficient with financial resources than men.[52] Plus women are better at preserving the environment. Therefore, the battle to empower women is now being fought at the highest levels. The recently commissioned World Bank study on the role of science and technology in agricultural development stressed the importance of women in agriculture.[53] The 515 or so scientists who authored the report argued that the focus of future agricultural development must empower women. The "governments [of fifty-eight countries] approve[d] the Executive Summary of the Synthesis Report." Three other countries (USA, Canada and Australia) "did not fully approve the Executive Summary of the Synthesis Report." [54] By clinging to the notion that agricultural development must be centred on technologies that profit industry, these countries are holding up progress. The food wars continue.

Peacebuilding—Hold the Poison, Please

Without pesticides, large-scale monoculture is impossible. Farmers who specialize in the production of only one or two crops need the pesticide industry to help them control weeds, diseases, and insects. As pests develop resistance to current pesticides, new pesticides are required. This is referred to as the pesticide treadmill, and it ensures that farmers are dependent on agribusinesses in the long term. Adopting more diverse and ecologically integrated farming systems reduces the need for pesticides, resulting in less dependence on multinational pesticide corporations for farm livelihoods.

Another problem with pesticides is that they are linked to sickness, in humans and in nature. Women who are flower producers in

---

52. Kanayo F. Nwanze, in conversation, April 17, 2013.
53. McIntyre and others, "Agriculture at a Crossroads," 75–80.
54. McIntyre and others, "Agriculture at a Crossroads," 81.

Honduras have confided to my female colleagues about numbness in their fingers and increased incidence of miscarriages. Many of these women are "kangaroo mothers," carrying babies on their backs during much of the work day. The effects of pesticides on child development are well established. Working in Mexico, anthropologist Elizabeth A. Guillette observed that children growing up in the presence of pesticides were not able to colour pictures as well and could not catch a ball as well as children the same age living where pesticides were not used.[55]

In one Nicaraguan community where I work, the mayor learned that the local university was testing pesticide levels in the local water supply. She received reports that a large local peanut farm had been using unregistered pesticides. The mayor asked that a sample of her breast milk be tested for pesticides. When the results came back positive for organophosphate insecticide, the community became alarmed and took action. They drafted and passed a new law regulating pesticide use in the area. When a cotton grower started contracting cotton in the area, these regulations were presented to the grower, who has been abiding by the rules, which has resulted in a peaceful coexistence between the company and the community. Without being proactive, this community would still be suffering pesticide poisoning.

Peacebuilding—Natural Systems Agriculture

Growing crops and animals is based on natural processes, where the ecosystem is the platform for the entire process. Damaged ecosystems are incapable of producing food. Therefore, we must make peace with the land itself.

Recently Jules Pretty summarized the capacity of natural or agroecological systems to "feed the world."[56] Using a meta-analysis of 289 agroecological comparisons involving twelve million hectares around

---

55. Elizabeth A. Guillette and others, "An Anthropological Approach to the Evaluation of Preschool Children Exposed to Pesticides in Mexico," *Environmental Health Perspectives* 106, no. 6 (1998), 351.

56. Jules Pretty and others, "Resource-conserving Agriculture Increases Yields in Developing Countries," *Environmental Science and Technology*, 40, no. 4 (2006), 1114.

the world, Pretty concluded that agroecological approaches increased food supply by an average 79 percent. Seventy percent is what the Food and Agriculture Organization of the United Nations (FAO) says we need to feed the ten billion people of the world. Indeed, by working in harmony with nature, we can secure food for future generations. When Olivier de Shutter, the UN special rapporteur for the right to food, brought this message to Canada in 2012, the Canadian government attacked him for his views. The food wars are exhausting!

Norman Wirzba suggests that nothing informs this aspect of peacebuilding better than Sabbath-keeping, where we allow the tiny organisms that contribute so much to food production to "be themselves."[57] Wendell Berry and Norman Wirzba argue that a "sense of place" is critical to sustainable ecosystem management. It is difficult to sense the requirements of an ecosystem when we continuously move our production to lower and lower cost of production centres.

Sometimes, ecological degradation is so bad that a wholesale restoration is needed. Ecological restoration refers to a process where entire landscapes are restored in order to jump start natural processes, including food production, again. John Liu is a documentary film maker turned soil scientist who has documented ecological restoration in China, Rwanda, Jordan, Russia, and elsewhere. His breakthrough occurred when he visited the Loess plain of northwest China, and eventually described the restoration work in a number of feature length documentaries. This is an inspiring story of peacebuilding in the landscape.[58]

Fortunately, these stories do not always fall on deaf ears. Some transnational agribusiness corporations are taking some notice of the issues described above, including the effects of pesticide overuse, ecological degradation, and lack of access to quality education. Companies such as Nestle, Danone, and Unilever have implemented the Sustainable Agricultural Initiative (SAI). The motivation for this initiative is European consumers asking questions about social justice in the food system. The SAI system initiative includes consideration

---

57. Norman Wirzba, *The Paradise of God: Renewing Religion in an Ecological Age* (Oxford: Oxford University Press, 2008), 34–40.
58. John Liu, *The Environmental Education Media Project.* (Accessed April 1, 2014.) http://eempc.org/.

of pesticide exposure in food and in farmers, but it also addresses the lack of schools and other social programs. While it is easy to be cynical, the SAI initiative represents an important truce in the food wars.

Peacebuilding—Seeds

Seeds represent a critical battleground in the food wars. Today, a few large transnational agribusiness corporations own most of the genetics for the major crops of the world. How these corporations gained control over the seeds is a worrying tale of influence peddling, intimidation, and pressuring poor countries. This issue requires a peaceful resolution since more than 1.5 billion farmers currently rely on farm-saved seed for their livelihoods.[59]

The question is, How can the issue be resolved? How do we make peace in a situation where farmers, and indeed nations, are losing sovereignty over their seeds? Do we pressure first world governments to address the issue? The decision by leaders of the Canadian government to reject the IAASTD report suggests this will not happen, at least not here. Would appeals to consumers to respect the sovereignty of the people in various cultures over their food varieties be effective? Perhaps. Should nations use the international courts to protect their genetic resources, like the case of Basmati rice in India? Definitely, yes.

Another approach involves supporting farmers who still have and want control of their seeds. This work takes many forms. In the developing world, local governments, often in partnership with NGOs, work to strengthen on-farm conservation of seeds. Supporting farmer-managed seed banks facilitates seed saving and farmer-to-farmer seed exchanges. USC Canada has been a leader in this work. Farmer variety selection and farmer participatory plant breeding efforts are now being promoted around the world, even in developing countries. But all this peaceful work will be for naught if international treaties allow transnational companies to own what is in the farmers' seed storages. When it comes to seeds, we need to be ever vigilant.

---

59. Personal conversation with USC Canada and other NGOs.

Moving the Peacebuilding Process Forward

In 2009, the Canadian School of Peacebuilding offered a Canadian first, a course titled *Our Contested Food System: Cultivating a Just Peace*. The four instructors, an Anglican priest, a food activist, a development scholar, and an agronomist, sought to bring people from within the food system together for a week-long dialogue.

The first day was spent framing the issue, including examples of compromises between industrial and agroecological approaches. The second day was spent in the field. Students were exposed to current conventional farming, organic cropping systems, and intermediate systems that use minimal external inputs but are not completely organic. A development worker demonstrated conservation agriculture as it is practised in southern Africa. We also invited commercial farmers to explain their systems. The farmers were a highlight. "I did not know that farmers knew so much," was one student's response.

Day three involved a look at the food system in an economically depressed urban area, and day four was spent at the Canadian Grain Commission building in downtown Winnipeg, the Canadian grain business centre. Presentations from the grain industry were interspersed with presentations of economic theory by a development scholar. A grain company representative explained the role of private business in the grain collection and export sector. Students gained a strong appreciation for the role of businesses in linking Canadian farmers with international markets.

Students in the 2009 class consisted mostly of food activists, small-scale farmers, and undergraduate students with strong views about agribusiness exploitation. Therefore, agroecology leanings were vastly overrepresented in the class. The two activities that challenged students most were the interactions with farmers and representatives from the grain industry. Students went away with a much greater appreciation for farmers and the need for businesses to link these farmers to markets.

The Canadian Mennonite University (CMU) peacebuilding experience demonstrated an unfortunate trend—that is the reluctance of industrial agriculture proponents to participate in meaningful dialogue. While rare exceptions exist, industrial agriculture appears fearful of being implicated in problems for which it may have to take responsibility. In order to remedy this situation, future peacebuilding events should allow a "safer" place for the discussions. Forums need to allow for discussion of difficult topics without laying blame, and away from media scrutiny. Such forums will be more welcoming if they are focused less on specific problems, and more on solutions. The work of the Canadian Foodgrains Bank comes to mind. In this case, large industrial farmers and small-scale farmers, gardeners, and even non-farming urban donors come together with a common purpose. Somewhat ironically, the solutions that the Foodgrains Bank supports to ensure food security in developing nations are agroecological ones.

Summary and Conclusions

This chapter, having set the topic in the peaceful state of love for people and place, focused on the nature of the food wars, offering some historical perspective on how we got here. Challenges and threats to those who seek to effect change were presented, with a focus upon inequalities in empowerment and the global shift from the particular to the abstract. Narratives that expressed the suffering of victims of food wars were followed by considerations of matters that are important in the peacebuilding process.

In some ways the food wars are just another class struggle. But, in two ways, the food wars are different. First they involve absolutely everyone; we all need to eat. Second, food wars truly constitute a world war. It is the global ecosystems; it is creation that enables food production in the first place. We need to remind ourselves that humans currently appropriate at least 40 percent of the products of global photosynthesis, much of it for food.[60] And this value does not include the food energy derived each year from oil. If we get it wrong, the whole earth will pay the price.

Establishing peace as a replacement for the food wars will require stronger enforcement of human rights, especially rights of women and children. Peace will require respect for minorities and rural communities. Because food has moral currency, peacebuilding in the food wars is entirely a moral issue.

---

60. P.M. Vitousek, and others, "Human Appropriation of the Products of Photosynthesis." *Bioscience* 36 no.6 (1986): 368.

Peace in the food wars will require strong rules of engagement, so experienced peace builders are needed. Do people qualified to tackle peacebuilding in the food wars even exist? The uniqueness and global reach of the food system suggests that qualifications for these peacebuilders are indeed unique. In addition to the usual skills in conflict resolution, food war peacebuilders require an understanding of agricultural sciences, ecology, rural sociology, and global political economy.

Bibliography

Carson, Rachel. *Silent Spring.* Boston: Harcourt Publishing, 1962.

City of Joy, DVD, directed by Roland Joffe. Culver City, CA: Columbia Tri-Star, 1992.

Diouf, Jacques. "Towards the World Food Summit and Millennium Development Goal Targets: Food Comes First." Foreword, *The state of Food Insecurity in the World 2005.* UN Food and Agriculture Organization (2005).

Farm Radio International. (Accessed March 31, 2014.) http://www.farmradio.org/about-us/history/.

Guillette, Elizabeth A., Maria M. Meza, Maria G. Aquilar, Alma D. Soto, and Idalia E. Garcia. "An anthropological approach to the evaluation of preschool children exposed to pesticides in Mexico." *Environmental Health Perspectives* 106, no. 6 (1998): 347–353.

Hayes, Tyrone B., Vicky Khoury, Anne Narayan, Mariam Nazir, Andrew Park, Travis Brown, Lillian Adame and others. "Atrazine Induces Complete Feminization and Chemical Castration in Male African Clawed Frogs (Xenopus laevis)," PNAS 107, no. 10 (2010). (Accessed March 31, 2014.) http://www.pnas.org/content/early/2010/02/12/0909519107.full.pdf +html.

International Fund for Economic Development. *Smallholders, Food Security and the Environment,* 2013. IFAD. (Accessed April 1, 2014.) http://www.unep.org/pdf/Smallholder ReportWEB.pdf.

Johnson, A. E. "The Rothamsted Classical Experiments." In *Long-term Experiments in Agricultural and Ecological Science,*

R. A. Leigh and A. E. Johnson, eds. Wallingford: CAB International, 1993, 9–37.

Liu, John. *The Environmental Education Media Project*. (Accessed April 1, 2014.) http://eempc.org/.

Lockertz, Willy. *Organic Farming: An International History*. Wallingford, Oxon, UK: Commonwealth Agricultural Bureau International, 2007.

Madhusree, M. *Churchill's Secret War: The British Empire and the Ravaging of India during World War II*. New York: Basic Books, 2010.

Mazoyer, Marcel, and Laurence Roudart. *A history of World Agriculture: From the Neolithic Age to the Current Crisis*. London: Earthscan, 2006.

McIntyre, Beverly D., Hans R. Herren, Judi Wakhungu and Robert T. Watson. *Agriculture at a Crossroads: International Assessment of Agricultural Knowledge, Science and Technology for Development Synthesis Report,* Island Press, 2009. (Accessed February 24, 2014.) http://www.unep.org/dewa/agassessment/reports/IAASTD/EN/Agriculture%20at%20a%20Crossroads_Synthesis%20Report%20(English).pdf.

Messer, Ellen, and Marc. J. Cohen. "Conflict, Food Insecurity, and Globalization," *International Food Policy Research Institute, Food Consumption and Nutrition Divisions Discussion Paper 206,* May 2006. (Accessed 2014 May 03.) http://www.ifpri.org/sites/default/files/publications/fcndp206.pdf.

Mohanty, B. B. "'We are Like the Living Dead': Farmer Suicides in Maharashtra, Western India." *The Journal of Peasant Studies*. 32, no.2 (2005): 243–276.

Patel, Raj. *Stuffed and Starved: Markets, Power and the Hidden Battle for the World's Food System*. Toronto: Harper Collins, 2007.

Pray the Devil Back to Hell, DVD, directed by Gini Reticker. New York: Fork Films, 2008.

Pretty, Jules N. A. D., Noble, D. Bossio, J. Dixon, R. E. Hine, F. W. T. Penning de Vries, and J. I. L. Morison. "Resource-conserving Agriculture Increases Yields in Developing Countries." *Environmental Science and Technology*. 40, no. 4 (2006): 1114–1119.

Smil, Vaclav. *Feeding the World: A Challenge for the Twenty-first Century.* Boston: MIT Press, 2001.

Statistics Canada. (Accessed March 31, 2014.) http://www.statcan.gc.ca/pub/96-325-x/2014001/article/11905-eng.htm.

UN-Habitat. The Challenge of Slums—Global Report on Human Settlements, 2003. (Accessed March 31, 2014.) http://www.unhabitat.org/pmss/listItemDetails.aspx?publicationID=1156.

Vidal, John. "India's Rice Revolution." *The Observer,* February 13, 2013. (Accessed April 1, 2014.) http://www.theguardian.com/global-development/audioslideshow/2013/feb/15/india-rice-revolution-audio-slideshow.

Vitousek, P. M., P. R. Ehrlich, A. H. Ehrlich and P. A. Matson. "Human Appropriation of the Products of Photosynthesis." *Bioscience* 36. No. 6 (1986): 368–373.

Wirzba, Norman. *The Paradise of God: Renewing Religion in an Ecological Age.* Oxford: Oxford University Press, 2008.

Wright, Angus. *The Death of Ramón González: The Modern Agricultural Dilemma.* Austin: University of Texas Press, 1990.

Additional Resources

Alavanja, Michael C. R., Matthew K. Ross and Matthew R. Bonner. "Increased Cancer Burden Among Pesticide Applicators and Others Due to Pesticide Exposure." *A Cancer Journal for Clinicians*, 15 Jan 2013. (Accessed: February 14, 2014.) http://onlinelibrary.wiley.com/doi/0.3322/caac.21170/abstract.

Araghi, Farshad. "The Great Global Enclosure of Our Times: Peasants and the Agrarian Question at the End of the Twentieth Century" in *Hungry for Profit: The Agribusiness Threat of Farmers, Food and the Environment.* Fred Magdoff, John Bellamy Foster and Frederick H. Buttel,, *eds.* New York: Monthly Review Press, 2000.

Bello, Walden. *The Food Wars.* London: Verso, 2009.

Janzen, Henry "Soil Science on the Canadian Prairies—Peering into the Future from a Century Ago." *Canadian Journal of Soil Science*. 81 (2001):489–503.

Patel, Raj. *Stuffed and Starved.* Melbourne: Schwartz Publishing Limited, 2009.

"Sustainable Agriculture Initiative." (Accessed February 14, 2014.) http://www sai platform.org/.

Weis, Tony. *The Global Food Economy.* Halifax; Fernwood Publishing, 2007.

WHAT CATS CAN TEACH US ABOUT IDENTITY AND PEACE THEOLOGY

—Harry Huebner

Introduction

R ECENTLY I WAS INVITED TO PRESENT a lecture at the University
of Qom in Iran on the topic of Christian ethics. I spoke about
peace and justice as important themes in Christian ethics and
especially in the Anabaptist/Mennonite understanding. During the
discussion someone asked why I considered the emphasis on peace
to be so important. Should not religious scholars rather place the
weight on justice? After all, peace is but a path; justice is the destination. Everyone likes peace and if it can get you to justice, great; but if it
cannot, then peace quickly becomes irrelevant. I responded by saying
that, as a Christian, I believe that peace names something more than
is implied in the question. Peace is a distinctive way of working for
justice even, perhaps especially, when it seems apparent that it cannot get us there. In most cases peaceful ways of resolving conflict are
abandoned far too quickly (usually because they don't get us there
quickly enough) in favour of violent approaches when there are still
far more peaceful options remaining. The questioner continued with
a second question, pushing his point that preoccupation with peace
neglects the need and the justification for imposing justice when
rational argument fails. Hence, to overemphasize peace is to risk per-
petuating injustice.

At this point the discussion got somewhat personal for me. I told the audience that, while there will always be conflict, I believe that God is opposed to violence and war as a way of resolving human conflicts. Moreover, I reminded them that I came from the West where the nations have identified them (the Iranians) as enemies. This meant that Western nations consider themselves justified in using whatever violence is necessary to bring about their view of justice against them. I was present with them to give voice to an alternative approach defined by a peace that refuses violence. After all, justice is not properly understood as "the interest of the stronger" as Trasymachus suggests in Plato's "The Republic."[61] No religion advocates that, and especially not monotheists who believe that God created the world as peaceful and that its current violent state is an aberration of original creation.

I continued my stumbling remarks since by now the large theatre had become rather attentive: I reminded them that there are legitimate differences in the understanding of justice and that how we negotiate these differences should be a matter of peace. And, when dialogic means are employed and discussions emerge that are genuinely open to the difference of others, a peace-informed justice will more likely result than when "the stronger" impose their "justice" violently. I suggested that the "peaceful approach" to justice was best modelled by engagement between friends.

Exchanges between friends include, by virtue of being friends, agreement that they will not kill each other regardless of the differences between them. The cultivation of friendship is therefore an important model of giving peace-informed justice a chance. Hence, I see peace and justice as inseparable, and only when they proof each other in openness to people of difference (even enemies as Jesus insists) can a peaceful and just polis (locally and internationally) flourish.

In June 2010 I taught a course for CSOP, *Mennonite Approaches to Peace and Justice,* in which we discussed selected literature on the topic. This essay has its roots in the subject matter of that course. But courses explore specific literature and they do so with particular students. This affects their nature. Moreover they are taught by specific

---

61. Plato, "The Republic," in *The Dialogues of Plato*, vol. 1, trans. B. Jowett (New York: Random House, 1937), 603.

professors. Notice the emphasis on particularity. It would be foolish to pretend that teaching is all about dumping truthful content onto the students' intellectual laps. It is but one take among others. It's an exploration! It's about bringing students to the table of past explorations. Hence the answer to questions that begin with What is …? or Who is …? must of necessity retain a *mysterium* since we cannot know all there is, even in what is named in the question, let alone in what is posited as the answer. Hence, unless one retains an honest pedagogical humility, teaching itself becomes violent.

Now, whatever is said about the mystery surrounding teaching and learning, at least as much should be said about the practical expression of one's knowledge. For who we are does not only determine what we can know, it also informs what we can and must do. Here pedagogy and ethics join hands.

To highlight the importance of the ambiguity of being I begin with a story. One day when I was about twelve years old something unusual happened. I walked into the big garage on the farm and looked into the hopper on top of the grain crusher. At the bottom was a rat and I quickly tripped the bottom trap door and caught it by its tail. It screeched and caught the attention of our big cat. So without much thought I picked up the cat and dropped it into the hopper because cats kill rats, right? She had demonstrated that many times. The cat protested as she slid down the shiny metal sides of the hopper. When the cat reached the bottom the rat bit the cat hard before she gained her footing to leap out to safety. I then realized that I had made a big mistake.

But what was my error? It never occurred to me that I might have violated the rule on cruelty to animals, for I was helping the cat do what it always did—catch and then eat rats. (Cat food in those days did not come from store shelves.) So what I did was a good thing, right? (Of course, I'm not speaking about the rat's fate—on a farm, morality didn't readily extend to rats.) But back to the cat! No, what I did was not a good thing. But it took me a long time to understand why. You see, in retrospect I now know that what I did was redefine the cat in my own image; I was not permitting her to be what she was.

Have you ever observed cats pursuing their prey? The first thing you'll notice is that they make themselves practically invisible and inaudible. They crouch way down with bellies dragging on the ground and shoulders protruding above their bodies. This gives them extra leverage for the big pounce. Then they measure ever so carefully the distance and the timing of the attack. When it's all just right, bingo, they leap and their jaws land with precision right where they immobilize their prey. But when any piece of this manoeuvre is even slightly compromised success is unlikely and the venture becomes perilous. And I had robbed the cat of all this catty setup that is essential for being a cat, at least a well-formed rat-catching cat.

But what does this have to do with Mennonite peace theology, both for its teaching/learning and for its practice? Well, it reminds us that not all can be remade in our own image; some things are given and are best received as given. And this requires the discipline of study, analysis, and understanding. It also reminds us that in this venture we dare not forget who (and whose) we really are.

Anabaptist Peace Theology

It would be wrong to suggest that there is a singular Anabaptist theology of peace and justice. There are several, and no one narration would be given the right to claim to have discovered the language in which such a theology must be written. Clearly the Anabaptists saw the problem of evil and injustice as a key social problem and, like other Christians, sought an ethic of faithfulness in response to it. Yet their stance toward the mainline churches' social ethic was at most dubious, and in practice it was rejected. Their own view of social sin was coloured by a separatist ecclesiology and by an eschatology rooted in their reading of what Jesus required of his followers in bringing about the new kingdom. They were not driven by pragmatics of outcome measured by immediate resolution; they were driven by fidelity to a cosmic cause of divine activity.

It is well known that the formation of pacifism had contentious birth pangs for the sixteenth-century Anabaptists. Some early Anabaptists were convinced that followers of Jesus should not use the sword in protecting themselves or others (e.g., Conrad Grebel 1498–1526). Nevertheless, within a very few years, there were those who could not resist the apocalyptic temptation to take up the cause to move history toward its idyllic end. This was the direct result of a struggle that came with placing themselves into the stream of events that made them instruments in bringing about the New Jerusalem. They saw, in the Jesus story, a real fulfillable promise to overcoming the injustices of the world. Not only that, they saw in this process a distinct agential role for themselves. C. Arnold Snyder states this tension between these "Münsterites"[62] and other Anabaptists by quoting two writers. "Conrad Grebel says, 'The gospel and its adherents are not to be protected by the sword, nor are they thus to protect themselves.'"[63] Some years later in 1535 Bernhard Rothmann, writing on behalf of the Münster rebels, states that the Lord desires

> ... that we and all true Christians in this time not only be allowed to turn away the power of the ungodly with the sword, but even more, that the sword be put into the hands of his people to avenge all that is unjust and evil in the whole world.... The time is at hand.[64]

The Münsterites did not have a different Christology from the other Anabaptists but they did have a different eschatology and ethics. They believed that they were living in the final dispensation and that the earthly teachings of Jesus no longer applied to them. Jesus was now calling them to live a different drama than he had in the pre-eschaton dispensation. They were now called to participate in ushering in the New Jerusalem because the end was near. How else could the new be born unless through the violent overthrow of the old? But they were wrong about their reading of history and their movement, and many people died tragic deaths.

The Münster experience was an important lesson to the Anabaptists, especially about how not to be political, which is different

---

62. For a helpful summary of the Münsterite story see *Mennonite Encyclopedia*. Vol. 3. Hillsboro, Kansas: Mennonite Brethren Publishing House, 1982.
63. C. Arnold Snyder, *From Anabaptist Seed: The Historical Core of Anabaptist-Related Identity* (Kitchener, ON: Pandora Press, 1999), 42.
64. Snyder, *From Anabaptist Seed*, 43.

from being non-political.[65] Absolute pacifism became the Anabaptist mantra and, for them, that meant nonresistance to the powers (endurance of politically caused suffering instead of violent resistance) and separation from the world. For the church to take charge and to violently (or even non-violently) impose the new kingdom agenda on earth was not the call of Christ. Nevertheless, Anabaptist political theology was not uniform. By far the majority of Anabaptists sought to separate themselves from the world and structure their existence in accordance with an ethic derived from Jesus's teaching. In other words, their politics was different from that of the world and, as they saw it, the two could not mix. They did not believe that it was their purpose to save the world; they saw it as their purpose to rescue individuals from the world and to have them join the body of believers separated from the world. All should become part of the new "body of Christ."

There were, however, some Anabaptists who saw the divide between church and world somewhat differently. For example, Pilgram Marpeck believed that the distinction could not be stated (nor lived) as exclusively as the others thought. He too believed that the church was to be a light to the world, which meant that the world ought to see in the church the promise of its own salvation. For the world had no ultimate reality as world; it was fallen and its true nature was to be seen in the politics of the church, where the hostilities of human relations could be overcome in Christ. However, for all this to happen the politics of the church should be clearly visible to the world; that is, the church should not separate from the world. The church and its members should live radically in the world, albeit *differently*.

It goes without saying that Christology was at the centre of Anabaptist theology, but that does not yet tell the entire story. For what does it mean to take Jesus seriously? How must we then live? Their answer: be the church as the new body that foreshadows the future of the kingdom which is not yet. But how (or where) to express this new kingdom was not so easily settled.

---

65. I say it this way because I do not believe that the Anabaptists chose between being political and not being political; they chose between being political in the way the Münsterites were political—that is, being violent—and being political in a non-violent way.

Recovery of the Anabaptist Vision

In the middle of the twentieth century a movement emerged in North America that sought to revive the vision and passion of the Radical Reformation and to state again, perhaps somewhat more clearly, what it meant to be faithful peacemakers. There was an effort to show that Anabaptist theology was neither Protestant nor Catholic and this was important since the common assumption was that Mennonite theology was merely a radicalized version of mainline Protestant theology.[66] In contrast, Walter Klaassen argued that the radical view of discipleship held by Anabaptists like Conrad Grebel and Menno Simons was uncompromising in ways that the mainline churches were not. This underwrote their views on pacifism, separation from world, and community. The Anabaptists believed that true believers could not be faithful by themselves and needed, in addition to the guidance of the spirit and the Word of God, fellow Christians with whom they covenanted openness to admonition and discipline to keep them from yielding to the worldly temptations that sought to break apart the passions of the heart, the words of the mouth, and the actions of the body. For if these three, passions, words, and actions, are not in unity, the witness of the body of Christ is compromised.

Before Klaassen's study, a seminal essay appeared in 1944 written by Harold S. Bender, in which he argued that "the Anabaptist vision included three major points of emphasis: first, a new conception of the essence of Christianity as discipleship; second, a new conception of the church as a brotherhood; and third, a new ethic of love and nonresistance."[67] This essay had a major impact on both Mennonite theology and life. It is possibly the most read theological essay in the Mennonite world. And only after the polygenesis project of re-reading the sixteenth-century sources and noticing a lack of uniform theological teaching was Bender's succinct summary questioned, but even then not profoundly.

---

66. See Walter Klaassen, *Anabaptism: Neither Catholic nor Protestant* (Waterloo, ON: Conrad Press, 1973).

67. Harold S. Bender, "The Anabaptist Vision." (Accessed February 3, 2014.): http://www.mcusa-archives.org/library/anabaptistvision/anabaptist-vision.html.

There are, however, significant Mennonite voices in the debate that seek to shape the view of peace and justice differently. And some of these arise from reading contemporary American theologians, especially the Niebuhr brothers, Reinhold and Richard. One way of narrating the influence is around the move from key words like "discipleship" and "faithfulness" to "responsibility." This may seem like a mere nuance, but it had big results. The language of responsibility, made popular by H. Richard Niebuhr,[68] emphasizes a Christian's relationship to the world that connoted a stance of being in charge of (responsible for) the state of affairs in the world. This was anathema to the Anabaptists/Mennonites in part because of the Münsterite experience. Yet it was strongly compelling for some contemporary Mennonite theologians.

Niebuhr emphasized that Christian ethics is best understood when moral agents see themselves as acting in response to what God is already doing in every situation. We are responders, not citizens under a law to be obeyed at all costs, and not artisans bringing about an end to be achieved at any cost. Niebuhr's approach, emphasizing responsibility, takes context and place far more seriously than did the Anabaptist emphasis on following Jesus. Hence, Mennonite theologians like J. Lawrence Burkholder and Gordon D. Kaufman, both professors for a time at Harvard University and both influenced by the writings of Niebuhr, challenged the somewhat sectarian-sounding ethic of Bender and Guy F. Hershberger.[69] Both Burkholder and Kaufman argued that the manner in which the church-world distinction gets parsed by the Anabaptists and their Mennonite recoverers is problematic. The church, even in its separation from the world, is not nearly as pure and spotless as is supposed, and the world in its sinfulness is not to be shunned but saved. Christians need to be in the

---

68. See H. Richard Niebuhr, *The Responsible Self: An Essay in Christian Moral Philosophy* (New York: Harper and Row, 1963). See also Harry J. Huebner, *An Introduction to Christian Ethics: History, Movements, People* (Waco, TX: Baylor University Press, 2012), 361–376.

69. See J. Lawrence Burkholder, *The Problem of Social Responsibility from the Perspective of the Mennonite Church* (Princeton, NJ: [np], 1958); Gordon D. Kaufman, *Nonresistance and Responsibility, and other Mennonite Essays* (Newton, KS: Faith and Life Press, 1979); Guy F. Hershberger, *War, Peace, and Nonresistance* (Scottdale, PA: Herald Press, 1944).

world with great passion helping it to be *responsible* minimally to live up to its own ideals. That is, we need to bear witness to what a peace ethic can offer the world as it is. For the Mennonites represented by Bender and Hershberger such language was new and dangerous. They believed that the world cannot be saved as world but must be transformed, and the church is called to keep itself pure as a beacon of light to the darkness of the world. The church is now what the world could be if it were faithful to the original vision expressed in the creation story; and the world as world has no permanent (ontological) status. It is a fallen form of good creation.

This discussion raised the question of the relevance of Jesus for social ethics. Following Jesus (discipleship) had been the focal point for Mennonite life from the beginning; but as more and more Mennonites moved to the cities and became bankers, lawyers, physicians, public university professors, and employees of governments, the challenge became what to do when the One whom we follow offers little apparent guidance on these matters. That is, it is one thing to follow Jesus when we remain unto ourselves in Christian community where we determine the framework and its limits but it is another to do so within the ambiguities of the world and its structures. So Mennonite ethicists asked openly whether there is a social ethic in the Jesus story that instructs Christians to live not only in Christian community but as Christians in a secular society.

Mennonite ethicist/theologian, John Howard Yoder, in his 1972 book, *The Politics of Jesus*,[70] assesses the theological underpinnings of the peacemaking imagination from which these concerns come. In his study he gives a new read of the Jesus story, new not in that he provides a unique perspective, but new in that he brings together the accepted scholarly readings of Jesus around the question of whether there is in this story a social/political ethic that can guide Christian life today. His argument is that Jesus lived by an ethic that was distinct from the accepted norms of his time and yet fully within the fray of social/political reality. And he did so by choosing from outside the accepted norms. This outside norm should guide Christians today.

---

70. John Howard Yoder, *The Politics of Jesus* (Grand Rapids, MI: Eerdmans, 1994 [1972]).

Two modes of faithful living in Jesus's time were represented by the Essenes and the Zealots. Both groups positioned themselves in relation to the injustices of the day. The Essenes believed that in order to be faithful to Yahweh they needed to withdraw from society (to the Judean hills, for example) to protect themselves from the worldly influences around them. They believed it to be important that there be a people who lived as a faithful-to-Yahweh remnant, concentrating on their own purity in order that people may see the contrast between the unfaithful and God's faithful. The injustices of the world were not their primary concern; that was God's doing, and the justice of God would be rendered by God in due time.

The Zealots, on the other hand, believed that social reform needed to take place with their direct involvement in the struggle. Hence they organized themselves into units of resistance and used whatever means necessary to seek to overthrow the Roman occupation.

Both groups believed that the Roman occupation was unjust and not willed by God. The Essenes believed that it was not their business to do the overthrowing—it was God's; the Zealots believed it was their business and hence needed to get involved in the revolution.

Those working with articulating the Mennonite understanding of faithfulness should find this dichotomy instructive. If the only option to living a withdrawn-from-society existence is the Zealot option, then their traditional commitment to the peace position is up for grabs. Then the Münsterites had it right all along.

However, Yoder's reading of Jesus is that these are not the options that faithful believers must choose between. Jesus struggled with them himself, only to reject both in favour of a third option which is characterized by the way of cross. That is, it is neither only God's business to make the world just nor only up to us to do so. Jesus was every bit as concerned about the social injustices as the Zealots and every bit as concerned about spiritual purity as the Essenes. But his way of the cross is characterized by a non-violent confrontation of the powers of injustice which was neither withdrawal nor violence.

Part of what's at stake with the way of the cross is the notions of power: What power is at work in the world to bring about the kingdom that Jesus envisions? Yoder addresses this issue in the following words:

The triumph of the right is assured not by the might that comes to the aid of the right, which is of course the justification of the use of violence and other kinds of power in every human conflict. The triumph of the right, although it is assured, is sure because of the power of the resurrection and not because of any calculation of causes and effects, nor because of the inherently greater strength of the good guys. The relationship between the obedience of God's people and the triumph of God's cause is not a relationship of cause and effect but one of cross and resurrection.[71]

Lots can be said about these sentences, but before I say more I will introduce several other voices into the mix in the hope that this might serve to embolden the debate.

The Challenge from Other Interlocutors

As Mennonite theologians sought to give an account of a viable Christian pacifism, they encountered many critical voices. I begin with another Niebuhr, this time Reinhold. In his famous essay "Why the Christian Church is not Pacifist," he says that most Christian views of pacifism are heresies because they operate under the illusion that they have discovered a method of eliminating violence from the political process. And that is impossible! There are, however, some pacifists who are not heretics, according to Niebuhr. He names them thus:

In medieval ascetic perfectionism and in Protestant sectarian perfectionism (of the type of Meno [sic] Simons, for instance) the effort to achieve a standard of perfect love in individual life was not presented as a political alternative. On the contrary, the political problem and task were specifically disavowed.... It is this kind of pacifism which is not a heresy.[72]

71. Yoder, *The Politics of Jesus*, 232.
72. Reinhold Niebuhr, "Why the Christian Church is not Pacifist," in *Christianity and Power Politics* (NY: Archon Books, 1969), 4.

Niebuhr's attempt to exempt Mennonite pacifism from his critique flattered and tempted some Mennonite theologians. But notice how Yoder's words suggest that Niebuhr's rendering of Mennonite pacifism relegates it to complete irrelevance, and hence Mennonite pacifism could not be Christian. Thus it turns out that Niebuhr's intended compliment is pacifism's greatest critique.

A Christian ethic that is for everyone, says Niebuhr, must be more realistic than pacifism can offer, one in which we recognize the limits of the human capacity that is circumscribed by sin. This is an ethic that may well endorse constraints on violence but requires it nonetheless precisely in order to curb the destructive power of sin. The love ideal that Jesus embodies is impossible for the human political/social process (even while it may be possible for individual Christians) and can only be approximated in human society. Nonresistance, which Jesus preached, and even non-violent resistance, which Niebuhr contends is falsely derived from Jesus, are no match for the power of evil in the world. In fact, for Niebuhr, nonresistance and non-violence are both forms of non-power and hence cannot really effect social change. Hence a commitment to pacifism implies that the unjust status quo will remain. This, argues Niebuhr, is heretical.

This is not the place for a detailed analysis of Niebuhr's thought,[73] but his assumption of the absolute dichotomy between a perfectionist and a realistic ethic has led to questioning from both sides: What is perfectionistic about non-violence and what does it mean to be realistic? These two questions are actually closely related in that both hinge on whose reality counts in the labelling process. For example, the perfectionist perspective has been seen as a spectator stance because active engagement with earthly structures *requires* something other than non-violence. But why attribute normativity to an ontology of violence when the Christian imagination tells the story, via the creation account, of an ontology of peace?[74] Indeed what has received

---

73. For a more extensive treatment of Niebuhr's thought see my chapter in *An Introduction to Christian Ethics: History, Movements, People* (Waco, TX: Baylor University Press, 2012), 345–360.

74. For a further discussion of the difference between an "ontology of peace" and an "ontology of violence" see John Milbank, *Theology and Social Theory: Beyond Secular Reason* (Oxford, UK: Blackwell Publishers, 1990), esp. 278–325.

a great deal of discussion in the past half century, and has taken on a kind of experimental practice in the peace movement, is non-violence as a *power* for political/social change. While this demonstration may not answer all the questions about whether violence is necessary in order to keep the peace within the social order, it does show that non-violence is a usable power for social change in a manner that Niebuhr did not foresee.

Many examples of non-violent peace activists/theorists could be cited. Perhaps the most obvious are Mahatma Gandhi, Gene Sharp, and Martin Luther King, Jr. They had much in common but came from profoundly different backgrounds: Gandhi, a Hindu civil rights leader in South Africa and India, Sharp, an American political theorist[75] and King, a Baptist minister and American civil rights leader. Yet all have shown the power of non-violent direct action as an effective power in resolving disputes and in changing unjust structures to more just ones. There is no denying that in the twentieth century non-violence came into its own as a political force that surprised even most religious pacifists like the Mennonites.

Yet we do not get careful *theological* reflection from this group of three thinkers on how to understand human participation in social change. What we get, however, is suspicion from some Mennonite theologians like Guy F. Hershberger who believe that the non-violent peacemaking vision of people like Gandhi has nothing to do with the pacifism of Christian faithfulness. So here we're back to the Essene-like withdrawal pacifism that cannot work in the real world. There seems here an embarrassment in associating with a power like non-violence, the assumption being that Jesus taught us to shun power. The dichotomous logic simply won't go away.

There are those who believe that with the advent of Liberation Theology there was new hope in the resolution of the problem of dualisms. However, here one finds dualisms by a different name. In a way Karl Marx states the dualism with his famous quote: "Philosophers

---

75. The works of Martin Luther King, Jr. and Mahatma Gandhi are well documented online and so will not be cited here. Gene Sharp's seminal study is *The Politics of Non-Violent Action: A Study Prepared under the Auspices of Harvard University's Center for International Affairs* (Boston, MS: P. Sargent Publisher, 1973.

have only interpreted the world, in various ways; the point is to change it."[76] This time it's between theory and practice. But this distinction is not so different from Reinhold Niebuhr's ideal/real distinction; theories are ideal and practices are real; pacifism is okay in theory, in practice you need something else.

Proponents of Liberation Theology were critical of the theory/theology emanating from the "Northern/Western" imagination and argued that it was preoccupied with correct theology (orthodoxy) at the expense of correct practice (orthopraxis). With the Exodus story as their paradigm they made liberation the determiner of correct practice. They recognized that, in the Exodus story, God was the primary liberator, but they resisted the traditional dichotomy of "God's domain" versus "human domain." So they drew human activities fully into the liberation nexus. This has made Liberation Theology very appealing to the Mennonite peace activists. Indeed it opened their eyes to a much more broadly understood view of violence—like the violence of structures, some of the very structures that peacemakers participated in, like the cherished economic, cultural, and social structures. Yet most Liberation Theologians are not pacifists for they cannot subordinate liberation to an ethic. In other words, the "how" of liberation must bow down to the "that."

These voices add new wrinkles to the Mennonite peace theology discussion that require a fresh take on our earlier analysis, especially on the delicate claim that we find ourselves speaking peace from the stance of implicated violence. Indeed the space we occupy is much more complex than we would like it to be. How then might pacifists position themselves as relevant peacemakers?

Theological Struggle — Take Two

After the impact of the above voices, Mennonites can no longer do peace theology pretending that the old categories work. As we have seen, those engaging in the discussion have struggled from the very

---

76. Karl Marx, "Theses on Feuerbach," in *Marx/Engels Selected Works*, (Accessed February 3, 2014.) http://www.marxists.org/archive/marx/works/1845/theses/theses.htm.

beginning with the temptations to withdraw in order to remain faithful on the one hand and to fully engage the exigencies of the world in order to demonstrate that God's peace in Christ is relevant in this conflict-ridden world that is our home on the other hand. And, in both cases, it hinges on a viable theology of power.

On December 16–18, 1986, an important event took place that reshaped the traditional understanding of Mennonite peace theology as it relates to power. Mennonites from several conferences and Brethren in Christ[77] held a conference at the Techny Towers in Chicago, Illinois, to debate how faithfully to understand the biblical mandate to Christ's followers to be active peacemakers in the world. The question focused on whether Christian faithfulness required a move from nonresistance to evil (the traditional language) to active non-violent resistance to evil. In other words, are people like Gandhi, Sharpe, and King our allies or our adversaries? The conference unanimously affirmed that they are indeed our allies.

The conclusion reached at the conference is captured with the following affirmations:

1. We believe the mandate to proclaim the gospel of repentance, salvation and reconciliation includes a strengthened biblical peace witness.
2. We believe that faithfulness to what Jesus taught and modeled calls us to more active peacemaking.
3. We believe that a renewed commitment to the gospel of peace calls us to new forms of public witness which may include nonviolent direct action.

---

77. The moderators and secretaries plus several theologians from the North American Mennonite churches (including representatives from General Conference Mennonite Church, Mennonite Church, and General Conference of Mennonite Brethren Churches) and Brethren in Christ met to discuss "active peacemaking." The discussion was initiated by Professor Ron Sider, from the Brethren in Christ, who gave an address "God's People Reconciling" at the Strasbourg, France, Mennonite World Conference in 1984. Here he challenged those gathered to a more active peacemaking stance in our violent world and called for the establishment of a Mennonite peace force that would be prepared and willing to go into violent regions to resolve conflict. See http://www.cpt.org/resources/writings/sider for a copy of his speech.

4. We believe the establishment of Christian Peacemaker Teams is an important new dimension for our ongoing peace and justice ministries.[78]

At one level this settled the matter—active confrontation of violent powers is understood as part of the biblical mandate; at another level questions continued. Is active peacemaking to be understood as the employment of non-violent strategies because they are more effective than violent strategies? What difference does it make that Christians believe that God is in charge of the peace of the world? How are we to understand Jesus's failure to overthrow the Roman occupation and set up his kingdom of peace? What difference does it make for us to recognize that we live in a sinful, broken world and that we ourselves are part of it? More nuance seemed necessary!

The quest to develop a deeper theological understanding moves us in the direction of how properly to see ourselves as agents of historical change. This seems to have been the issue for Mennonite peace theology all along. And to go there requires that we say more about a key sentence in the Yoder quote above: "The relationship between the obedience of God's people and the triumph of God's cause is not a relationship of cause and effect but one of cross and resurrection." The affirmation of the use of non-violent direct action as a power for social change can be understood in two quite different ways. One is as a new kind of warfare where violence is not required to bring about our desired goals of history; it can now all be done using non-violent techniques to move history in the right direction. The other way to affirm non-violent direct action is as a peace witness—as a sign that although we are not in charge, the One who is in charge calls us to undermine the powers of evil by refusing allegiance to them. This is the alternative to violence—a way to say that peace is the desire of God from the very beginning of creation.

Yoder helps us to see that the pacifism that is rooted in the story of Jesus Christ (life, death, and resurrection) is not one that suggests that we can achieve with non-violent means all that war promises

---

78. Known as the "Techny Call" and is quoted from *Christian Peacemaker Teams: Discussion Guide* (Waterloo, ON: Institute of Peace and Conflict Studies, 1985), 1.

to achieve. Although non-violence is always better than violence, Christian peacemaking is not best understood as a new kind of warfare. Says Yoder:

> That Christian pacifism which has a theological basis in the character of God and the work of Jesus Christ is one in which the calculating link between our obedience and ultimate efficacy has been broken, since the triumph of God comes through resurrection and not through effective sovereignty or assured survival.[79]

The ultimate challenge is therefore not one of strategy at all, but one of training ourselves to be certain kinds of people; people who are willing to give up striving to attain an elusive peace and who learn what it means to participate in Christ. This permeates all aspects of human existence and all earthly structures; surely it means refusing to obey the state when it calls us to war, but it also means refusing to pay, through our taxes, for the wars the state can fight without us joining in actual battle. It also means challenging the structures of poverty, the structures that marginalize peoples, oppress races, exclude voices, and so on. It means we should talk about violent and peaceful ways of rearing children, violent and peaceful ways of growing and eating food, violent and peaceful ways of relating to enemies, strangers, and the earth, of living with difference, even of seeking the truth. Perhaps most important of all it means coming to see the insidious nature of violence residing in places and structures we wish to hold pure. Just because we are not in charge does not mean we are not involved. Christian peacemaking is not a spectator sport; nor is it solely about winning! And it can call existing violent structures to peace because the very grain of the universe is peaceable and not violent.

But how are we to play the game of life when what drives us is not the achievement of the end toward which we strive? The answer is delicate one but important. To "be in Christ" cannot be captured by seeking to bring about a goal like the kingdom of God; nor can it be summarized by obeying a law. To participate in Christ is to be drawn into the very spirit and demeanour of Christ and live the life

---

79. Yoder, *The Politics of Jesus,* 249.

of radical openness to the divine. In this life there is no necessity to kill or hate or do violence. For even if our non-violent posture should bring suffering upon us, God is not defeated by violent earthly forces, even the force of death. So the pacifist is placed between the cross and the resurrection; our suffering does not *produce* new life, yet our hope in God's mercy empowers us to trust in redemption beyond what seems graspable. The *mysterium* of being is the stance from which we live Christ's peace.

When God created the world it was given as a beautiful garden of peaceful coexistence of animals and vegetation. When the Apostle Paul presents a picture of Jesus he envisions him as restoring the peace of original creation.[80] Mennonite peace theology can therefore no longer be ghettoized to an anti-war stance; it must encompass all of life. This is because we have learned that violence too cannot be narrowly defined; it permeates every structure of life. Hence, so does the search for and the practice of peace.

Conclusion: The Cat Came Back

So why should we care about the well-being of others and the world if it is not up to us to fix it? We care because of whose we are. To be Christ's, or to be in Christ, is to care as Jesus cared—he called down those who were abusing their power; he healed the sick; he taught those willing to listen to the way of peace; he confounded the legalists; and he called the little children models of the kingdom. He pushed his hearers to see unpeace in places they long ago thought all was settled. (See the Sermon on the Mount, Matthew 5ff.) The issue for Jesus did not seem to be what we could accomplish but rather who we give voice to by what we say, by the place we occupy, and by how we express our identity.

In 1983 I returned from two years of MCC service in Israel/West Bank, having worked as a peace worker in that conflict-ridden region. Shortly afterward I gave a report to a local Manitoba Mennonite church. When I was done I was asked a penetrating question by one of the listeners: "Who do you think you are? God is working out his purposes there and you dare to interfere?" Hmmm! Although it was

---

80. Rom. 8:18–25 and Col. 1:15–20.

a painful question, nonetheless, it was the right one. Who did I think I was as a peace worker? That does make all the difference. For the questioner, I suspect, it was a rhetorical question suggesting I had no right to try to make peace in that conflict. It was not my arena of faithful activity. It was God's business alone. The old dichotomy! But surely we must say more—nothing more that would make it less God's business. But does not the invitation by Jesus to "take up the cross and follow" invite every faithful follower into the very activities of God's peacemaking work? The question is not, Whose task is it— God's or ours? The question is rather how we can become the kind of people who are able to participate in the divine peacemaking activities of which we are not in charge. It requires being a particular kind of people trained in the art and strategies of peacemaking, offering alternatives to violence that are too often defended as necessary, even when we and our efforts are rejected. What kind of people we are is indeed the right question.

I am writing the conclusion to this essay during the week of Israeli leader Ariel Sharon's death and burial. For me personally it is reminiscent of an experience in Jerusalem in 1982 during the time Sharon was Israeli defence minister and in charge of the war in Lebanon. On the day the story of the Sabra and Shatila massacre[81] in southern Lebanon broke in Jerusalem I happened to have a dental appointment with my Israeli dentist. When I entered the examination room and met the dentist, he did not respond to my "Shalom" greeting. I knew he was distraught! We had a friendly rapport even though he was an avid Zionist from New York doing his Jewish duty to reclaim Eretz Israel for his people and I was an MCC peace worker with the Israeli and Palestinian peace movements often calling Zionist Israelis to task for unpeaceful practices. We respected each other even though, by

---

81. The Sabra and Shatila massacre took place September 16–18, 1982. It involved the slaughter of (762–3,500 civilians in these two refugee camps near Beirut who were mostly Palestinians and Lebanese Shiites. The massacre was conducted by a Lebanese Christian militia under the control of Ariel Sharon's military. Later in an Israeli conducted enquiry (the Kahan Commission) Ariel Sharon was held personally responsible, and although Prime Minister Menachem Begin refused to fire him, Sharon was forced to resign but remained in the Israeli cabinet as minister without portfolio. Later (in 2001) Sharon was elected Prime Minister of Israel.

conviction, we were miles apart. That morning he did not speak until I was sitting back in his chair with my mouth open. Then he said simply and emotionally, "We did not do this, you know. We are not that kind of people." Although he was later proven wrong when an Israeli government enquiry held Sharon personally responsible for the massacre, the dentist was grappling with the right question—What kind of people are we?

Who are we? Or, perhaps better asked, whose are we? These are the questions that are so crucial in imagining and practising peace; to answer these questions correctly is to have put in place key building blocks for a peace theology relevant for our time and worthy to bear the name of the Prince of Peace. Remember, cats, when permitted, require enormous setup to be *good* cats; so, I contend, do faithful peacemakers.

Bibliography

Bender, Harold S. "The Anabaptist Vision." (Accessed February 3, 2014.) http://www.mcusa-archives.org/library/anabaptistvision/anabaptistvision.html.

Christian Peacemaker Teams: Discussion Guide. Waterloo, ON: Institute of Peace and Conflict Studies, 1985.

Burkholder, J. Lawrence. *The Problem of Social Responsibility from the Perspective of the Mennonite Church.* Princeton, NJ: [np], 1958.

Hershberger, Guy F. *War, Peace, and Nonresistance.* Scottdale, PA: Herald Press, 1944.

Huebner, Harry J. *An Introduction to Christian Ethics: History, Movements, People.* Waco, TX: Baylor University Press, 2012.

Kaufman, Gordon D. *Nonresistance and Responsibility, and other Mennonite Essays.* Newton, KS: Faith and Life Press, 1979.

Klaassen, Walter. *Anabaptism: Neither Catholic nor Protestant.* Waterloo, ON: Conrad Press, 1973.

Marx, Karl. "Theses on Feuerbach," in Marx/Engels Selected Works. (Accessed February 3, 2014.) http://www.marxists.org/archive/marx/works/1845/theses/theses.htm.

Mennonite Encyclopedia 3. Hillsboro, KS: Mennonite Brethren Publishing House, 1982.

Milbank, John. *Theology and Social Theory: Beyond Secular Reason.* Oxford, UK: Blackwell Publishers, 1990.

Niebuhr, H. Richard. *The Responsible Self: An Essay in Christian Moral Philosophy.* New York: Harper and Row, 1963.

Niebuhr, Reinhold. "Why the Christian Church is not Pacifist," in *Christianity and Power Politics.* Hamden, CT: Archon Books, 1969.

Plato. "The Republic." *The Dialogues of Plato* 1. Translated by B. Jowett. New York: Random House, 1937.

Sharp, Gene. *The Politics of Non-Violent Action: A Study Prepared under the Auspices of Harvard University's Center for International Affairs.* Boston: P. Sargent Publisher, 1973.

Sider, Ron. "God's People Reconciling" (lecture, Mennonite World Conference, Strasbourg, France, July 24–29, 1984), (Accessed February 3, 2014.) http://www.cpt.org/resources/writings/sider.

Snyder, C. Arnold. *From Anabaptist Seed: The Historical Core of Anabaptist-Related Identity.* Kitchener, ON: Pandora Press, 1999.

Yoder, John Howard. *The Politics of Jesus.* Grand Rapids, MI: Eerdmans, 1994.

Additional Resources

Berry, Wendell. *Blessed Are the Peacemakers.* Berkeley, CA: Counterpoint, 2005.

Berry, Wendell. *What are People For?* New York: North Point Press, 1990.

Hauerwas, Stanley. The *Peaceable Kingdom: A Primer in Christian Ethics.* Notre Dame, IN: University of Notre Dame Press, 1983.

Huebner, Chris K. *A Precarious Peace: Yoderian Explorations on Theology, Knowledge, and Identity.* Waterloo, ON: Herald Press, 2006.

Huebner, Harry J. "The Church Made Strange for the Nations," *Echoes of the Word: Theological Ethics as Rhetorical Practice.* Kitchener, ON: Pandora Press, 2005.

Huebner, Harry J., and Hajj Muhammad Legenhausen, eds. *Peace and Justice: Essays from the Fourth Shi'I Muslim Mennonite Christian Dialogue.* Winnipeg, MB: CMU Press, 2011.

Reimer, A. James. *The Christian and War: A Brief History of the Church's Teachings and Practices.* Minneapolis, MN: Fortress Press, 2010.

Yoder, John Howard. *The Original Revolution: Essays on Christian Pacifism.* Scottdale, PA: Herald Press, 1971.

Žižek, Slavoj. *Violence: Six Sideways Reflections.* New York: Picador, 2008.

Coming Back Home: The Awakening of a Feminist, Buddhist, Anti-Oppression Peacebuilder

—Ouyporn Khuankaew

M Y LIFE HAS BEEN DEFINED BY peacebuilding. I have worked to relieve the suffering that women, minority groups, and other disempowered people experience. I have worked to relieve the suffering experienced by abusers, particularly men who were reared with unhealthy ideas of power and ownership; and I have worked to provide tools that empower people to challenge and to change institutions and social structures that, often unknown to the powerful, are the sources of most—if not all—abuse. It is important for us to recognize the fact that disempowered people do not make up a minority group; they are in the majority. The peacebuilding work described here has occupied most of my life, but my life did not begin that way.

I grew up very poor, in a violent family located in a farming village north of Chiang Mai, Thailand. The suffering from poverty and domestic violence paved the way for me to work for peace and justice. Despite never receiving the message from any adults in school, from the temple, or from neighbours, I knew—and kept telling myself— that my father was wrong, that things were not right in our family. And when some of my older siblings just sat and let my father beat them up, I would run away, believing that it was not right and that I did not deserve that beating. My survival mechanisms then were focusing on making good grades in school; helping my parents, especially my mother with any household chore; and spending as much time as I could outside our home. Later on, when I looked back at my childhood, I believed that the beautiful natural surroundings—rice fields, mountains, and the river that runs through our village where my friends and I went swimming every day— must have helped hold my suffering so that I did not go insane.

Domestic violence, for me, is like a war within the family. Many women, like my mother, have to live through danger on a daily basis, and their children have to grow up with hurt, fear, shame, and anger. Growing up through this war, and witnessing the suffering that is still present in the lives of my family members, makes me hold this issue as a big part of my peacebuilding work.

Like most of the poor farmers in the village, we did not own a rice field. Each year we would experience bad floods that often took away all our harvest. I remembered many times at night when my mother quietly walked out of our house to the house of a neighbour with a woven basket in her hand, signalling that we needed to borrow the rice grain for the next few days. She told me that before I was born they lost their piece of land. It was given by her parents to a rich old lady in the village when they could not pay back a small loan. When I first went to the district town and sat resting on the concrete stairs of the Chinese Thai shoe shop, whose owner later came out to sweep the floor as a signal for me to get out of her shop, I knew that was wrong too.

Around 1976, when I was thirteen years old, a group of student activists came to stay in our village. They helped us harvest rice during the day time, and at night they talked to some of the farmers and to a youth group about being part of the national farmer movement to bring down the military dictatorship government. I remember going to the temple, where they had a meeting with the adults and we, the children, learned to sing revolutionary songs. It was the first time that I heard the words "oppression" and "injustice."

A year after that, when I went to a secondary school in a district town, I would spend lots of time alone in the library. With thirst and enthusiasm I read about slavery in the United States of America and about Anne Frank. With the support of the two teachers who were part of the students' movement from Bangkok, I did an internship at our school. I was involved in producing an underground newspaper that told stories about the suffering of the poor farmers and about being part of the revolution. A few months later the newsletter was found by the school discipline master, who condemned our activities in front of the all the students and teachers after we finished singing the national anthem. I knew then that my life in the future would somehow end up working to challenge authority.

My only brother went to work in the Middle East in order to support me to go to the well-known, middle-class, Christian high school in the city, where I studied for just one year. I had a deep awareness of my working-class roots just from seeing how much money other friends brought to school and that their parents could pay after-class tutoring fees for them to study French or English. I must have been the only student, at least in the entire batch of students attending that year, who came from a poor farming family. That year I felt isolated, alone, and disconnected.

Domestic violence and class oppression were the two main direct forms of suffering that taught my childhood conscience that things need to change. At home, fear and worry were my constant companions, with me not knowing when my father would start violence. At school, from the secondary level all the way to university, I felt disconnected, unsatisfied, and often worried about not having enough money. Formal education did not help me understand any of these matters, so I found ways to pass school quickly. I took a special test so that I did not have to study the second year of high school, and passed another test that allowed me to go straight to university. I spent only three and one-half years finishing university in order to save money and to get out of the system.

Inside of me I often felt the resistance, disagreement, and questioning toward things that were going on, but I did not have anyone to share them with. I found that things of interest to my classmates were nonsense and meaningless: talking about their boyfriends, chatting about movie stars or their favourite singers. I realized, later on, that the reason high school English was my favourite subject was that reading things in English helped open the doors for me to know, or even to escape to another world that was so different than the one I actually was living in. My major in university was English and American literature, and I would indulge myself in reading all the assigned books and poetry and finished them all soon after the semester began. I had found nurture, happiness, and peace from reading since I was very young. I would read even the English dictionary over and over on a bus to school.

In 1984, after I graduated from Chiang Mai University, I went to teach English as a Second Language in the Indochinese refugee camps situated along the Thai and Cambodian borders. Working with the refugees and hearing their stories of violence, loss, and despair made my personal suffering from poverty and domestic violence seem very small. Every one of the students had lost someone, or many loved ones, in war. I remembered the session that I taught them about family, in English, using coloured wooden rods to help them talk about their family members: their names and ages. There would be moments when some of them could not say anything, when they laid down some of those rods or pulled them away signalling the ones that were dead or left behind in their home country. Many of the old ones who had never been to school in their own country had to struggle— with faces of depression and fear—to pronounce words and phrases in English.

Domestic violence and war share common root causes: the male-dominated culture that teaches people to believe and accept that power is about owning, and about controlling and conquering. These two forms of violence are interrelated because men learn and practise violence inside their homes, with the support from the collective silence of neighbours and of our culture. So every time that I can prevent or stop domestic violence I believe that I am, at the same time, preventing the big war from happening. Because if you are ignoring the war in your neighbour's home you will naturally ignore, or not know how to stop, the big war.

After three years of working with the refugees I returned home because my father passed away suddenly. I returned home to support my depressed mother, who lived with one of my sisters, a sister who neither had a paid job nor a healthy mind. Her mental problems had developed as a result of being the one who intervened in my father's violence when the other older siblings left our home.

In Chiang Mai I worked with the Thai-German Highland De-velopment Project, a bilateral rural development project between the Thai government and the German Agency for Technical Cooper-ation. The project involved promotion of the tribal communities in Chiang Rai and Mae Hong Son provinces to improve their living stan-dard in health, education, and agriculture. The project was intended to influence the tribal population to change from growing opium to growing other cash crops and to be part of the mainstream Thai rural development model.

My job was to design and conduct training courses for the field staff and government officers who worked in the field of education and public health. It was here that I learned the concept and theory of adult learning, the participatory methods and approaches that sup-port adults in acquiring knowledge and skills that will change their behaviour. This job helped to form me, to ground my future work as a trainer. It also helped me understand the difficulty in working with the centralized, male-dominated, hierarchal bureaucratic structures in Thailand. It was clear to me then that such an environment would be neither a place for me to work for social change nor for me to ex-perience personal growth or learning.

In 1992 I graduated with a master's degree in non-formal educa-tion from Chiang Mai University. These studies helped me understand the failure of Thai rural development. Their development approach partnered with the education system to align everything to sup-port economic development. This approach would make Thailand an industrialized country. I learned about the views and activism of many prominent thinkers and activists in Thailand and abroad. These thinkers were critical of this kind of development. Even though none of them included gender inequality in their views and actions, I was inspired. I gained more understanding of social problems, their common root causes, and the different alternatives that thinkers and activists around the world have explored and used to create changes. I was very impressed by the work of Paulo Freire.[82]

My connection with the grass-root groups and Thai social move-ments began in 1994 when I lived and worked in the Buddhist activist

---

82. Paulo Freire, *Pedagogy of the Oppressed,* Trans. Myra Ramos (New York: Herder and Herder, 1970).

community called Wongsanit Ashram, located two hours northeast of Bangkok. I went there after I experienced difficulty in my marriage and needed a place to stay to sort things out. It was also the time that I was looking for work that would connect me to the non-governmental organizations that, in those years, played a vital role in catalyzing various social movements in Thailand. Those movements emerged to respond to the impact of the centralized governmental policies and projects that were designed to make Thailand an industrialized country. When I lived and worked there I identified myself as a feminist activist even though I had never worked with any feminist organization before.

The Wongsanit Ashram was created to support social activists who experienced burnout; to allow these activists to rejuvenate and to reflect on their lives. It was intended to apply both Buddhist and Gandhian principles in a commune where residents were living and working for social justice. Even though I lived at the Ashram for only six months, I found that it was a place that paved and grounded my life for the journey as a Buddhist peace activist trainer. It was a place and time that supported me in one of my most important life transformations. It was a place that brought me back home to my two roots, a Buddhist and a working class life.

The Ashram leaders' commitment to simple living helped transform my deep sense of shame and my low self-esteem, caused by class oppression, into a sense of belonging and gratitude for having been born poor and having grown up in simple village life. I remember the first night—lying on a simple mattress in a bamboo house with a thatched roof—and the words that came out of silence were "You are coming back home." Tears ran down my cheeks. The marriage that I later left invited me to the life of comfort, convenience, and often luxury. I enjoyed and benefited from those privileges, but I always lived with a sense of betrayal to my family members and to other fellow poor folks in our country who still live hard lives.

The Ashram was founded by Sulak Sivalaksa, a world pioneer and prominent Engaged Buddhist activist and scholar. He was the first person to awaken me to Engaged Buddhism. My attention was awakened by one of his lectures, delivered at the Ashram in 1995, when he said, "Buddhism teaches about suffering and the way to confront suffering, not to run away from it." I have learned about Engaged Buddhism through working with the International Network of Engaged Buddhists (INEB), a network of Buddhist activists and scholars who focus on grassroots social movements in Asia and who have connected their work with other national, regional, and international faith-based groups. Before studying Engaged Buddhism, I never knew that there could be a connection between religion and social justice, between a spiritual life and an activist life.

This was also the place that I first learned the value and the aim of meditation. It was the time that I began to be aware of the lack of peace within me, chaos that was a result of the deep anger and fear that I had accumulated from my turbulent childhood, my lonely adult life, and my marriage. I did not know that I had been living with deep anger, disconnected from my father, and how that had been affecting me. I did not know how to relate to men in general and, especially, to trust them. When you cannot trust your own father, the man who is supposed to give you love, to protect you, and to make you feel safe, how would you know how to develop those feelings with any other man? Through meditation practice I acquired tools to reconnect and to reconcile with my father, twelve years after his death.

The experience of meditation practice helped me see my father in a bigger picture, as a whole person, not just an angry and abusive father. I remembered the picture of my father being a lonely man most of his life. None of us wanted to be near him. I also felt grateful for the kindness and generosity that he had toward me, and toward other people, when he was not in ignorance. I saw those qualities of him in me and my other siblings. This transformation also helped me to provide proper care for my mom, who lived through depression and fear for a long period of her life.

My feminist understanding was deepened by an encounter with Kathryn Norsworthy, a feminist psychology professor from Rollins College, Orlando, Florida, who has been practising Buddhist meditation for many years. We connected through our work in a class on sexuality, feminism, and Buddhist spirituality. Kathryn taught me a great deal about violence against children and women, about gender and sexuality, and about trauma healing. We started working together in 1996, with women from Burma, Thailand, India, and Cambodia, leading workshops on feminist leadership, violence against women and children, as well as feminist counselling. Kathryn and I became very close friends and we continue working together in this region.

Through feminist analysis and Buddhism, and through meditation practice, I came to understand how men who grow up in a patriarchal culture can easily use violence against women, even in their homes, because they are taught to do this and there are social systems that support them in doing so. For example, in Thailand a husband and wife fighting is considered "teeth and tongue" that often collide, so that is not a problem. A man also learns that, as the head of the family, he owns the wife and his children; and with those views he is allowed to use control over the family. So if I was born as a man I may have done the same things my father did, or even worse. This helps me see the root cause of the violence, beyond the person. Rather than seeing only the individual person, I see that patriarchy, or any other form of ignorance such as racism, sexism, class oppression, or homophobia, are created and supported by the social institutions in our society and in our world. And I need to change and challenge those social institutions, not the person. Violence is something we learn and that we are supported to do directly and indirectly; it does not come with our birth.

I realized later on that feminist theory and the concepts that I learned from reading for my master's degree thesis gave me a framework to understand the oppression of women and male privilege at the individual and structural level. But it is the Buddhist teachings and meditation practices that gave me tools for reconciliation and healing. Most of all, Engaged Buddhism shifted me from working for justice that was motivated from anger and discontentment to working for change that was grounded by compassion and peace within. To become a peace activist I needed to do peacebuilding within myself. I needed to transform my own deep suffering that was a result of being a survivor of childhood domestic violence and class oppression.

There are a few peacebuilders whose ways of dealing with great suffering inspire me both for peace work and for my inner life. The first one is Maha Ghosananda, the Buddhist monk from Cambodia who lost almost all his family members and relatives to the Cambodian civil war that killed more than a million people.[83] I heard that, while he was being trained as a monk in the forests south of Thailand, the news that civil war had broken out in his home country had brought great suffering to his mind and heart. He wanted to go home and help. However, his teacher, a Thai monk, told him that if he went home then, there was not much he could do to help, but if he continued to meditate and practice, when he went home at the right time he would be able to help his people. As the master said, when the right time came he returned home and initiated an annual peace walk into dangerous areas controlled by the Khmer Rouge, who had not yet given up arms. One year, during the walk, a few people were killed, but he continued to lead the walk amid the deep fear, the wounds, the hatred, and the division among the Cambodians and their opposition to the government.

During that time I worked as an independent trainer with many Buddhist women, monks, nuns, and grassroots activists around the region, to train them in social work for peace and justice through the INEB network. The work was intense and demanding. I felt isolated and alone living in a village and in a family that was dysfunctional. I was alone with the feminist work I was doing at that time. I did not yet have a strong spiritual foundation, because I had not found a meditation form, apart from sitting with closed eyes, which I later realized was not a technique that works well for a trauma survivor. I did not look for a meditation teacher to help me as I did not feel, at that time, that I needed one.

I was the only one in my family who provided financial and emotional support to my mother, who lived with severe depression and fear, and to my sister, who used alcohol as a way to cope with lupus and her childhood trauma. They lived a few steps from my house.

No one in the village, not even my family members, really understood what I was doing for a living. None of my siblings had made it beyond primary school; thus I had no intellectual connection with them. Our conversations were limited to the family issues or to stories that were not much beyond the village life and its borders. I was the

---

83. Maha Ghosananda, *Step by Step: Meditations on Wisdom and Compassion* (Berkeley, CA: Parallax Press, 1992).

first person in the local area who travelled abroad and went to graduate school.

Most of my friends from primary and secondary school were married and lived their lives as farmers or working in jobs in tourism, the major income of Chiang mai province. In the city, I knew of some local non-governmental organizations, but most of their work was focused on rural development or environmental issues. I had not heard of any feminist activists or activists who were interested in spirituality. In those days, when you were interested in meditation or when you became religious, people would assume that you had been diagnosed with cancer or you had experienced a relationship break-up. Because I worked as an independent trainer, I had no support from an organizations and I did not have colleagues to share my work on a daily basis.

I was the only woman within and among the circle of the Ashram in Thailand who identified publicly as a feminist; I often challenged the gender roles and sexist culture within the community. Although there were many other women activists around, I could feel a sense of discomfort and a distance from them when the word feminist was spoken.

This distance was a result of the term "feminist." A feminist was mistakenly understood to mean one who hates men or does not want to work with them. I sensed that heterosexual women were uncomfortable with the term primarily because of fear of how it would affect their relationships with men. Resistance from older male activists was very common, often expressed in the form of a joke. However, I was strong and outspoken, which attracted younger women in the community who could not challenge the sexist culture there. So, when I came down to the Ashram, these younger women would come and sit around me. An older male activist said to the younger women, "Do not hang around with Ouyporn; you will lose your Thai women's gentleness and sweetness." This was one of the main reasons that I left the community. Though I was unhappy with the lack of Thai feminist allies, the Ashram and INEB friends were the only community that supported my Buddhist peace activist journey.

I met Maha Ghosananda in 1997 during the INEB conference organized in Thailand, when I was the INEB coordinator of the women and gender program. I was captured by his calm and radiant presence. He was available and ready to meet whoever came to him with love and compassion, not showing a single sign of someone who had lost all the members of his family and not showing a trace of burnout or stress from leading dangerous peace walks.

I went to ask him for advice on how to handle all the challenges I was facing with work and family responsibilities. He stood up, after giving advice to many Cambodian activists sitting next to his chair, and asked me if I could show him the way to the bathroom. I pointed the way, but he said let's walk there together. He walked pretty slowly for my pace but very mindfully, not saying anything. When we were close to the bathroom he paused and turned toward me saying, "Like this, Ouyporn. Do it step by step, one at a time," and walked into the bathroom. I stood there speechless. His words penetrated right into my mind and tears just came down. I've never forgotten that great moment of his teaching.

Those of us who work for peace and justice can easily be overwhelmed by the stories of suffering and injustice that we hear from the people we are working with. Because of the constant exposure to suffering we are unaware that we take the suffering of others into our whole being. We feel a big burden and feel that we cannot stop working or even stop thinking or talking about it. This can result in reacting to every problem we encounter, a sign of burnout and stress. But we would feel guilty if we would take a break or if we were to work less. These are the experiences I have gone through in my early years of working with many marginalized groups from Burma, Thailand, and India.

I have to note here that gender roles have more influence on the personal life of female activists than they have on male activists. For us, the women, aside from working to care for the well-being of others, we also have to take care of the well-being of our family members and do house work. In recent years, we have witnessed female activists experiencing more stress and more burnout than our male colleagues. And we, the women, experience guilt at not being able to take care of our families as a result of spending more time and energy at work. It took me many years to overcome guilt over my choice to give more time for work than I gave to taking care of my mother, to overcome my assigned role as it was defined in my culture, in which the youngest daughter has to take care of aging parents.

In 1997 Maha Gosananda told me to take one step at a time. His messages got into my head, but without mindfulness practice and self-care built into my daily life, I ended up being very sick for a few months in 2001. I had severe back pain, and for those few months I could not sit for more than half an hour. I went to see more than ten doctors, who gave me different diagnoses. The more doctors I saw, the more confused my mind was, so I stopped seeing them. One night I sat quietly in front of a book shelf and pulled out a book written by one of the most well-known Thai Buddhist monks, Payutt Yutto. He wrote *Buddhist Economics: A Middle Way for the Marketplace.*[84] Initially I intended to browse through that book in order to pass the night. But the first page that was open was the beginning of the chapter that has big printed phrases saying, "When your body is sick, do not let your mind be sick." That was a great awakening that made me drop into a deep silence with clear light coming out. I realized that, although my back had been in severe pain, my mind was in greater suffering from not knowing what really caused the back pain and how and if I would recover from this illness. I was also a person who could not say "no" to work demands, and if I did say "no," then later I would feel guilty. So instead of stopping and resting, I continued to work at almost the same pace. I have learned since then, slowly, to love and care for myself, my own needs, and my welfare.

The core teaching of Maha Ghosananda, which he repeatedly told people during his peace walks and through his life, is that there is no enemy outside. The only enemy that we have is our own fear, our own ignorance. And only compassion can overcome this enemy from within. The ignorance I had at that time was a separation between the peace and well-being of others and the world, and my own peace and well-being. I was ignorant of the fact that I could easily have compassion for others while not seeing and having the same thing for myself.

Maha Ghosananda's teaching is the same as the stories I received from the Tibetan refugees living in northern India, where I have been

---

84. Ven P. A. Payutto, *Buddhist Economics: A Middle Way for the Market Place* (Badge, CA: Torchlight Publishing, 1996).

offering leadership training to the nuns and other women since 1999. Many of these women left Tibet and travelled to India to be with His Holiness, the Dalai Lama who was heading his community in exile in that town. Some of them came alone and have never seen or heard from their family since. A few of them lost their family members from sickness during the escape. Those women told me their stories during the workshop about the hardship of crossing the freezing terrain of the Himalayan Mountains on foot with the possibility of being captured by the Chinese soldiers, but I saw no signs of trauma among them. I have worked with refugees from Indochina and Burma, and I knew the common signs and symptoms that refuges have as a result of war and the difficulties from leaving their homeland and family. But I did not see those signs among the Tibetan refugees walking along the narrow roads of Dharamsala. So, during one of my trips there, in my ignorance assuming that there were traumatic people somewhere, I walked to the refugee-processing centre and asked people working there if there were such people who needed counselling. I was told that if people need such help they would go see the Lama. I was not satisfied with that answer, so I asked one of the nuns in my workshop to visit the Tibetan nuns who used to be tortured in jail because of their non-violent active resistance to the Chinese government occupation in Tibet. The nuns took me to see the head of the nunnery, who not only showed no signs of trauma but was compassionate, and clear light radiated from her presence. I asked her how she had transformed her suffering. She said that she transformed her suffering through compassionate meditation for herself and for the Chinese authorities and through the meditation of impermanence of the body that was being violated. That encounter totally transformed my understanding of the way to support female trauma survivors who have experienced violence such as rape, of the way to heal their pain at the spiritual level.

In my work with female trauma survivors I found that using feminist power analysis to understand violence perpetuated by men who were trained in a patriarchal culture is a very important framework, but that was not enough. I needed another tool operating at a deeper level, at the level of the heart and the spiritual level in order to really transform and heal the women. The Tibetans always inspire me and give me a sense of hope when I am working with issues of deep-rooted injustice and violence. Their steady effort, the commitment to non-violence, and a patience derived from daily spiritual practice make them my best, most peaceful and hopeful teachers of peace, despite their long experiences of suffering and struggle.

Besides the connection with grassroots work and engaged Buddhism I also learned the concepts, theory, and practice of non-violence and non-violent actions as alternative tools for social change from Quaker peace teachers. I learned from, and was inspired by, the Quakers' activism and by observing them living as models of peace activism who walked their talk. But for me the major lessons learned from these teachers were the concepts and skills for transformation through a concept called "experiential learning." I learned this through being a translator and co-facilitator with them during many workshops that they led in Thailand and Cambodia from 1996-2003. I also went a few times to attend their training courses in Philadelphia.

In 1997, I co-created a women and gender program within INEB. The program involved work with Buddhist nuns around the Asian region. The women and gender program was a result of my participation in the 1995 INEB conference, when I saw only one woman speak in front of the gathering, while the rest of the women—lay and ordained—either sat and listened to male speakers or did all of the administrative work during the entire three-day conference. I said to myself, "Something is wrong here." Thus I helped create the INEB women and gender program. The program works primarily with Buddhist women in south and southeast Asian communities in Thailand, Cambodia, Sri Lanka, and India (including the Tibetans in exile). It was eye-opening for me to understand the oppression of women, and in particular the oppression of nuns, within Buddhist institutions and culture. This was the time when I started to be part of an international circle of feminist women who helped me learn more about Buddhism and feminism and which later led me to call myself a Buddhist, feminist activist. After a few years of working to empower nuns in Thailand and India, particularly the Ladakh nuns and the Tibetan nuns living in exile in India, I began to see the need to work with monks, helping them to become aware of the suffering of the nuns so that they can be good allies to them. For about seven years I worked in Thailand with other Thai trainers—both monks and lay people—aiming to support the ordained community in applying Buddhist teaching to respond to the modern social suffering in our society. Today I still work with the Himalayan nuns in India because they are more open to feminism. I believe that feminism will save Buddhism from corruption and further ignorance.

When I returned to my home village in 1998, I had a vision to build an Ashram so that women peace activists could live and work together. This vision was influenced by the experiences from living in the Wongsanit Ashram. I wanted to combine spirituality, activism, and communal life. I had a belief that a feminist anti-oppression framework with Buddhist and Gandhian principles would be possible and could be lived out in an alternative community. Such a community would permit me and other women who share these values to live and work for social justice on a journey in a setting where internal and external change can meet each other. But I had neither financial resources, nor friends in Chiang Mai who shared these values, to help me start the women's Ashram. So I continued to work as an independent feminist Buddhist trainer with various grassroots women's groups in Burma, Thailand, and India as well as with Tibetans in exile in Cambodia. Between 1996 and 2001 I grounded my understanding and confidence in the use of anti-oppression feminist collective leadership, non-violence and spirituality, and experiential training styles. Month after month, year after year, I tried to embody these principles and methods in the various courses I taught to women's groups. These experiences helped me find fulfillment, to find a happy place as part of the social movements that were active around the region.

This work gave me answers to the many unhappy questions I had in my childhood and early adult life: how to stop violence, how to change class oppression, and how to be out of the systems and to work as the outsider in order to change those systems. Most importantly, I learned how to help make peace outside myself, but to also know how to come home to find peace from within. For a decade, the friends and teachers from the Ashram, and especially the International Network of Engaged Buddhists, continued to be the main community that supported my learning, my spiritual life, and my activism. It is very important that, as activists and searchers for alternatives, we have a community of good friends and teachers to support, to guide, and to help strengthen our journey.

In 2002 I co-founded the International Women's Partnership for Peace and Justice (IWP) with Ginger Norwood, a feminist activist from the United States who has been working for some years with refugee women from Burma. With the shared vision of connecting feminist anti-oppression work and Buddhist spirituality we started providing an in-house training course for the women of Burma. We rented a retreat centre belonging to the Catholic nuns in Chiang Mai. There we hosted participants who came from inside and outside of Burma. Hidden on top of Chiang Mai hills, the retreat centre served us well because it was safe for our participants, all of whom were un-documented. When we could no longer rent that centre, we had to house all of the participants in a small two-storey house next to mine, a house that I had built from the small amount of money I received when I left my marriage.

Later on, one of my sisters donated a small piece of her land to us. With money we had saved from the revenue from previous train-ings we began to build a new building that we used both as a dorm and a training space. Starting in 2004, we began to operate a regional training program on Buddhist peacebuilding, inviting the Buddhist women that I had been working with separately, to come and learn together for six weeks.[85] The expansion of the centre occurred slowly because we had decided from the beginning of our project that we would be a free, donor-driven organization.

We built our meditation hall, our first adobe building, in response to the experience of taking our participants from Burma to meditate at the local temple, where the residential monk told the women to sit in rows behind the men and away from him. The lesson I learned from this encounter with the residential monk was that, if you want to be alternative and make change, you have to stay away from the old structure, and you have to create your own, different structure. In our temple we sit and meditate in a circle; we talk about our enlighten-ment as well as our activist life and our sexuality.

---

85. Ouyporn Khuankaew, *Leadership for Social Change: Training Manual* (Thailand: International Women's Partnership for Peace and Justice, 2005).

IWP integrates feminist anti-oppression, spirituality, and non-violence concepts and practices in each of our training workshops. We also travel to other parts of the region to teach workshops on topics as diverse as feminist leadership; gender and sexuality; violence against women and other sexual minorities; non-violence and peacebuilding; trauma healing; and mindful activism. We also train activists who are interested in using experiential training styles and in integrating spiritual practices in their training programs. We promote simple living, non-violent activism, and the cultivation of relationships with other like-minded groups and individuals based upon a power-sharing practice.

Through the past twenty years of this journey I have learned that peace and justice work needs both a feminist power analysis to understand dominant systems and compassion toward the people with power and privileges who suffer in their roles in the dominant culture. As a Buddhist I believe that those with the wrong use of power and privileges have lost an opportunity to gain enlightenment. When working to challenge people with power and privileges we need the wisdom to help us see the social conditions that support their ignorance.

No human being was born with an intention to harm, to take advantage of others. Besides, those who commit harm will go through natural suffering like all of us: aging, sickness, loss, and loneliness; and they also need love, happiness, and forgiveness like anyone else. With this awareness, our hearts can begin to open and can guide us to take wise and compassionate actions to stop violence and injustice. This, for me, is peacebuilding that shapes my activism and my daily life. The compassion and wisdom that guided me in my early peace activist life to transform my childhood trauma has become a foundation of my activism and has sustained my daily well-being.

In Buddhism we believe that every human being was born with the inherent Buddha nature, a seed of enlightenment. This teaching has helped me to deal with a person or a group that has committed violence. It also motivates me to intervene in a violent situation, be it direct, like domestic violence, or structural, such as war or any form of oppression and injustice because I believe that everyone can gain enlightenment. To stop violence is not only to stop suffering itself; it is also to protect the seeds of enlightenment in each person and support him or her to grow.

As years go by, meditation helps me to see and to use the truth of impermanence, a core teaching of Buddhism. I use the truth of impermanence to deal with hopelessness and despair, both in taking care of my family members who suffer from long-term trauma and in helping other women activists to deal with their obstacles. When we were establishing our project, I thought that the work of our centre to end gender inequality and homophobia, and to heal women who experience trauma, would never yield positive results. An awareness of impermanence helps me focus on being in the present moment. This awareness allows us to do the best we can to create conditions to end or to reduce, even in a small way, an injustice while removing the obstacles that block the path to goodness and peace.

An awareness of interconnectedness helps me see that all the conditions needed to transform long, deep-rooted, collective ignorance are not necessarily in my hands, in my control. Thus I cannot be driven to work for change with a self-centred mind and self-centred action because the cessation of social suffering needs allies, time, patience and effort.

Working and living among "Kalyanamitra"—good friends who share the path and are committed to spiritual practice—is also foundational in my efforts to prevent isolation and disconnection in my activist work. In the early time of my Engaged Buddhist work, in the late 1990s, we created a group called the Rainbow Weavers. The group met once a year and took time to cook, to meditate, to share our personal stories, and to inspire each other. Even though the whole group did not last long, the friendships among a few of us continue to the present. Friends who share the same path have become my spiritual family because my biological family cannot relate to the work I am doing. Even among my circle of feminist activists, most are not interested in inner work or spiritual practice. For me, without good spiritual friends on the path, I feel that my work and life would not have come this far. Spiritual support is needed more these days because the structural ignorance that we want to transform requires collective wisdom, creativity, and cooperation so that we can make effective change.

In my daily life I practise meditation through yoga. While practising yoga I constantly bring my mind back to the breath and body, the same way I do when walking in the rice field. Because I usually think a lot and because I experienced childhood trauma, sitting meditation with eyes closed does not work for me. Other women who experienced trauma report that they also found that sitting with closed eyes brought the trauma back to them. So I train myself and the workshop participants to use our breath and the returning to our bodies as a way to ground ourselves when our own strong emotions rise or when we are swept away by negative or useless thoughts. The analogy of coming back home, coming back to the breath and the body, is also a technique I use when helping others to work through their trauma. It is a meditation form that we can use anytime, anywhere as long as we have our body and our breath. This is an important change and a challenge to the traditional form of eyes closed meditation that, I concluded later on, fits only male monks who have many privileges, men who do not have to worry about cooking, cleaning, or any family responsibility, and thus have time to sit and meditate.

Here I also want to note importantly that, through IWP, I have been working to deconstruct the wrong mainstream Buddhist teachings that oppressed women and sexual minorities through the notion of karma of a previous life. The wrong teaching would say that the female form is inferior to the male form; one was born female as a result of karma from a previous life. One of my sisters who internalized this message deeply, devoted her life to support the monks and the temple so that, in the next life, she hopes, she may be born in a male body. In that way she can become a monk who will have more support for enlightenment. The wrong teaching also includes the belief that gay, lesbian, and transgendered people are people who, in their previous life, broke the third Buddhist precept, the committing of sexual misconduct. In our workshops we brought back the true teaching; the participants then know that karma literally means "actions" and that whatever form of suffering we are going through—be it natural or socially caused—is a result of conditioning factors of this life. Thus we can focus on transforming the present conditions in order to reduce or eliminate the suffering.[86]

---

86. Ouyporn Khuankaew, "Buddhism and Domestic Violence: Using the Four Noble Truths to Deconstruct and Liberate Women's Karma," in *Rethinking Karma: The Dharma of Social Justice,* ed. Jonathan S. Watts (Chiang Mai: Silkworm Books, 2009), 199–224.

I was trained by Thich Nhat Hanh in his disciplines of practice: mindfulness, joy, and happiness through walking meditation.[87] I live in a rural village surrounded by rice fields. My daily walks for several years not only saved me from burnout, disconnection, and loneliness; they taught me a very simple way to experience peace, joy, and happiness in daily life. I also intentionally live in solitude and in silence for a period each day, and this helps me sustain well-being, healthy life, and activism. I have taken a vow to not let negative views and emotions stay in my heart and mind overnight. The commitment to transform any ignorance that arises in my daily life is an important reminder for my peace work.

Peace activists can easily be trapped in the attachment of ego, a self-satisfaction of being a good person, working to save the world, and everything else that we identify with as "me" and "mine" or "our" work. We are not free from any form of ignorance, greed, anger, and self-centredness that we see easily in others whom we think are part of the violent or unjust systems. If we do not cultivate this awareness of self we can easily get caught up in fame, delusions of power, and a corrupted mind, the same things we want to challenge out there. These corruptions are rooted in wrong thinking about the self.

For me, only through meditation practice, and mindful daily living, can I engage with a non-self experience. This non-self state of mind helps me to see things the way they are, and thus, to be able to accept the limitations of myself, of others and of the situation. It enables me to live and work with a cool and calm mind, the nirvana of the here and now experience. This is the core foundation in my understanding of living and working for peace. I strongly believe that this state of mind, grounded in wisdom and compassion in daily life, will sustain my activism and help me experience peace and happiness within while working for outer change.

Aside from the Buddhist peace teachers I mentioned earlier, there are a few others from whom I learned about the framework and

---

87. Thich Nhat Hanh, *Peace Is Every Step: The Path of Mindfulness in Everyday Life* (New York: Bantam Books, 1991); *Touching Peace: Practicing the Art of Mindful Living* (Berkeley, CA: Parallax Press, 1992); *The Miracle of Mindfulness: An Introduction to the Practice of Meditation* (Boston, MA: Beacon Press, 1987).

the content for peacebuilding that I later adapted to fit the people and the social context in our region. I learned a great deal about peace-building, non-violent actions, and living in peace and equality both in organizational and personal life, from the Quaker teacher George Willoughby and his wife, Lillian Willoughby, who came to teach us. These veteran Quaker peace activists and teachers from Philadelphia came to teach us about community building. What I admire and re-member about them was when they told me, as a translator, that in a community-building workshop, it is important to get the leaders of the organization to attend the workshop. They said the leaders are often the obstacles to democracy within the group. Besides the lack of feminist and gender equality within the organization, the problem we were facing at that time was the hierarchal structure that supported centralized power with the male leaders of organization. George Lakey, the director of Training for Change, located in Philadelphia, who was the main Quaker teacher from that organization, for many years trained me in non-violence and training for transformation.[88] He and Karen Ridd came to teach from 1996 to 2000; those ongoing training courses helped create a pool of Thai trainers that continue to provide transformational training throughout Thailand.

The first core teaching that we, the IWP, use when teaching peacebuilding is power analysis. We identify sources of power that individuals, groups, institutions, and nations have. With the vari-ous sources of power there are two ways that they can be used. These sources of power can be used over others that have fewer sources of power, in order to take advantage, to control, or to exploit; or the sources of power can be shared by supporting or making decisions with others.

Along with ways to use sources of power, we also learn about power within, which every individual or group already has or can develop. Marginalized groups such as women have internalized the belief that they do not have any power. For them power has been de-fined only as external elements such as wealth, position, social status, and being part of an institution, which most marginalized people do

---

88. George Lakey, *Facilitating Group Learning: Strategies for Success with Adult Learners* (Mississauga, ON: John Wiley & Sons, 2010). See also Karen Ridd in this volume.

not have access to. Also, the people in these groups do not want to be involved with that kind of power as it is often related to abuse, to control, to corruption, or to politics. But when we discuss power within—power such as courage, wisdom, patience, faith in justice and integrity, and compassion, that they and other marginalized people all over the world already have and use to respond to injustice and violence—this gives them a new framework to look at themselves as well as ways to change the conditions suppressing them.[89]

This kind of power analysis has become a powerful tool for marginalized groups, yet "power over" concepts remain a problem. Marginalized groups report that outside allies, such as middle-class activists—people with good intentions who work to support the grassroots people—often unconsciously use the "power over" method in their support. These allies' "power over" actions indirectly diminish the power of those they intend to help. In particular, grassroots women and other marginalized groups, feel that the "power over" concept and framework help them see root causes of injustice that are inherent in the "power over" culture; and they see the vision of a new model of living and in building a different society.

Understanding structural violence is a way to see a problem beyond the individual or the group and to see the need to organize and mobilize the power of people to influence change. In order to help participants directly experience how social change works, we use an exercise showing ways in which social institutions and groups that form pillars of society work together to support violence. These social institutions may support domestic violence, gender or class oppression, ethnic oppression and conflict, the suppression of dictator-led governments, or exploitation by multinational corporations. We emphasize the fact that direct violence, or any form of injustice, is a result of structural violence. Seeing the interconnectedness of these conditions helps participants see the ways they can reduce their cooperation and support of any form of injustice and ways in which they can create

---

89. Joanna Macy, *Coming Back To Life* (Gabriola Island, BC: New Society Publishers, 2009); Riane Eisler, *The Power of Partnership: Seven Relationships That Will Change Your Life* (Novato, CA: New World Library, 2003); Starhawk, *Dreaming the Dark: Magic, Sex, and Politics*, 15th Anniv (Boston, MA: Beacon Press, 1997).

conditions to challenge the institutions or groups holding power. The understanding of structural ignorance helps participants deconstruct the belief in individual or group karma or faulty faith principles that they are often taught by religious institutions and to deconstruct cultural myths that suggest that violence and injustice are the faults of the victims.

We explore non-violent principles as well as non-violent actions, skills, and strategies to effectively intervene or challenge offending individuals, groups, institutions, or governments to change their wrong use of power and create a just, safe, and peaceful situation.

One core skill that supports acceptance of the framework of power sharing and power within is deep listening. This is a fundamental skill in peacebuilding which sometimes is called listening from the heart or compassionate listening. It is a skill that I learned from the Buddhist Master, Thich Nhat Hanh[90] and the anti-oppression feminist counselling model taught by Kathryn Norsworthy.[91] To me, deep listening is a powerful tool to help restore confidence and to empower marginalized people because, in the dominant society, no one listens to their voices. The emphasis of deep listening is to listen with the heart open, without judgment, without the need to think about ways to help or to fix the victim's problem. It is about being a witness to an individual or group who is experiencing suffering, to affirm the victim's truth and to be with the victim. It is also a fundamental skill when dealing with violence or conflict situations so we do not react with confusion and anger. When working with Buddhist activists I often call deep listening practice "a meditation in action." It is a method that combines understanding from seeing things the way they are and being present with the heart open.

Deep listening needs a foundation of mindfulness. Mindfulness practices are the main skills that we train peacebuilders to use to

---

90. Thich Nhat Hanh, *For a Future to Be Possible: Buddhist Ethics for Everyday Life* (Berkeley, CA: Parallax Press, 2007).

91. Kathryn L. Norsworthy and Ouyporn Khuankaew, "Women of Burma Speak Out: Workshops to Deconstruct Gender-Based Violence and Build Systems of Peace and Justice," *The Journal for Specialists in Group Work* 29, no. 3 (September 2004): 259–283; Ellyn Kaschak and Kathryn L. Norsworthy, eds., *Global Border Crossings: Feminist Activists and Peace Workers Collaborating Across Cultures* (Abingdon: Routledge, 2012).

cultivate peace. We train people in the awareness of the body, or knowing the body through sitting, walking, movement, and breath. In our residential training, practising yoga is part of the daily course. These different mindfulness practices are not just self-care but are the core foundation of peacebuilders and peacebuilding work. Cultivating daily mindfulness aims to help participants ground themselves in body and breath to that they learn how to be present, and to experience peace and stability of the mind.

Deep listening is not just a skill but, when grounded in mindfulness, allows the listener to be present with a stable and calm mind, and thus able to respond to a difficult situation wisely and compassionately.

Peacebuilding combines head, hand, and heart work. We need to learn head work to engage deeply in the analysis and understanding of structural injustice and inequality that causes all kinds of suffering and violence. Seeing this, we know that we need a new model, a new culture, a partnership model for all forms of relationships. We need to practise power sharing, reawakening our power within and across identities, engaging issues through non-violent actions to change the old power over model and create a peaceful and just world. We also need hand work: all the skills necessary to help us carry the content and framework into action. We need heart work: the compassion to see humanity in ourselves and in others who hold power so that we take actions that create no more harm. The heart work brings joy, happiness, and contentment that makes the path and the goal of peacebuilding become one: whole and real. This spiritual work, cultivating from the peaceful heart and mind makes us live as one harmonious being, a peacebuilder inside who does peacebuilding out there.

My experience of teaching about women and peacebuilding with the Canadian of School of Peacebuilding in 2012 helped confirm my understanding and confidence in peacebuilding. The Canadian School of Peacebuilding is committed to making connections between individual and structural peace, the spiritual and social life, the outer and inner life. The program values personal experiences in connection with theory so that peace is not something we just study and analyze; it is also something that we practise. This program is thriving in its efforts to include women in the peacebuilding world. These are the important elements, I believe, in making peacebuilding work: the Canadian School of Peacebuilding produces programs that are inclusive, whole, and practical and thus are effective in creating change.

Bibliography

Eisler, Riane. *The Power of Partnership: Seven Relationships That Will Change Your Life*. Novato, CA: New World Library, 2003.

Freire, Paulo. *Pedagogy of the Oppressed*. Trans. Myra Ramos. New York: Herder and Herder, 1970.

Ghosananda, Maha. *Step by Step: Meditations on Wisdom and Compassion*. Berkeley, CA: Parallax Press, 1992.

Hanh, Thich Nhat. *For a Future to Be Possible: Buddhist Ethics for Everyday Life*. Berkeley, CA: Parallax Press, 2007.

———. *Peace Is Every Step: The Path of Mindfulness in Everyday Life*. New York: Bantam Books, 1991.

———. *The Miracle of Mindfulness: An Introduction to the Practice of Meditation*. Boston, MA: Beacon Press, 1987.

———. *Touching Peace: Practicing the Art of Mindful Living*. Berkeley, CA: Parallax Press, 1992.

Kaschak, Ellyn, and Kathryn L. Norsworthy, eds. *Global Border Crossings: Feminist Activists and Peace Workers Collaborating Across Cultures*. Abingdon: Routledge, 2012.

Khuankaew, Ouyporn. "Buddhism and Domestic Violence: Using the Four Noble Truths to Deconstruct and Liberate Women's Karma." In *Rethinking Karma: The Dharma of Social Justice,* edited by Jonathan S. Watts, 199–224. Chiang Mai: Silkworm Books, 2009.

———. *Leadership for Social Change: Training Manual*. Thailand: International Women's Partnership for Peace and Justice, 2005.

Lakey, George. *Facilitating Group Learning: Strategies for Success with Adult Learners*, Mississauga. ON: John Wiley & Sons, 2010.

Macy, Joanna. *Coming Back To Life*. Gabriola Island, BC: New Society Publishers, 2009.

Norsworthy, Kathryn L., and Ouyporn Khuankaew. "Women of Burma Speak Out: Workshops to Deconstruct Gender-Based Violence and Build Systems of Peace and Justice." *The Journal for Specialists in Group Work* 29, no. 3 (September 2004): 259–283. doi:10.1080/01933920490477011.

Payutto, Ven P. A. *Buddhist Economics: A Middle Way for the Market Place*. Badge, CA: Torchlight Publishing, 1996.

Starhawk. *Dreaming the Dark: Magic, Sex, and Politics*. 15th Anniv. Boston, MA: Beacon Press, 1997.

Additional Resources

Alternative to Violence Project. www.avinternational.org.

Buddhist Meditation Retreat Center at Plum village, France. www.plumvillage.org.

Buddhist Peace Fellowship. www.buddhistpeacefellowship.org.

Dhammayietra-Peace Walks in Cambodia. Center for Peace and Nonviolence.

International Network of Engaged Buddhists, (INEB) Bangkok. www.ineb.org.

International Association of Buddhist Women. www.Sakyadhita.org.

Training for Change, Philadelphia. www.trainingforchange.org.

Feldman, Christina. *Women Awake: Women practicing Buddhism*. Berkley: Rodmell Press, 2004.

hooks, bell. *Feminism is for Everybody: Passionate Politics*. Cambridge, MA: South End Press, 2000.

Kotler, Arnold (editor). *Engaged Buddhist Reader: Ten Years of Engaged Buddhist Publishing*. Berkley: Parallax Press, 1996.

Riane, Isler. *Sacred Pleasure: Sex, Myth and the Politics of the Body-New Path to Power and Love*. San Francisco: HarperOne,1996.

Rothberg, Donald. *The Engaged Spiritual Life: A Buddhist Approach to Transforming Ourselves and the World*. Boston: Beacon Press, 2006.

Pray the Devil Back to Hell. New York: Fork Film, 2008. http://praythedevilbacktohell.com/filmmakers.php.

Courage Is Acting Even though We Are Afraid

—George Lakey

I LOVE, AND AM INSPIRED BY, photographs of great peacemakers. One of the things I have realized is that, in most of the information we get about these people, they don't appear to be very scared. That realization leads me to share stories of some people I know who, to my mind, are great peacemakers, partly because they are scared and do it anyway.

I was once on a speaking tour in the Netherlands. My host in one town was a man, who, although at that moment was a museum curator, told me that his previous career had been as a lion tamer. I was agog because I had never met a lion tamer before—yes, tigers, lions, large—you know—bears, that kind of thing. I said to him, "I'd love to know more about what that was like for you." He replied, "I'll show you my scrapbook."

He had the scrapbook open; I was looking through the pages; and in one of them his head was in the mouth of this enormous lion. I was flabbergasted. I said, "You must be the most courageous man I've ever met." He said, "Sorry to disappoint you. I don't happen to be courageous." I said, "What do you mean? I see this head of yours in the mouth of a lion." He replied, "To be courageous, you need to be scared, because it's in the ability to do something even when you're scared that you get to exhibit courage. It happens that I've always liked kittens. As a little boy, I was very attracted to cats and I always had cats around me. For me, these enormous animals are really just tabbies;

they're really, at heart, kittens. So I got to play with them and I made a living out of playing with these grown up tabby cats. I have to find other ways of developing my courage, because this way didn't turn out for me."

I would like to talk about a couple of people who helped me to understand what courage is. The first is a woman named Barbara Smith, who is an African American leader. She has passed away now, but she gave tremendous leadership in Philadelphia for the peace cause, and also for neighbourhoods standing up for themselves when they were very oppressed. Her neighbourhood was a very low-income African American neighbourhood in Philadelphia, at a time when the drug trade had pretty much taken over the area to the degree that police were hesitant to arrest people, even if they were selling flagrantly on the street. The police were either paid off or intimidated. Barbara Smith was disgusted by this situation, but she knew that the people were completely intimidated as well. She talked a couple of her friends into going with her to one particular street corner, which was a market for drugs, carrying brooms and a plastic bag. She came up to these guys saying, "Oh, excuse me, but it's so littered here and we're just trying to clear this up." So they were just sweeping and picking stuff up. The drug sellers were like, "What…?" But you do not actually kick around a woman who could be your mother when she's with a broom and a bag cleaning up. So these three women got away with it.

There were people looking out the windows at that end of the block, seeing these women do this work in the middle of this environment and getting away with it. The three then passed the word around, "Come to the basement of the Baptist church down the street and we'll talk about it." A bunch of people showed up, partly out of curiosity, like "I can't believe these women would do this." They had a good talk about why it is that they were putting up with this. The women said, "Next Monday night, we'll be there again." So, the next Monday night they all showed up again, with their brooms and their plastic bags cleaning the street. Barbara decided it was time to up the ante a little bit. Out of her purse she pulled a little notebook and a pen, stepped back a little bit, and started writing. Well, immediately the atmosphere got tense. She told me later she was not actually writing anything. She was too scared to write any words. She was just moving the pen, you know, and they got away with it. The guys with the Uzis and the AK47s decided not to do anything because, after all, "She could be my mom, and who knows what she's writing?" As a result, many more people came to the basement of the church that week asking, "What is this?" "What are you doing?" "How can you get away with this?" Week after week after week more women joined them, to the point that the drug dealers had to move to another corner.

When life is that marginal you celebrate every victory. So they celebrated the drug dealers moving to another corner as a victory and said, "Next week we want a mass meeting. Let's fill the basement of the church." They did not fill the basement of the church, but they did get a lot of people at the meeting saying, "What else can we do? You chased those people off the corner. What else can you do?" They replied, "Well, there are probably several corners that we can hold at once. Let's try that." So they did. There were little squads of women, again, looking very unthreatening. The result was they chased the sellers off those particular corners, too.

These church basement meetings, still attended only by women, were getting very feisty and very bold. The police had said that if the women would tell them where there was a car with the trunk open and a large stash of money, they would take the car. The women said, "That's a good deal. We see that kind of thing all the time." So they spread the word around the neighbourhood, "If you happen to be looking out your window and you see a car open and money put in, call the police." People started making the call, and the police, avoiding a direct confrontation because there was nobody at the car, would basically steal the car, pulling it away with a tow truck. More and more tension in the neighbourhood started to be felt from the drug sellers who were part of the neighbourhood. Everybody kind of knew everybody else or knew somebody who knew somebody. Nevertheless, they kept going with the actions, step by small step. Eventually they decided, "It's march time. Let's go marching." They would march in the evening when the drug selling would be most active. At first they avoided the busiest corners, until they got their energy and their boldness up. Soon they started going down the streets where the drug sellers were active. The marching crowds got so large the police got bold enough to start arresting people along the line of the march. The police would actually arrest drug sellers they saw, because they were emboldened by how many people were supporting them.

This, by the way, is a not very well-known fact: police will enforce laws much more effectively if they actually experience community support than if they do not.

This movement kept building and, of course, the men of the neighbourhood had to get into it, right? There was action and everybody was talking about it. You can't be a real man if you are not in on the action! The men started coming to Barbara saying, "Okay, Barbara, you women, you've done all right, but now it's time to move on to the big time, so what do you want us to do?" She fully expected this, so she replied, "Oh, we've been saving the most important job for you. And that is," she said, "there are these houses that have been taken over and made into crack factories, to turn cocaine into crack. We want to reclaim those houses. On our next march we'd like you guys to go first, put on hard hats, so we can really see you brightly, and in fact," as she held out a hat, "here's an example." She had previously made a hard hat with the initials "MAD" on it, because the neighbourhood was called Mantua so the acronym stood for "Mantua Against Drugs." Of course, everybody also knows what "mad" means. She continued by saying, "You guys will be there with sledge hammers, and when we come to the house, you smash down the door and go inside." The men of the community replied, "All right, we can do that." By then there were three hundred people going down the street and up on the porch: smash, smash, smashing down the door and entering the crack house. The people inside were running out the back door. The men were suddenly heroes and, well, men want to be heroes too.

These actions became a neighbourhood insurgency against the drug traffic. Other neighbourhoods, upon hearing about this action, came to Barbara asking, "How can we do the same?" She taught them how to do it.

That is my friend, Barbara Smith. Barbara never became a highly sung hero. I do not think her picture is to be found on any walls but she is such a great example, for me, of going into a situation of great danger, figuring out the margin of relative safety; and, although the risk was still very great, working that margin, building confidence, building allies, and making a difference right there in her own neighbourhood. This is my nod to Barbara, who is probably listening.

The other story I will tell briefly is of the people around me who have helped to form a new group called the Earth Quaker Action Team (EQAT—pronounced "Equate"). I am a Quaker, and the Quaker community has a history of confrontation, of going directly up against the principalities and powers. In more recent times, however, Quakers have got pretty lazy or timid or something like that, and the legacy remains much more in the past than it is active in the present. There are not many Quakers, at least in the USA, who are willing to take on direct action to confront those powers and principalities. There is, though, a group in my area, in Philadelphia, who became so stirred up when we started talking about the crisis of climate change that they said to each other and to me, "We would like to do something about that now. We would especially like to focus on climate change since it is going to destroy so much of life, as we know it, for our grandchildren and our great grandchildren, who are going to inherit a wrecked world unless we take responsibility very soon." These friends of mine, realizing the reality of climate change, said, "Let's take on the Quaker legacy of non-violent direct action." It is fear time.

We started by deconditioning ourselves with regard to the fear. The first step was just to go to a flower show, which was sponsored by PNC Bank. It is important to know that the PNC Bank is the fifth largest bank in the United States and is the number one funder of what is called "mountain-top removal," which is the removal, literally, of mountain tops to mine coal. Over five hundred mountains in Appalachia have been destroyed so far in a region already decimated by coal mining. It is one of the accelerators of climate change in the USA.

Our group decided to target, very clearly, a particular thing to see if we could win. That is why we went after the PNC Bank by going after the flower show. Why, you might wonder, would we choose that to focus on? The reason is that on their website the PNC Bank says it is the "greenest bank you'd ever want to meet." Therefore, of course, you should bring your deposits to the PNC Bank. They are very vulnerable because of the way they present themselves, which is great for us. Those of us involved in these actions need to go after a place where people in institutions that are doing harm are going to feel it. So we went to the flower show and sang songs. We were a little scared, so we undertook a very modest action: we sang songs. "Where have all the flowers gone ... in Appalachia...."[92] Even that was a bit fear-building because we were not sure what the security guards would do and what the police would do when we moved further inside to push the envelope wider.

I am happy to report about these folks who were new to it. I have a history of this kind of direct confrontation. Some of you may know that the first time I was arrested was in a civil rights demonstration, so I go way back. It might be possible to dismiss what I have been doing because I am used to it. These friends were taking these actions for the first time. We built ourselves up to the point that we went into a bank in Washington, DC, in September of 2010. (The Canadian border people brought that up when I came into the country to teach at the CSOP. They said, "We see on our computer an offense in Washington, DC, in September of last year." I just want to let you in Canada know that your tax money is going to a good cause; keeping track of George seems to be one of the ways that your tax money is being used.) In any case, there we were at a PNC Bank near the White House. One of the wonderful things about this particular bank is that it is so close to the White House. It has a history of being "the president's bank." Presidents have cheque books, too; they have to pay bills like the rest of us. Presidents in the USA have tended to use this particular bank, so there are a lot of oil paintings on the walls, kind of like a museum.

We walked into the bank with our gang of Quakers and with Reverend Billy and his gospel choir, with whom we had made an alliance for the day. You perhaps know him as "Reverend Billy of the Church of Life After Shopping." He is an actor who puts on the persona of a televangelist with bouffant hair and so on; he is quite a character and a wonderful man. He and his gospel choir walked casually into the bank with us Quakers.

At the agreed-upon signal Reverend Billy pulled out a tarp and put it on the gorgeous marble floor. We all took out the baggies full of dirt that we had put under our sweaters. We ran over to the tarp and piled up the dirt so we have created a little mountain top. We put on

92. 93A brief video showing EQAT's civil disobedience action at the PNC-sponsored flower show in Philadelphia (Accessed: May 26, 2014.) http://www.youtube.com/watch?v=u_ovXRd-beM.

the mountain top a little sign that says "Stop," and a few cones. Once we had done that we sat down around the "mountain" to conduct a worship service to celebrate God's creation. While we were doing this the gospel choir members pulled out bags with their gospel outfits, which were green robes. Reverend Billy started to walk around the lobby proclaiming the day of the Lord. The bank manager, as you might imagine, was totally freaking out. "Get that stuff off my floor!" and so on.

In my experience, one of the ways that peacemakers deal with fear is to make good plans ahead of time, which we had done. We had decided that two people would deal with the freaked-out bank manager. As soon as the rest of us were doing our tarpaulin thing, building our little mountain, there were—right away—two people zooming over to the bank manager using de-escalation tactics while he was screaming and yelling. Basically they were talking him down through active listening, "Oh, you're upset. I can tell you're upset." He was engaged in it, but the next thing you know he is on the phone calling the police. We fully expected this to happen: we were singing gospel songs, praying, and testifying in the middle of a bank.

The next thing you know the police came in. It happens there were only two police because in town that day there were about two thousand people, all there because of mountain-top removal issue. There was an action at the White House, an action at the Environmental Protection Agency, and the one we were doing at the bank. The police were feeling a bit overwhelmed, so, only two police showed up at the bank.

We had people delegated to meet the police—again, planning being a part of handling our fear. Our two people went right over to the police, where a police officer said, "Are you folks planning to do any violence?" Our people responded, "What? What do you think of us? Of course not. We're a non-violent demonstration and you can count on it absolutely." They responded with, "Oh, good, we'll be back." Then they left! (In all my years of doing these kinds of actions I have never seen police leave the scene of the crime.) Their departure gave us more time to worship. We had a grand afternoon. We did song sharing with the gospel choir and a lot of very deep sharing about our mutual experiences of nature.

By this time the bank manager was so calmed down that he apologized to us for being so harsh in attacking us for demonstrating at his bank. So there we were having a big love-in. In the meantime, the bank manager did not want customers in there, so he had locked the door. The police came back to find a locked door to the bank. Of course, we unlocked the door allowing the police to enter.

The police said to our police liaisons, "Sorry, but we can't arrest anybody more today. We just have too much going on."

Our people replied saying, "Oh, but that's not acceptable. We are sending a signal to the leadership of the bank, the national leadership, that we are escalating this struggle. We are willing to sacrifice a lot, to do jail time, and whatever it takes to get their attention. We really want to send the signal that we are increasing our commitment to the people of Appalachia, and to their mountains. You have to arrest us!"

The police officer replied, "No, we can't make an arrest. There is so much going on in town today, our jails are full, and we have no place to put you: we just can't do it."

Our people replied, "You must arrest us."

There we were having an intense negotiation. Some of you know negotiation theory well, so you know that sometimes negotiating parties end up with a compromise. The police suggested, "How about four of you?" After consultation, our group said, "All right. We will accept that."

The police officers moved over to the sixteen of us sitting on the floor, who were available for arrest. Our team said, "They'll take four. Who will the four be?" In about thirty seconds we figured out that would be the oldest and the youngest, with gender parity. I got to be one of them because I was the oldest. It is definitely a benefit to be an old person engaging in civil disobedience projects, because you can pull rank with, "I deserve it, I deserve it!"[93]

Those are two stories about the question of fear and courage. There is nothing more human than that we feel fear when we are risking taking a new step, especially something that we have not done before, like confronting authority. Even if we have a particular view that suggests

---

93. A brief video showing the EQAT civil disobedience action in Washington, D.C.. (Accessed: May 26, 2014.) http://www.youtube.com/watch?v=b3EGBoPHKwU.

authority has not been well earned or used responsibly by a particular individual or group, still it is kind of scary to confront authority. There is nothing to be ashamed of about that hesitation to confront authority. Probably Daniel in the lion's den had a certain amount of pit-pat going on in his heart. The important thing is to know we are going to work with the fear and anger. Notice that Gandhi was both scared and angry at various points in his life. A journalist once asked Gandhi, "You are a great Mahatma of Asia. How do you transcend your anger?" Gandhi replied, "What do you mean, transcend my anger? I'm up against the British Empire. Anger is energy. I need all the energy I can get. Why would I want to transcend that?" A significant part of peacemaking seems to me to be to make peace with the reality of who we are as human beings. We have a lot going on inside us when we contemplate these actions: we have fear; we have anger; and we have a lot of other things going on, too.

How to bring that energy together with our friends, our beloved community, is to act together so that even if, in the beginning, as in Barbara's case, it is only two friends, it will grow and grow. That is how the early Christians did it. It is how we can do it.

THE USE OF ART IN SOCIAL CHANGE: A CASE STUDY OF THE PONTANIMA CHOIR IN BOSNIA-HERZEGOVINA

—Ivo Marković

IN THE SPRING OF 2007, PONTANIMA[94] was invited to sing for the elementary school children from the Serbian and Bosniak (ethnic Muslim) communities in Srebrenica, a small city in eastern

---

94. In 1996, after the 1992–1996 war in Bosnia-Herzegovina among peoples whose souls were religious, and in a place where religion had been abused for the purpose of war, a choir was formed to show the positive peacebuilding potential of religions. This choir, Pontanima, was formed to show that music can contribute to the healing of suffering people and it can direct them to the future and to the authenticity of faith. The purposes of Pontanima included witnessing to members of all religions and beliefs in Sarajevo. The choir's repertoire included music from each of these traditions. Thus, in spite of the terrible war, a Symphony of Religions emerged, a symphony which came into being in Sarajevo, in Bosnia, which for centuries has been a cross-roads of cultures and religions.

Even though this project was built on the purest peacebuilding, ecumenical, and interreligious standards, Pontanima, whose name is from the Latin words *pons*=bridge and *anima*=soul, was both a provocation and a stumbling block for those who were slaves to exclusivity, defensiveness and hatred. Despite these challenges, from the beginning Pontanima found a way to go out and sing where there was pain and hatred, and where divisions were strongest. During seventeen years of activity, Pontanima has undertaken

Bosnia. During the war, Serbian military units committed genocide on the Bosniaks in Srebrenica, killing roughly eight thousand people.[95] Not surprisingly, reconciliation between these two groups has been an extremely difficult process. Even in 2007, at the time of the concert, the two communities were sharply divided, and bringing them together was a particular challenge. However, one peace-focused non-governmental organization (NGO) was successful in bringing together almost 250 children and their parents.

Before the concert, in the theatre hall, the parents from each community were obviously trying to avoid eye contact and conversation with the parents from the other ethnic group. The parents were in a depressed mood but the children, as always, were happily chatting and playing. Trying to connect with some of the parents, I greeted

---

more than 400 performances and has made six CDs. Two documentaries have been made about Pontanima, and it has been featured on major television and radio stations around the world. It is fair to say that Pontanima has been one of the best ambassadors for the new face of Bosnia-Herzegovina. The music of Pontanima—the shocking and powerful musical symphony of Abraham-Ibrahim-Avram ecumenism of Judaism, Orthodoxy, Islam, and Catholicism—has allowed injured Bosnians to be healed and turned toward an unexpected and hopeful future.

The work of Pontanima has been recognized by numerous organizations. In 1998, the New York-based Tanenbaum Center of Interreligious Understanding awarded the founder of Pontanima the first *Peace Activist Award*. In 2004, the Washington, DC-based Search for Common Ground awarded Pontanima a *Common Ground Award*. In 2006, the city of Sarajevo presented Pontanima with the *April 6th Award of the City of Sarajavo*. And in 2011, Pontanima became the recipient of a *Pax Christi International Peace Award*.

95. In 2005 the US Congress House of Representatives passed resolution 199 stating that "... the policies of aggression and ethnic cleansing as implemented by Serb forces in Bosnia and Herzegovina from 1992 to 1995 with the direct support of Serbian regime of Slobodan Milošević and its followers ultimately led to the displacement of more than 2,000,000 people, an estimated 200,000 killed, tens of thousands raped or otherwise tortured and abused, and the innocent civilians of Sarajevo and other urban centers repeatedly subjected to shelling and sniper attacks; meet the terms defining the crime of genocide in Article 2 of the Convention on the Prevention and Punishment of the Crime of Genocide, created in Paris on 9 December 1948, and entered into force on 12 January 1951."

one Serbian mother with two children, eight- and twelve-year-old boy and girl. It was apparent that the Serbian mother despised the Muslims who were there; she despised their presence, ornaments, language, and perfume. I asked her how she was feeling, and she answered openly that she didn't like this gathering. She explained that it was very difficult for her to endure the gathering, but that she was at the concert because of her children. I then asked her a provocative question, "Could you imagine yourself, during the concert, singing an Islamic *ilahi*, or words like the Islamic greeting *As-salamu alaykum?*" Her answer was an emphatic and repulsed, "Never!" accompanied by a dismissive hand gesture. Then she asked me, "You will not have it in program, will you!" I offered my apology. I knew that her revulsion was a defence mechanism common to Balkan Christians resulting from the Islamization of the Balkans during the centuries of occupation under the Ottoman Empire. That defensive negative energy had been systematically manipulated, amplified, and misused as a weapon in the recent war. Now this woman stood in front of me, uncomfortable with what was happening. The recent war had prepared her to live divided from Muslims, but now her expectations were being challenged as she was brought together with Muslims and was faced with the possibility of reconciliation.

During the concert, the choir Pontanima sang its prepared program of music from each of the Abrahamic traditions. One of the pieces was a Sephardic song sung in the Ladino language. The melody of the song was adopted by Muslims and had become a popular song among the Bosniaks. So, during the concert, the children and their parents sang this song back to the choir. When the audience was engrossed in the music, Pontanima introduced a variation on the Beatles line "All we are saying is give peace a chance" and invited the audience to dance, clap, and sing along to the revised version of this line: *Shalom aleikhem, As-salamu alaykum, Peace be among us.* The audience joined in and the whole theatre was a single choir. As we were singing I looked for the woman I had spoken to before the concert, and I was surprised to see that she was participating fully. She was dancing, clapping, and singing the words, *As-salamu alaykum.* We waved to each other across the theatre.

After the concert I found this woman again. She was joyful, with a wide spontaneous smile and, in her eyes, I saw a trace of tears of joy because of the power of music, art, and spirituality. She tried to express herself with broken phrases like "Thank you.... Now I see where I was.... There is hope... hope for my children.... Through your music it all becomes different...."

In this chapter I will examine the impact that music had on this woman. What is the magical structure within music that transformed this woman's mind more effectively than any words could have? How does music remove prejudices? How does it heal and transform minds and souls from hatred to trusted acceptance in a reconciled world?

Pontanima, in its mission in Bosnia-Herzegovina, has endeavoured to create a solid foundation and to have a clear vision and orientation to use music as a positive influence on humans and on the social state. Therefore I will begin by exploring the nature of art and, in particular, by analyzing the *V-Effekt* described by Berthold Brecht and the theory of game developed by Hans-Georg Gadamer. Special attention will be drawn to the place of art in human spirituality before returning to Pontanima to examine the genesis of this choir and its work in post-war reconciliation in the Balkans.

The Nature of Art

The ancient Greek understanding of art, as formulated by Aristotle in the fourth century BCE is that the purpose of art is to evoke emotion and thereby purify the human spirit. For Aristotle, art was *mimesis*, or imitation for the purpose of *catharsis*, which is a cleansing of emotions through the experience of compassion and fear. Greek tragedy demonstrated for Aristotle the importance of fear as a cathartic tool to purify the human spirit.

This understanding of art is important in a special way because it was adopted by Christianity and came to dominate Christian thinking about art. Art was understood as serving mostly a hedonistic aesthetic purpose; we enjoy art and beauty, which refines and ennobles human beings. We pay to go to the theatre and concerts, to view beautiful pictures and exhibits because we enjoy the experience and because it ennobles our emotions. Because of the importance of compassion and fear as cathartic emotions, art was consistently understood within Christianity as creating feelings of sublimity or elevation. The ancient Greek philosopher Longinus (c. 213–273 bce) wrote a treatise on sublimity

(Περὶ ὕψους, perì hýpsous; ὑψόω = elevate, ὕψος = elevated) that had a strong influence on Christian preaching. This sublimity periodically achieved the level of caricature. For example, preachers would seek to stir emotions so that the congregation would cry, thereby cleansing their hearts with holy emotions. The goal of art was to fill humans with a sublime, heavenly feeling that purified the human spirit.

With Immanuel Kant (1724-1804), the nineteenth century marked the beginning of a new romantic view of art in which aesthetics became understood as a subjective experience. Kant was not occupied with the question of what art is but with the effects of beauty and the sublime. He reduced art to personal taste; an aesthetic experience is a response to a natural or created form.

Kant understood art to be a purely personal experience. This view became widely accepted and led to a separation of art from the dynamics of daily life. For instance, most artists, from the Romantic era until the present day, have not been concerned with how others would experience the artwork. The artists simply have worked to depict their own realities.

In Pontanima we found that some compositions, though beautifully composed, failed to communicate with the audience. When hearing such pieces, the listeners were calm and equanimous. In contrast, the works of composers like Andrija Pavlič (*Alleluia, Missa Bosniensis*), or Aleksandar Vujić (*Kyrie, Our Father*) from Belgrade, although composed with strange musical tools, communicated with the listeners because these composers integrated their creativity with real life.

The German writer Berthold Brecht (1898–1956), in contrast to both Aristotle and Kant, argued that art is a tool for social change. He argued that the most dangerous human temptation is laziness about life, in which one accepts ideological stereotypes and prejudices that tolerate spiritual and moral disintegration. Brecht discovered within art a mechanism that he called *Verfremdungseffekt,* or the *V-Effekt.* The German word *Verfremden* means to discover that something is different than we thought: astonishing, unusual. It differs from *entfremden,* which means to alienate. The V-Effekt then, is that element within art which astonishes or shocks the audience, thereby unmasking stereotypes and inaccurate assumptions to reveal the truth.

Through the V-Effekt of the art, the audience becomes ashamed of its moral degradation· and is inspired to change. Even though this understanding of art has its origin in the communist revolution, it has more in common with the Christian notion of conversion than with Aristotle's hedonistic aestheticism. Brecht's understanding of art has influenced Christian theology and preaching.[96]

Art, as an important tool for social change through its power to astonish, has been manifest repeatedly in the work and experience of Pontanima. In the Balkans, people of different religions and cultures have always lived together, but always under the dominance of one group and with the goal of converting the other groups. In response to this oppression, people developed defence mechanisms. These defence mechanisms were often unconscious but led to contempt, to avoidance, and to disgust of the other groups and their religions.

Ivo Andrić, the Nobel Prize winning writer, argues that hate is the *secret of Bosnia:* "Bosnia is a country of hatred and fear.… That is Bosnia.… But in secret depths underneath all this, hide burning hatreds, entire hurricanes of tethered and compressed hatreds.… And thus you are condemned to live on deep layers of explosive which are lit from time to time by the very sparks of your loves and your fiery and violent emotion."[97] For example, according to one study, 70 percent of Catholic Croats and Orthodox Serbs have negative associations to the word "Allah."[98] In such an environment, offering people a glimpse of the purity of spirit and the beauty of those who oppose them enables them to experience the *V-Effekt.* The music unmasks their prejudices and enables them to face the other.

The theory of art espoused by the German philosopher Hans-Georg Gadamer (1900–2002) is very helpful for understanding

---

96. Hans Dieter S. Bastian, "Verfremdung in der Verkündigung," Bruno Dreher, Norbert Greinacher, Ferdinand Klostermann, *Handbuch der Verkündigung I* (Freiburg: Herder, 1970), 97–119.

97. Ivo Andrić, *Letter from 1920.* (Accessed: May 26, 2014.) http://www.diogenpro.com/uploads/4/6/8/8/4688084/ivo_andric..a_letter…from_1920…pdf (12.112013), 2–3.

98. Ivo Marković, "Studenti Franjevačke teologije, Pokušaj sustavnog istraživanja" (Students of Theology of Franciscans Sarajevo, An Attempt of Systematic Research), *Bilten Franjevačke teologije*, XII-XII (1987): 43–66.

Pontanima's Symphony of Religions.[99] Like Brecht, Gadamer resisted Kant's aesthetic subjectivism. Gadamer claimed that art is not only subjective consciousness, but also that "art is knowledge and experiencing an artwork means sharing in that knowledge"[100] which integrates everyday human life and, for humanity, brings structure into an atomized and chaotic world. The investigation of the influence of art on human life led Gadamer to an analysis of play, whose importance had been discovered earlier by Dutch psychologist Johan Huizinga (1872–1945).

In Gadamer's understanding, play, aesthetics, and culture are deeply interconnected. Play is an essential and integral component of each human being and is passed from one person to another. A person is both *homo sapiens* (wise human) and a *homo ludens* (playing human). Johan Huizinga, in his book, *Homo Ludens,* coins this term and argues that it is a basic human characteristic. There is a "fun-element that characterizes the essence of play."[101] Play is free, without any agenda, and serves as a digression from ordinary and real life. A positive aspect of play is that it creates order,[102] which Gadamer terms a *structuralized entity.*

Art is a higher degree of play, which is particularly evident in music. There are numerous "elements that music and play have in common" and a there is a "bond between play and music."[103] However, "from poetry, music, and dancing to the plastic arts ... the connections

---

99. Andrew Packman published an article, "Pontanima Interfaith repertoire, A Bosnian choir sings reconciliation," in *The Christian Century,* May 31, 2012 (accessed June 15, 2012, http://www.christiancentury.org/article/2012-05/ interfaith-repertoire), and now has been writing his doctoral dissertation applying the redemptive mission of Pontanima to the theory of art of Hans-Georg Gadamer.

100. Hans-Georg Gadamer, *Wahrheit und Methode* (Tübingen: J.C.B. Mohr, 1965), 92.

101. Johan Huizinga, *Homo Ludens: A Study of the Play-Element in Culture* (London: Routledge & Kegan Paul, 1949), 9. The direct quotes in English translation were taken from the English translation: Gadamer, Hans-Georg, *Truth and Method,* second, revised edition. Trans. Joel Weinsheimer and Donald Marshall. (New York: Continuum, 2004).

102. Huizinga, *Homo Ludens,* 16.

103. Huizinga, *Homo Ludens,* 164.

with play are becoming less obvious"[104] because they are "always subjected to the skill and proficiency of the forming hand."[105] Culture originates from play; in fact, the entire book *Homo Ludens* is focused on "culture *sub specie ludi*" (under the guise of play). "Play is older than culture, for culture, however inadequately defined, always presupposes human society, and animals have not waited for man [sic] to teach them their playing."[106]

The idea of digression (French *écart*, German *Abweichung*) is important to fuller understanding of play and art. Play begins as a digression from reality and the creation of a virtual reality.[107] For example, in linguistics a digression from ordinary, literal language—a word, a sentence or a meaning—results in the creation of stylistic or rhetorical figures; in metaphor the meaning of one word is conveyed to another. This digression from reality leads to polysemy of relations, intentions, and meanings. In play, the player digresses from himself or herself; the player "loses himself in the play" … "in playing, all those purposive relations that determine active and caring existence have not disappeared, but are curiously suspended."[108] The digression is evident also from the fact that "human play requires a playing field [which] sets off the sphere of play as a closed world."[109] The reason for the digression is to overcome a limited view of reality, to look at life from a different point of view, and to deepen one's understanding of reality, with the final goal being to create a reality that is better understood, more structured, and beautiful. Therefore play and art are advanced exercises, which offer exposure to an unknown future, imagination, frivolity, and risk. Play and art open one up to something new and unknown, which allows growth in one's own identity. "The attraction that the game exercises on the player lies in this risk." Through play, a player surrenders himself to the mystery of play, and "the game masters the players." In other words "the real subject of

---

104. Huizinga, *Homo Ludens*, 171.
105. Huizinga, *Homo Ludens*, 166.
106. Huizinga, *Homo Ludens*, 1.
107. Jacques Dubois and others, *Allgemeine Rhetorik* (München: W. Fink, 1974), 29–30.
108. Gadamer, *Wahrheit und Methode,* 97–98.
109. Gadamer, *Wahrheit und Methode,* 101–102.

the game ... is not the player but the game itself."[110] Digression is an essential aspect of play and art, and is more accurate and is a more useful understanding of play than some other theories, including the theory of play described by Brian Sutton-Smith in his book, *The Ambiguity of Play.*[111] Understanding play to have an ambiguous relation to reality misses the main motives of play. Play is a basic human need to rid oneself of the slavery of a determined reality, to awaken suppressed abilities and powers, and to discover new perspectives in the chaos of reality.

In play, the player looks for a co-player and together they surrender to the game. The audience is included and becomes a part of the game. When everyone involved surrenders to the game an independent entity comes to exist, a structuralized reality. The play becomes enchanted, like a life with its own dynamics. When the players finish their game and the audience scatters, the enchantment of the game remains as something living and lasting. What remains of the game now is an echo of reality, a truth about all participants, expressed in unexpected discoveries and insights. New and shocking possibilities are suddenly revealed, and the truth invigorates life, making it better. When the sport clubs from two cities or countries surrender themselves to the game being played in front of the spectators in a stadium and in front of television viewers, then the entire event is transformed in its structure. The structure of the game contains interactions between the cities or countries, their past, their conflicts and friendships, their loves and hates, and their hopes and fears. Through the game, all of this is unmasked and transformed, allowing for a new perspective, and an openness to a new relationship. It is as if all of reality is under a new beam of light.[112] This theory can also be applied to art. The visitor views, reads or listens to the artwork and discovers what the artist had put into the piece of art. The visitor gradually enters into a silent dialogue with the artist. This dialogue is mutual and forms a structure of spirit around the artwork, containing new knowledge about the participants in the dialogue and about the human condition. Artwork can have its own life, independent of the artist. This understanding

---

110. Gadamer, *Wahrheit und Methode,* 101–102.
111. Brian Sutton-Smith, *The Ambiguity of Play* (Cambridge, MA: First Harvard University Press, 2001).
112. Gadamer, *Wahrheit und Methode,* 97–127.

of art, developed by Hans-Georg Gadamer, is helpful in elucidating the effects that Pontanima's music has had on those who have heard the Symphony of Religions in concerts on radio, television or from recordings, particularly in terms of transforming the circumstances and emotions created through the war in the former Yugoslavia from 1991 to 1995.

The Place of Art in Human Spirituality

The methodical building of spirituality is a complex and multidisciplinary process. Figure 1 shows the stages of the development of human spirituality; beginning with the superficial impression of reality, through learning, research, science, model, and theory, to the higher levels, such as law and principles. This is followed by the stage of play and sport, which is followed by art that leads to the ultimate stages of human destiny and transcendence, namely revelation and God. Through these stages an integral human spirituality is formed.

SPIRITUALITY
14. GOD, GRACE
13. REVELATION, THEOLOGY
12. CULTURE, CIVILIZATION
11. ART, AESTHETICS
10. PLAY, SPORT
9. PRINCIPLES, ETHICS, MORALS
8. LAW (PARLIAMENT)
7. THEORY
5. MODEL (RETAKEN THEORY)
4. RESEARCH, SCIENCE
3. LEARNING
2. EXPERIENCE
1. IMPRESSION
REALITY, PRAXIS, LIFE, PROBLEM

Figure 1: Stages of the Development of Human Spirituality

Spirituality and praxis can be properly related only if one passes through each of the stages of spiritual development to arrive dialectically back at the beginning so that the spirituality can be verified in reality. Through this dialectic, spirituality and praxis are coordinated and improved.[113] If the growth of spirituality is stopped prematurely, and an incomplete spirituality is applied to life and praxis, there is a risk that the incomplete spirituality will produce a dangerous ideology.

Art and Religion in War and Reconciliation in the Former Yugoslavia

Balkan History and Context

Christianity and Islam have always been inexorably linked with conflict in the Balkans, and these religions have been drawn into every level of the conflict. Islam was the religion of the Ottoman Empire, and so Islam penetrated the Balkans on the wings of the Ottoman conquest. Likewise, as the primary religion of Europe, Christianity was used as a tool to create a block of resistance against the penetration of Islam. The complex Balkan situation is moulded by these memories, as are its people and their identities. A united Europe and increasing globalization in the Balkans have gradually become the dominant factors moving the region toward reconciliation.

The 1991–1995 war among Croats, Serbs, and Bosniaks started as Serbian aggression in response to the declared independence of Croatia and Bosnia and Herzegovina. Very soon, the crux of the problem emerged: Serbs and Croats (Catholic and Orthodox—that is, the Christians) waged war against the Bosniaks (Muslims). Serbs and Croats, although at war with each other, consistently cooperated in their policies in the war against the Muslims.

Religious identity in the Balkans is the basis for ethnic identity; each of the three main ethnic groups developed from a particular religious group; the Serbs are Orthodox, the Croats are Catholics, and the Bosniaks are Muslims. The primary content of ethnic identity

---

113. Clodovis Boff, *Theologie und Praxis, Die erkenntnistheoretische Grundlagen der Theologie de Befreiung* (München: Kaise-Grünewald, 1983), 330–339.

for Croats, Serbs, and Bosniaks is religious identity and their religious group. Faith tradition is the soul of the ethnic nation. This is the starting point for the theocratic tendencies of Orthodox Serbs, Catholic Croats, and Muslim Bosniaks alike. In their strongest form, these tendencies among the Bosniaks are exhibited in the tenet that non-Muslims cannot be full-fledged members of the nation. Such tendencies are also voiced by Catholic Croats and Orthodox Serbs.

National expansion and imperialism, and the growth of religions, are closely connected in the philosophy and the goals of the conquering nation. Thus, national expansionism incorporates the spreading of religion. Under the hegemony of the Ottoman Empire, the authorities tried to convert the Christians (Catholic and Orthodox) to Islam and they partially succeeded. However, one effect of this policy is that Christians developed deep, subconscious, myth-based defence mechanisms against Islam that provide lasting and dangerous memories. The Catholics saw the Austro-Hungarian Empire as a force that was able to prevent the penetration of Islam and a way of retrieving what had been lost. This resistance had a similar effect on the Muslim population, who were antagonized through continued contact with the powerful and aggressive civilizations of the West. The Old Yugoslavian Serbian Orthodoxy, animated by the ideal of pan-Slavism, aimed to convert members of all the nations to Serbian Orthodoxy, first imposing the Serbian language, then culture, history, and memory, and finally Christian Orthodoxy, thus paving the way for a pan-Yugoslav Orthodox soul.

All these dangerous spirits in the Pandora's box of the Balkans were repressed through social control during the rule of Tito's communism. However, after Tito's death, the skillful warriors educated by the Yugoslav National Army broke into nationalistic groups and were extremely effective in awakening this dangerous inner energy of the Balkans. Thus began a terrible war that could be stopped only by outside intervention.

In the 1991–1995 war, the nationalists made great use of religion as an extremely effective tool of war. In religious communities, the majority of believers and religious leaders were at one with the nation. The majority of religious leaders aligned their work more closely with the interests of their own nation than with the foundational understandings of their own religions. The war in the Balkans was not a religious war but an ethnic war. However, religion played an integral role insomuch as religious tradition is the soul of the nation.

The Role of Art in Mobilizing for War and in Bringing about Reconciliation

Art is powerful tool and can be used both to foment a nation for war and to bring two sides back together in post-war reconciliation. Figure 2 (below) illustrates the progression of conflict as it occurred in the collapse of the former Yugoslavia. Use of art in the development of conflict starts on levels seven and eight of the progression (left side of the figure) and helps to mobilize a group for war. Early in the progression of conflict, artists are occupied with the values of their own group, and art serves to awaken solidarity, to build community, and to solidify group identity. As fear grows and the level of conflict escalates, artists become more and more occupied and obsessed with the enemy.

In 1991, in the beginning of the war in Croatia, popular Croatian singers were invited to Band Aid to sing the song *My Homeland*.[114] Croatian writers and poets wrote patriotic texts; the composers wrote music; and the visual artists painted pictures inspired by love of their homeland. This art was then sold to raise money for war expenses and humanitarian relief. Similar artistic activities were carried out by Serbs in Serbia and in Bosnia by Bosniaks.

After the conflict progresses to level twelve, art turns from the love of homeland to contempt and hate of the enemy. The goal is to demonize and dehumanize the enemy. Art depicts the men in the opposing group as stupid cretins and reduces the women in the group to sexual objects. Symptomatic of this pattern is the Croatian song *Oh, My friend from Belgrade*: "Pretty lasses of Belgrade / Oh how skilled you were in kissing, / Yet I remember blond hair / of my wench from Novi Sad." The Serbian side responded with the song *Oh, My friend from Zagreb*: "Good cat-girls of Zagreb / Were for us playthings / O, my friend from Zagreb / It was sexy." But, of course, this is the misuse

---

114. Damir Lipošek and Husein Hasanefendić, *Moja domovina*. (Accessed: May 26, 2014.) http://www.youtube.com/watch?v=dZmLgeGOrI4.

of art. It is the misuse of art for the purpose of war. Once the fighting erupts, art must keep silent. The old Latin proverb "Among arms, the muses fall mute" is true. But art is also a very effective tool to awaken responsibility and sensitivity in those people who may be able to influence the resolution of a conflict.

This figure depicts the stages of increased dehumanization of the perpetrators of war (the left half of the figure) along with the stages of re-humanization that attend reconciliation (the right half of the figure). A state of total war is depicted at the top of the figure, and a state of total peace is depicted at the bottom. The left side of the figure depicts the release and the enhancement of the evil elements of the human spirit, shown to progress through fifteen stages, reaching a point of dehumanization of the enemy, with concomitant dehumanization of the perpetrators. On the right, stages of de-escalation of evil human acts are depicted: a series of actions that release the virtuous side of the human spirit. The reader will notice that much of the de-escalation is accompanied by—is stimulated by—external interventions. These external stimuli, it is asserted herein, are closely tied to the muses, to the awakening—the inbreaking—of the human spirit of goodness that is found in the arts.

The place for formal and systematic use of music in the process of post-war reconciliation begins at level seven or eight (right side of the figure). The time for music comes only after the fighting has stopped, the soldiers, with their weapons, have withdrawn to military barracks, the roads are re-opened for travel, after the exchange of prisoners has begun, and after those in the helping professions return to performing their healing missions. Then it is the right time for the use of music. In the Balkans, rock and roll was the first type of music used for reconciliation because it is popular worldwide and unifies the younger generation all over the world. Before the start of the millennium, shortly after the end of the war, rock singers from all over the world were invited to perform in locations in which young people from all over the former Yugoslavia could gather, such as Budapest, Ljubljana, and Montenegro.

Next in the efforts toward reconciliation through music were pop singers from all sides of the conflict who sang a type of world music and who were not involved in the promotion of nationalist agendas. The exchange of such singers between the national groups stimulated

WAR—conflict-based disaster, total destruction of others, catastrophe—WAR				
	maximum violence		**no peace**	
15	Humans reduced to war instincts, full dehumanization	Help coming from the third side is coming to a standstill	1	↓ Reconciliation / rehumanizing ↓
14	Darkness of humanity, assassination on reason	Warrior groups separation	2	
13	Humans transform to warriors, full armament	Withdrawal of soldiers and weapons to military barracks	3	
12	Mutual attacks, killings, full enmity is deepening	Organizing of societies for peace and democratization	4	
11	First attacks, attacks cause revenge	Prisoners of war exchange	5	
10	Fanatics, endangerment, threat	Reparation of mutual systems: roads, water supply, rivers …	6	
9	Fear predominates—fear is a mystery of war	Road opening: train, air transport, open market	7	
8	Accusations, repulsing, satanization	Silent to more open contacts and communication	8	
7	Strong identification with own national or religious group or excommunication of traitors	Peace initiatives from outside and from inner groups	9	
6	Division into interest groups, mobilization within the groups	Vocational healing of humans, physicians, teachers, social and religious workers	10	
5	Breaking of interaction and communication	Cultural and religious initiatives, trends in music, life, various groups …	11	
4	Negative tensions prevail—open conflicts emerge	Fear and tensions reduced	12	
3	Focus shifts from problems to people	Mutual discovering of suffering and revival of compassion	13	
2	Positive tensions are growing and helping to solve conflicts	Mutual discovering of human face of enemy	14	
1	Complex social situation—unsolved conflicts accumulate	Normalization of life	15	
	no violence		**maximum peace**	
PEACE—normal life—conflicts are being resolved and integrated in life—PEACE				

↑ Violence / dehumanizing ↑

Figure 2: Progression of Violence and Reconciliation

a spirit of connection among the people on all sides of the conflict. Journalists and filmmakers played important roles as they travelled to the enemies' territories. But not all musical genres were useful in the reconciliation progression.

The official state-operated and financed music of concert halls and religious organizations didn't play a significant role in reconciliation because it was too expensive and because overcoming the necessary obstacles in official relations between states was very complicated. The most negative music is folk rock. It is music generically connected with hunting societies, and exclusive, primitive, macho groups. Very often such music has racist and fascist connotations that are masked in religious language and language about destiny. These singers use texts and melodies of passionate racism, together with references to religious traditions and nationalist motifs to narrow the perspective of closed groups. This music serves to keep these groups defensive and enslaved by fear and prevents them from being able to normalize their lives following the war.

One example of a musician who misused religion to promote a nationalist agenda is Croatian singer Marko Perković. He adopted the stage name "Thompson," which is the name of a submachine gun. He wrote this name as THO-MP-SON, which clearly alludes God's name in Greek, *THeO,* and SON in English connected with his initials, MP. So, with this stage name, he is both alluding to a weapon and subtlety communicating the phrase "Marko Perković, son of God." These connections are emphasized during his concerts as he dresses in a style that is reminiscent of a Promethean priest. He carries a large sword shaped in cross decorated with a Saint Benedict coat of arms. In front of him on the stage he has a table that represents an altar on which he stabs his sword-cross. Marko Perković sings primarily ethnic Croatian songs. At times these songs sympathize with fascism and the holocaust. This has resulted in his music being banned in many countries all over the world.

However no representative of the Catholic Church in Croatia or Bosnia-Herzegovina has ever spoken out against such blasphemy. On the contrary, many Catholic leaders spoke publically in support of THO-MP-SON's spiritual mission. THO-MP-SON received more opportunities to provide music for Catholic celebrations than were provided to Pontanima. Those who did speak out against his music as a misuse of religion in the service of nationalism were labelled as traitors. Examples of similar misuses of religion for the promotion of nationalism can be found in Serbia in the music of bands such as *Riblja Čorba* (Fish broth) and in the folk music of the Serbs and Bosniaks.

In contrast, musical groups, painters, poets, sculptors, and film-makers, from within and without the Balkans, created art in the Balkans as emissaries of faith, non-violence, and reconciliation in the region, during and after the war. Among them were Susan Sontag and Zubin Mehta, who conducted the Philharmonics of Sarajevo in the midst of shelling and other strife.

A leader among these artists, for the past seventeen years, Pontanima has been promoting a culture of peace by celebrating and singing the rich spiritual diversity present in the region. Pontanima has worked toward interreligious understanding and peace, and has used religious music as a powerful cathartic, healing, and peace-making force, removing prejudices and initiating the fascinating play of human creativity. The vision for Pontanima was carefully and thoughtfully developed and Pontanima has adjusted its mission, its orientation, and its methods to respond to changing circumstances in the region. Pontanima has many years of experience combining art and spirituality as a tool for social change and can serve as a model for reconciliation in other troubled regions.

Recent Shifts in Interreligious Relations in the Balkans and Around the World

One of the fundamental elements of the postmodern era, in which we currently live, is the importance of mutual understanding and appreciation among religions. This is a dramatic shift from the individualism that was the quintessential quality of the thinking within the modern era. Individualism means the separation and isolation of an individual to become a Promethean hero concentrating all power within oneself without considering connections between others, nature or God. Within the postmodern era, this individualism has been transformed so that an individual is seen as connected to and reflected in all things. In the shift from modernity to postmodernity, an exclusive culture is being replaced with an acceptance of plurality and spontaneous inclusivity. Within the postmodern framework, exclusivity is untenable and counterproductive.

Members of religious communities must co-operate with members of other religious communities if they wish to retain the credibility of their mission. Each must communicate with the others, and each proponent of a religious project is required to appreciate religious plurality. Without conversations with members of other religions now, it is impossible to be a mature believer in one's own religion. Today, members of traditional religious groups often have difficulty in accepting the truth and value of religious plurality and, in particular, struggle to accept that other religions produce the fruits of faith. Creative religious initiatives can help such religious people to overcome these transitional difficulties. This can be done by emphasizing the fact that God has the initiative in faith and that all believers surrender themselves in hearing and following that call to faith. Religious plurality enables religions to distill the essence of religion so that the believers may hear the message of any religion.

Both of the dominant religions in Bosnia-Herzegovina, Christianity (Orthodox, Catholic, and Evangelical) and Islam (both Arab Sunni and Iranian Shiite), experienced a passage into modernity out of a colonialist period. This caused religious exclusivity to develop into missionary imperialism, exacerbating interreligious relationships so as to make a conflict of civilizations seem inevitable. After these religions had been drawn into a hundred modern conflicts and wars, however, and it had become quite obvious that such relations were pushing our world toward a catastrophe of total destruction, there came about a fundamental, Copernican, break in their way of relating to one another.

Christian exclusivity was based upon the belief that God's salvation lies in Christ Jesus alone, which renders all other religions extraneous and leaves the conversion of the world as the only possible mission. A critical break with this understanding took place at the Second Vatican Council, with the Declaration on the Relation of the Church to Non-Christian religions *Nostra Aetate*. Today some theologians claim that the conciliar fathers would never have issued this document had they been aware of its consequences. A U-turn was made within the very heart of Christianity ; the divine gift of salvation through Jesus Christ was no longer only for Christians; rather, Jesus had mounted the cross for all people. All of humanity is embraced within the divine perspective.

Out of this new inclusivity, the question then arises as to how God speaks to those who are outside the revelation and the church, and the answer is, through other religions. This encapsulates briefly the new approach that Christianity as a whole, not just the Catholic Church, has adopted toward other religions. The pogrom against the Jews during the Second World War woke the Christian world from its slumbers, and the Christians and the Jews have begun to clean out nearly 2,000 years of accumulated distrust.

The sea change in Christian and Jewish relations has been epochal, and the positive results have so mounted up so that they are difficult to enumerate. The Jews have begun to feel themselves as the custodians of the entire Abrahamic ecumene, researching the historical Jesus as a Jew and looking upon Islam as part of its own monotheistic heritage. Similar results are also evident in the relations between Christianity and Islam.

The shocking events in New York on September 11, 2001, and the Pope's notorious lecture at Regensburg on September 12, 2006, exacerbated tensions and misunderstandings between the Islamic and Christian worlds but also served as the impetus for innovative initiatives to work at problems and improve understanding between Muslims and Christians. In spite of the many burdens and obstacles to positive relations between the Islamic and Christian worlds, profound processes are taking place throughout the world that already provide an intimation of an entirely different future and of a world in which there is very little room for Huntington's perspective.[115]

In the Balkans, and more generally in Europe, conflicts are frequently labelled as religious conflicts when, in fact, they are conflicts between cultures. For example, in Europe providing plenty of places for Muslims to pray is not problematic. However, if Muslims wish to raise a mosque with a minaret, it can be problematic, not because it is a place for Muslims to pray, but because is an architectural sign of that culture.

---

115. Ivo Marković, "Interreligious Culture and Relation in Bosnia." *Forum Bosnae*, no. 55 (2012), 5–12. See also Samuel Huntington, *Clash of Civilizations* (New York: Simon and Shuster, 1996).

A Case Study: Pontanima

The Roots of Pontanima

The initial motivation for Pontanima grew out of the Spirit of Assisi meeting which took place on October 27, 1986, when the Franciscans succeeded in gathering representatives from all the world's religions in Assisi, together with Pope John Paul II, to pray for peace. That day symbolized the historic shift in the relations between religions.

The idea for Pontanima emerged because of this shift in interreligious perspectives and because of the spirituality of the Bosnian Franciscans and their work with music during the time of Yugoslav socialism. The Franciscans are one of the oldest institutions in Bosnia-Herzegovina, with a history in Bosnia of more than seven centuries. The spirituality and traditions of the Franciscans are a fundamental part of Bosnian society. This spirituality, along with the memories and traditions of the Franciscans, are well suited to living among different religions and to providing leadership in difficult circumstances. The orientation of Franciscan spirituality is suited to times of upheaval because it is a spirituality focused on serving others to meet their concrete and urgent needs. The idea of an interreligious choir was inspired by the Franciscan peacebuilding response to the state of the Abrahamic religions in Bosnia-Herzegovina after the war ended in 1995.

Further inspiration for the formation of Pontanima came from a similar project in Zagreb between 1992 and 1995. There was a community of students from Bosnia who were studying in Zagreb, named *Heart of Bosnia*. The community had a small choir open to people from other religions, beliefs, or ethnic groups. Success for this choir was difficult in that context because Zagreb was more ethnically homogeneous than Sarajevo; and at the time Zagreb was fully mobilized for war. However, even in these circumstances it was possible for a group of the singers from this community to visit Islamic or Serbian centres and to sing there with surprisingly impressive and powerful effects. The Franciscans realized that this type of choir would likely have even greater success in Sarajevo after the war, since it was a location and time more conducive to this kind of peacebuilding work.

The Pontanima choir began in 1996 in the Franciscan monastery of Saint Anthony in Sarajevo, and was nurtured in the heart of the Old Town, which is the centre of all three dominant Abrahamic (Croatian)- Ibrahimic (Bosnian)- Avramic (Serbian) religions in Bosnia-Herzegovina. The Franciscan order recognized that the idea for Pontanima was a good fit for the Bosnian Franciscans and supported them in this work.

The idea was to form a choir that consisted of people from all of the religions and beliefs in Sarajevo, people who, together, would sing a symphony of religions as a way of realizing the vision for positive relationships among religions. The building of Abrahamic ecumenism in Sarajevo began in 1996 with an invitation to women and men from all religions and beliefs to join the choir. It was a blessing that people responded to this idea and took it on. Naturally, in the existing environment, some assumed that there must be a hidden agenda; perhaps a covert Franciscan Catholic proselytizing mission. The members of Pontanima very quickly recognized, however, that this was an honest ecumenical, interreligious, peacebuilding project that respected the identity and prior convictions of members of the choir and members of the audience. The underlying Franciscan theological inspiration was clear: God is the one with the initiative in matters of conversion, faith, and basic orientation; it is blasphemous to disturb such a splendid work of God. Our mission is, rather, to be a blessing to all peoples, so that everyone can be happy because they have met us. Dialogue, understanding, and the complete acceptance of others as they are, and not as we wish they were, is the only authentic way to move toward God's coming. Pontanima was conceived as an answer to God's call in contemporary circumstances and as a form of service to our world.

Pontanima initially began singing Catholic and Jewish songs. Although, after the war, the pressure of enmity weighed on the souls of choir members and made it difficult for some to sing these songs, Pontanima was therapeutic, above all for its own members. Already in mid-1997, the choir integrated Orthodox liturgical songs written in Old Slavic and Jewish songs written in Hebrew into the Catholic liturgy. Pontanima travelled around Bosnia, singing for Catholic masses and giving concerts in churches. Thus, Pontanima's mission was first carried out within a Catholic space.

Numerous examples can be drawn from the experience of Pontanima to illustrate how its Symphony of Religions removes prejudices. In 1998, Pontanima was scheduled to sing a mass in a church in Zagreb. Included in the program were some Orthodox songs in Old Slavonic, the language of the Serbian composers. At that time, some parts of Croatia were still occupied by Serbs, and the wounds and trauma of the war had not yet healed. When some priests from the hosting church saw the program for the mass, they disapproved and asked Pontanima not to sing the Serbian songs out of respect for the wounds and pain of the believers participating in the mass. They argued that believers don't come to mass to be exposed to the aggression of their enemies' spirituality and culture, and that we ought to spare them from it. Despite repeated attempts to explain that the prepared program might produce unexpected results, we were prohibited from distributing the program and singing the Serbian songs. I personally presided over the mass and right at the beginning of the mass I decided to transgress the promise I had given to the priests. I told the choir that we will be persistent and faithful to our mission. The prepared programs were distributed to the believers and the program was performed as it had been planned. The Serbian Orthodox songs were very beautiful; one was *Angel Song* by the Serbian composer Stevan Mokranjac. The songs filled the church with typical Orthodox splendour and a celebration of God. It was apparent that believers were impressed with the songs; they listened to it with abandon. After the mass, not one of the thousand believers in the church reproached us. In fact, many expressed their satisfaction and thanks because of the experience of celebrating God with the songs of their enemies.

Something similar happened in 2001 after the integration of the city and region of Vukovar into the borders of Croatia. In this place, Pontanima performed in the ruins of the Saint Philip and Jacob church. Believers with deep wounds and traumas experienced the cathartic power of the spiritual songs of their enemies. Many of those who listened to these songs were opened to a new perspective, to peace, and to the normalization of life.

Entering into the Islamic paradigm was particularly challenging because of the difference between Christian and Islamic religious and musical traditions, and especially because of the bitter conflict between these two groups in the Balkans. To begin, we researched Islamic spiritual music extensively. It was necessary to integrate traditional Bosnian praise songs (*ilahis*), sung strictly in unison, into our repertoire of polyphonic, multi-vocal Christian, and Jewish songs.

We were worried that simply including Islamic music—in which unaccompanied melody serves the text—among the powerfully harmonized works from other religions might convey an impression of lesser respect or cultural inferiority. This worry was assuaged by Mario Katavić, who was unsurpassed in his ability to grasp the intonation of Pontanima. In his arrangements of Islamic music, pure unison singing alternated with harmonized tones in hauntingly beautiful polyphony that would grow slowly into a fully polyphonic chord, a musical encounter between the Islamic East and the Christian West. Katavić arranged an impressive *ilahi* "Allahu ekber," which was first performed in 1998 for the Day of Assisi in October, in the Church of Saint Anthony in Sarajevo; it was a stumbling block. It became evident that the antagonistic relationship between Christianity and Islam in post-war Bosnia-Herzegovina was too great; at that point, many people experienced our performance as a source of dissonance, rather than an opportunity for interreligious encounter and reconciliation through dialogue.

The difficulties with incorporating Islamic music into our Abrahamic symphony became a substantial barrier to Pontanima's growth. Defence mechanisms sprang into action and criticism proliferated. Although the goal was to help, Pontanima was accused of failing to respect the pain of the sufferers. The choir was also accused of New Age syncretism even though it was built on the firmest foundations of dialogic, ecumenical, and interreligious cooperation. Pontanima was accused of being nostalgic for the old days of Yugoslavia and of failing to respect ethnic and religious divisions. The traditional religions tend to respond defensively by isolating themselves and were very cautious in the face of new ideas or approaches. One religious leader reproached Pontanima, asking, "Why do you sing our songs when we have our own choirs? Please, invite them to sing it!"

In building the Pontanima community it was important that the members believed in Pontanima's mission, which was to

- work at peace and reconciliation
- create interreligious and intercultural understanding
- remove prejudices and obstacles to communication
- connect people from different ethnic and religious groups
- use music to heal the trauma and wounds caused by the war

In post-war Bosnia, such an idea was powerful, and the people were ready to sacrifice themselves for it. The word "community" in the Bosnian language is *zajednica* and is composed of the words "for" (za) and "one" (*jedno*). Community means to live for something; it contains the concept of connecting people into the community. Music is powerful tool, both to transform an individual and to connect people. Music connects choir members, forming them into a community. From the beginning, Pontanima had two rehearsals per week and roughly thirty performances each year. This means that each member of the choir enthusiastically donated more than one month of his or her own life each year without any compensation other than the joy of singing and good fellowship.

To further the mission of Pontanima within a religiously closed and nationalistic society it was important to solicit the help of journalists. Without the help of those in the media, particularly television, it was impossible to get the publicity needed to broadcast and amplify Pontanima's message. To enlist the help of the media, the members of Pontanima adopted the following principle: knowing that smart journalists would be good allies, whenever a choir member read a good article or saw an excellent TV show, the choir members would invite the writer or filmmaker to accompany and co-operate with Pontanima. It was an excellent and successful idea.

In 1997, one year after the establishment of Pontanima as a project of the Franciscan Saint Anthony Monastery, Face to Face Interreligious Service was established as an independent branch of the Council for Justice, Peace, and Creation by the Franciscan Province Bosnia Argentina.[116] The Franciscans took on this work because civil society was not functioning well in Bosnia at that time. In 2007, Face to Face Interreligious Service was established as a non-governmental organization. Until 2009, Pontanima worked in the Saint Anthony Monastery, but at that time there was a shift in the Bosnian Franciscan Province so that it no longer had a vision for interfaith understanding, peace, and reconciliation. This shift was a response to the general institutional crisis within the worldwide Catholic Church in which

---

116. The Franciscan order is divided into geographical regions, called provinces. The province of Bosnia Argentina got its name because it began in the city of Srebrenica in the fourteenth century. Srebrenica means "silver" city and the Latin word for "silver" is "argentum".

the reforms of the Second Vatican Council were abandoned. Prior to this shift, the Franciscan Bosnian Province operated up to 90 percent of the interfaith projects in Bosnia. However, after divesting themselves of Pontanima and other interfaith projects, the Province settled into mediocrity and pietism that, not surprisingly, led to tragic consequences. Fortunately the Franciscans are democratically organized and so there is hope that this decadence will not last long. Meanwhile, after working through the transition, Face to Face began to work as a civil society organization. In its beginnings Interreligious Service Face to Face was helped by Canterbury Diocese and later by Mennonite Central Committee and Ministries for Culture of Canton Sarajevo.

The choir members understood the vision of Pontanima, believed in it, and followed it with enthusiasm. Conflicts are a normal and positive part of life and Pontanima strategized to have those members with charisma and a strong understanding of the situation work with the conflicts that arose. Pontanima's goal was to provoke those who connected nationalism and religion but, at the same time, to stay in communication with national political and religious leaders. It is fair to claim that these leaders didn't like Pontanima's mission, but they respected it.

Because of an understandable distrust between religions, during the start of the twenty-first century, Pontanima decided to show special respect to each individual religion by performing a concert with only the songs of each respective religion, even though we felt that diminished Pontanima's mission. In this way we hoped to demonstrate our honest respect and honour to each community. Only at the very end of each concert did we discreetly hint at the Abrahamic symphony by choosing songs in which every religious tradition could participate.

This approach meant a lot for the growth of the community of Pontanima itself, and for its enculturation into the spirituality of each religious tradition. It was also a research enterprise; we procured hundreds of compositions from the various religions, learning to know the pulse of each spiritual paradigm through its music, history, and mutual influences. We discovered surprising common threads, such as the incredible closeness between the Christian hymn and the Islamic *ilahija* stemming from encounters in Spain and in the Arabic world.

Cross-border work emerged from a decision in 2001 that Pontanima should extend its work to Republika Srpska[117] and Serbia. The choir's mission had brought abundant results in the Federation, and across Europe and the US, but it had not succeeded in entering Republika Srpska or Serbia, nor the most war-affected regions of Croatia, except through the media. It really was high time for this to happen. After long preparations, discussions, assurances, and negotiations, Pontanima managed to hold a full-length concert of Symphony of Religions in Banja Luka at the beginning of 2001.

Jim Satterwhite, professor of history at Bluffton College, Ohio, USA, after the concert in Banja Luka, wrote:

> It is not often that a historian gets to be present at an event that is truly historical. I had such an experience this last Saturday, when I traveled with the interreligious choir from Sarajevo to Banja Luka in the Serbian part of Bosnia.... It was the first time since the war in Bosnia that an interreligious group from the Muslim-Croat federation had gone to sing in the heart of the Serbian area. It is important to remember that "interreligious" is the same thing here as "interethnic," that the war in Bosnia was fought among the three main ethno-religious groups, and—as in Ireland —religion provided the basis for cultural identity. So, this concert was important because it was an INTERRELIGIOUS choir singing music from ALL of the religious traditions of the area. The members of the choir come from the Orthodox, Catholic, Protestant, Muslim, and Jewish faiths, and sang music from these traditions. Some of the choir members describe themselves as atheists or agnostics, which underscores the fact that religion, per se, is not the main issue. Also, the fact that people who had suffered at the hands of the Serbs during the war were willing to put their heart into singing Serbian Orthodox church music made an impression on many. The

---

117 Bosnia and Herzegovina is divided into two political entities: Republika Sprska, which is the Serbian entity, and the Muslim-Croat Federation, which is the Bosniak and Croatian entity.

war was fought here on the principle that people of different ethno-religious backgrounds cannot live together and, among many Serbs, Islam carries negative associations from the 500 years of Ottoman Turkish rule. Banja Luka was the place where not only were non-Serbs ethnically "cleansed" from the area during the war, but 30 mosques, including one that was a Bosnian cultural and historical treasure, were dynamited by Serb paramilitary extremists early in the war so as to remove any vestige of the Muslim presence in the area. Unlike in Germany after the Second World War, there has been very little attempt by any side to critically examine its own actions during the war, so since Banja Luka remains a stronghold of Serbian nationalism there was some apprehension among some of the choir members about how the concert would be received. Would the fact that music from "enemy" groups was featured going to be a problem?

As it turned out things went quite well. The group was welcomed, and the music was appreciated. The Islamic music that was sung received a lot of applause, and some people in the audience remarked later that there should have been more Islamic music. The seemingly ordinary event, an ecumenical concert, thus served as a kind of milestone on the way to reconciliation.[118]

Pontanima invited and encouraged musicians to write and arrange music for Pontanima, and performed these compositions, especially of younger composers that included a deep spiritual message. The most famous compositions written for Pontanima are *Bosnian Te Deum*, composed by Mario Katavic and performed in 1999 with the orchestra *Arion* from Banja Luka, and *Missa Bosniensis*, composed by Andrija Pavlič and performed in 2008 with Sarajevo Philharmonic Orchestra. Roughly twenty original compositions were written for Pontanima, and a number of existing compositions were arranged specifically for the choir. Numerous soloists from all over the Balkans,

---

118. Jim Satterwhite, (Accessed 28 May 2014.) www.danielpearlmusicdays.org/uploads/profile/3718/citatiionsonpontanima-eng.doc+&cd=1&hl=en&ct=clnk&gl=ca.

Japan, the USA, and Europe also performed with Pontanima. These contributions by composers and solo performers served to amplify Pontanima's mission.

That same year, Pontanima performed in the Madlenianum Theatre in Zemun, the area of Belgrade in which Serbian nationalist hardliner Vojislav Šešelj first won elections. Numerous well-intentioned people suggested that the Islamic *ilahis* be removed from the program because the situation in Zemun was not ready for this type of communication. Some singers from Pontanima didn't dare to travel to Belgrade, and some of them secretly wore bullet-proof vests in case of attack. Tensions were high; the bodies of the singers were cramped; and the voices performing the *ilahis* were restrained. The singers, frightened of an attack or protest, kept glancing at the audience. But shockingly, the audience thoughtfully and curiously listened to powerful exclamations *Allahu Ekber* and, at the end of the song, the audience erupted into frenetic applause. This applause surprised not only the choir but also the audience, who looked at their clapping hands in some surprise. Some of the singers couldn't believe what was happening and asked me if the audience was mocking us or trying to provoke us. They couldn't believe that applause came from the heart of the audience. However, the audience had discovered that Islam and Muslims are not what they had previously thought. Through singing *ilahis,* Pontanima shattered the prejudices of the audience, and new perspectives suddenly were opened for the listeners. The music turned them from a closed past to an open future.

Conclusion

The Symphony of Religions that Pontanima sings does not exist in the world in which Pontanima lives. That symphony is the hope, vision, foresight, and longing of humanity that the strongest spiritual energies of humankind not be used up in quarrels and conflicts but turned toward shared goals, that in mutual respect they may help make possible the resolution of our most crucial problems: the cataclysmic might of weapons, the destruction of the environment, social inequality (and its consequences of injustice, oppression, hunger), and the violation of basic human rights.

In contrast to that hope, reality is nearly the opposite—absurd and depressing, Huntington-esque—whether one looks from the perspective of the September 11, 2001 tragedy in New York, from the hellish Balkan or Iraqi wars, or from the manipulation of religion that feeds enmity all over the world. In the face of this reality, Pontanima has decided to bring about its vision in a musical symphony of the most beautiful fruits of religious faith expressed in music.

In the highest achievements of human creativity, differences fade away, enmity finds reconciliation, and space for enculturation is created—space in which we experience as our own everything that is good and beautiful. The supreme works of creativity within various spiritual frameworks are connected in a mosaic of fine art, in a symphony of music, in the architecture of cities, in the mysteries of language; they reveal a common Origin, a forgotten common Root. These works of art guide us toward a Vision as the mirror of the Origin. And in this lies the secret of Pontanima and the reason why its symphony is so powerful.

At Pontanima's concerts, audiences are shocked, but in a positive way: that which was once completely different, unknown, foreign, that which generated fear or even enmity, is suddenly discovered as something similar, intimate, enriching, a chance to look more closely at oneself and the dynamic of one's own growth. Pontanima's symphony of religious music awakens listeners and touches their most intimate longing for happiness, peace, and love. Pontanima is not about hedonistic pleasure found in music; rather, it challenges listeners to change. Pontanima is a community that both lives out this truth and witnesses to it, and this living witness greatly amplifies Pontanima's message.

Bibliography

Andrić, Ivo. *Letter from 1920*. (Accessed: May 26, 2014.) http://www. diogenpro.com/uploads/4/6/8/8/4688084/ivo_andric..a_letter_ from_1920…pdf (12.112013), 2–3S.

Bastian, Hans-Dieter. "Verfremdung in der Verkündigung," in B. Dreher, N. Greinacher, and F. Klostermann, *Handbuch der Verkündigung*. Freiburg: Herder, 1970.

Boff, Clodovis. *Theologie und Praxis, Die erkenntnistheoretische Grundlagen der Theologie de Befreiung*. München: Kaise-Grünewald, 1983.

Dubois, Jacques, and others. *Allgemeine Rhetorik*. München: W. Fink, 1974.

Gadamer, Hans-Georg. *Wahrheit und Methode*. Tübingen: J.C.B. Mohr, 1965. (The direct quotes in English translation were taken from the English translation: Gadamer, Hans-Georg. *Truth and Method*, second, revised edition. Trans. Joel Weinsheimer and Donald Marshall. New York: Continuum, 2004).

Huizinga, Johan. *Homo Ludens, A study of the play-element in culture*. London: Routledge & Kegan Paul, 1949.

Lipošek, Damir, and Husein Hasanefendić. *Moja domovina*. (Accessed: May 26, 2014.) http://www.youtube.com/ watch?v=dZmLgeGOrI4.

Marković Ivo. "Studenti Franjevačke teologije, Pokušaj sustavnog istraživanja" (Students of Theology of Franciscans Sarajevo, An Attempt of systematic Research), in: *Bilten Franjevačke teologije*, XII–XII,1987.

Marković, Ivo. "Interreligious culture and relation in Bosnia." In *Forum Bosnae*, no. 55, 2012.

Sutton-Smith, Brian. *The Ambiguity of Play*. Cambridge, MA. First Harvard University Press paperback edition, 2001.

Imagining Peace: Indigenous and Contemplative Pedagogies in Transformative Peace Education

—Maxine Matilpi

You may say I'm a dreamer
But I'm not the only one
I hope someday you'll join us
And the world will live as one[119]

My Tai Chi teacher says, "Do what you can, when you can, with what you've got." The Cowichan Elder who works with my First Nations studies class advises us to share our gifts. A fellow dancer remarks, "Don't hold back. The world needs what we have to offer." My colleagues in the Holistic Lawyers Association advocate open-hearted teaching/facilitating. I take all this advice and put it into practice and later—much later—try to sort out the corresponding theory.

It's kind of ass-backwards as methodology goes. While some people work from theory to practice, my method is the other way around. Trust yourself; use your gifts; fill in the theory and science afterwards. This method lets me use my intuition, something I had to suppress through most of my formal education.

---

119. John Lennon, "Imagine" (1971).

I had become aware of developing my intuition years ago when I practised midwifery and also when my now-grown children were babies. As well as a former midwife, I'm also a former lawyer and Chief Negotiator in the British Columbia Treaty Process, a dancer, artist, community organizer, and to my good friends, a "re-creation doula." As a professor, I bring a nonconventional set of tools to an academic classroom: creativity and intuition, emotional intelligence *inter alia*. For the most part, these tools aren't valued in academia,[120] and I've learned to keep them under wraps, hidden from science/object-ive-based programs and institutions. However, I got an opportunity to use these tools—to bring my whole self—when I was invited to teach at the 2013 Canadian School of Peacebuilding (CSOP).

The CSOP offer to teach *Human Rights and Indigenous Legal Traditions* came unexpectedly when the scheduled teacher was unable to fulfill her contract. I had just finished teaching—or more accurately, I'd just finished *facilitating—Resistance, Resilience, and Solidarity,* a First Nations Studies "special topics" course at Vancouver Island University. This special topics course turned out to be very special indeed as it was January 2013 and our focus was Idle No More. [121]

Just a few months before, this Indigenous-inspired mass movement had exploded into the collective consciousness, inspiring hundreds of teach-ins, rallies, and round dances all across Turtle Island, and beyond. The movement "calls on all people to join in a peaceful revolution, to honour Indigenous sovereignty, and to protect the land and water"[122] in Canada. The overarching issue being addressed by Idle No More is expressed in its Manifesto: " The spirit and intent of the Treaty agreements meant that First Nations peoples would share the land, but retain their inherent rights to lands and resources. Instead, First Nations have experienced a history of colonization, which has resulted in outstanding land claims, lack of resources and unequal funding for services such as education and housing.[123]

---

120. See for example, Heinz Klatt, "Embarrassed by 'drivel ... poppycock." *CAUT Bulletin: Canada's Voice for Academics*, 59, No. 2, February 2012.
121. *Idle No More.* (Accessed June 13, 2013.) http://www.idlenomore.ca/.
122. "The Vision," *Idle No More.*, (Accessed: 2014 June 14.), http://www.idlenomore.ca/.
123. "The Manifesto," Idle No More. (Accessed. June 14, 2014.) http://www.idlenomore.ca/.

The goal of the organization is focused upon a rich understanding of peace: "We believe in healthy, just, equitable, and sustainable communities and have a vision and plan of how to build them."[124]

My goal for the special topics course was an examination of Idle No More and other contemporary social movements, and I wanted to facilitate the creation of a learning community and to engage in some practical activities with theoretical and academic goals. Learning would be hands-on and would encourage service, deep observations, and listening in order to create oneness.

In the course I experimented with Open Space facilitation,[125] and in order to be responsive to the immediate context, used a constantly evolving course syllabus. I relied on talking circles, Indigenous pedagogies,[126] Forum Theatre,[127] Paulo Freire,[128] and laughter yoga. This wasn't what education typically looks like in our society. I was working without a safety net, and, importantly, I brought my whole self. Because a significant aspect of my pedagogical goal was to build community, I requested and received permission from the university registrar for the class to be ungraded. Grading and competition, I asserted, would disrupt connection, and my goal in teaching this course would be to create oneness.

But going to Winnipeg for CSOP would be different. I'd be using someone else's already-prepared syllabus and reading list; and, for administrative reasons, any deviations from this plan would have to be limited. Still, I felt a freedom that came from the fact of being the substitute teacher; filling in at the last minute brought some licence.

As I was preparing to go, I wondered about the pedagogical possibilities and about creating a learning community with such a rigorous

---

124. "The Manifesto." (Accessed June 14, 2014.) http://www.idlenomore.ca/.
125. "Open Space" is a "self-organizing practice of inner discipline and collective activity which releases the inherent creativity and leadership in people. By inviting people to take responsibility for what they care about, Open Space encourages inquiry, reflection, and learning, bringing out the best in both individuals and the whole." See Anne Stadler, *Doing Open Space, A Two-page Primer*. (Accessed June 13, 2014.) http://www.openspaceworld.org/tmnfiles/2pageos.htm.
126. Based on the work of Lorna Williams, Faculty of Education, University of Victoria.
127. "Forum Theatre" is from the work of Augusta Boal, *Theatre of the Oppressed* (New York: Communication Group, 1974).
128. Paulo Freire, Brazilian educator, philosopher, and critical theorist. See Paulo Freire, *Pedagogy of the Oppressed* (New York: Continuum Books, 1970).

schedule and an ambitious set of readings. It seemed we would be engaging in a lot of intellectual head (brain) work, and that's not usually what I do when I teach—or at least it's not what I like to do when I teach. Relying on my intuition, I got brave and exposed myself by sending out an email "prayer" to the entire class:

Subject Line: Preparing the Field
June 14, 2013.

Dear Participants,

As we prepare for our upcoming Human Rights and Indigenous Legal Traditions course, I want to invite you to join me in creating spacious intention for our time together at the Canadian School of Peacebuilding. We are in a field of energy that is informed by all of us. If you feel moved to do so, you can begin to shape that field now.

Some examples of ways that we can focus attention and intention are:

- *reaching out to the physical place before you arrive to connect to all living things there;*
- *envisioning all participants traveling there safely;*
- *opening to all of your being and intelligence so that your experience there is informed by your wholeness and a beginner's mind;*
- *being available to whatever arises while simultaneously holding spacious intention that our work and play through Indigenous pedagogies tunes us to the highest good for all (conscious, creative and collaborative process and outcome).*

Again, this is an invitation only. Please follow your own wisdom and heart. I look forward to meeting you all in Winnipeg.

Warmly,
Maxine

Maxine V.H. Matilpi, J.D., LL.M.
Instructor, Canadian School of Peacebuilding 2013
http://www.nianow.com/matilpi-maxine
Sent from K'omoks/Pentlatch Territory

I'd learned this non-denominational prayer from Jane Faulkner,[129] who'd sent it to participants of a conference for Holistic Law. I received Jane's email prayer a few days before travelling to the California conference and I remember, as I was preparing to travel, feeling this was not going to be typical continuing legal education credits. Jane's prayer set a tone that excited me, and I hoped CSOP students would feel the same. At the very least, they'd get a bit of a "heads-up" about me.

A few days later and I'm in Winnipeg getting my orientation at the Canadian Mennonite University with a co-director for CSOP. The gothic-style building looks like a Harry Potter set: big old stones, ornate gargoyle creatures holding up corners, and down the hall, an auditorium with leaded windows, a gigantic pipe organ, and a grand piano.

We're walking through the building under the high, arched ceilings when I let out a "Wow!" as we enter the expansive "Great Hall," where, starting the next day, students and faculty will gather for coffee breaks and conversations. The co-director, Valerie Smith, hearing my "Wow!" remarked, "The architecture of this building isn't the typical Mennonite style. The South Campus is more typical of Mennonite style. It's functional, simple."

I'd noticed the aesthetic contrast between the North and South campuses earlier. My apartment on the South Campus—which is student housing during the school year—is functional but very plain, nothing on the walls. Because I'm exhausted from the day's travelling, the Winnipeg heat and humidity, and the intensity of preparing class materials, I happily accept plain and unadorned, consider it calming, restful.

"As Mennonites," Valerie says, "we come out of a tradition of seeking to live simply. I think this is an important value. But one year I celebrated Easter in the Notre Dame basilica at the University of Notre Dame, and I couldn't help but notice the difference between the Easter decorations there compared to a typical Mennonite church.... I've thought that, for Easter—the season of resurrection and triumph—we are, perhaps, a bit too restrained."

She makes this comment not with scorn or shame, just a factual observation.

---

129. Jane Faulkner, lawyer, facilitator, coach, Seattle, WA. (Accessed June 13, 2014.) http://janefaulkner.net/.

Our conversation leads me to consider the cross-cultural context in which I'll be teaching, and I begin to worry that in my preparations I haven't given this enough thought. Maybe my intuition is about to fail me. I'm an outsider in someone else's territory and, in this moment, I'm feeling concerned about offending Mennonite students or administrators.

Some of my pedagogy will involve playing a card game, and it occurs to me a card game might offend Mennonites. I worry, too, that maybe I should have reviewed the university policy on this. Later, I seek out Jarem Sawatsky, the other co-director, for advice, to ask if it's okay for Mennonites to play cards. He lets me know it likely won't be a problem; perhaps to some of their grandparents it might have been forbidden, but he assures me it should be fine.

The card game, Barnga,[130] is set up with students divided among five or six tables. At each table, the rules are similar but different; importantly, players don't realize there are different rules at each table. The game is played in silence and because the game requires players to move to different tables with each round; they must use non-verbal communication to understand slightly different rules at each table. As a consequence, Barnga is useful for communicating about cross-cultural issues and helps participants experience differing viewpoints to see how cultures perceive things differently or play by different rules. Players learn through this game that they must understand and reconcile these differences if they want to function effectively in a cross-cultural group.

At the University of Victoria Faculty of Law, we'd used the game with first-year law students to get them talking about the new law school environment and the kind of community they'd like to create over their next three years. I've come to appreciate how, during the debriefing of the game, participants get an opportunity to talk about their feelings. Not very often are students—especially law students—asked

---

130. Barnga by Sivasailam "Thiagi" Thiagarajan, 1980. (Accessed June 13, 2014.)   http://www.google.ca/url?sa=t&rct=j&q=&esrc=s&frm=1&source =web&cd=1&ved=0CBwQFjAA&url=http%3A%2F%2Fwww.uk.sagepub. com%2Fparker%2FCHAPTER%25207%2FBARNGA.doc&ei=CnqcU4jkI 9SjyASLzIKwCQ&usg=AFQjCNFz3wAWiv5o3RpKPxgPmNp3DvTHqg. With gratitude to Gillian Calder, University of Victoria, Faculty of Law for introducing me to the game.

to talk about their feelings. The playfulness of Barnga also assists in my pedagogical goals as it helps students get out of their heads and into their bodies through non-verbal communication. They learn how difficult communications demand sensitivity and creativity; and because "communication is foundational to community,"[131] the game moves us toward oneness.

Over my years of teaching, a principle guiding my work has been this: Everything is one.[132] I try to work toward oneness; however, when I first started teaching, I had no word to describe it. Sometimes after a class, I'd go home and tell my husband that, today, the class "really came together" or "it felt really good." Sometimes I noticed this oneness energy in the middle of the semester, but more often it appeared near the end of the term. Once or twice, it didn't arrive until the very last day of class, and one year it wasn't there at all. Years later, I learned from Lorna Williams the Lil'wat term, *Kumucwalha*, "the recognition of our having a common goal, of being present to self and others, of everyone feeling as though they belong."[133] But until then, I didn't really focus on my role as a teacher in actively encouraging it, or about why oneness is important in the teaching and learning environment. I thought it came by accident or luck, or that it was something out of my control all together. Now I know differently.

As a learner I've been positively affected by oneness energy and I realize there are ways as teachers (or facilitators, or members of communities) we can consciously assist each other in finding and developing oneness so we can move forward together in a good way. In a classroom, finding oneness means working together, building respect, enhancing relationships, and recognizing coalitions. One particular element for developing oneness in the classroom is through making space for all voices, my own and those of the students.[134] We can encourage all the voices through talking circles, for example.

---

131. Roberto Dansie, *Communication and Community.* (*Accessed June 13, 2014.*) http://www.robertodansie.com/articles/communication.htm.
132. See, for example, Umeek/E. Richard Atleo, *Tsawalk: A Nuu-chah-nulth Worldview* (Vancouver: UBC Press, 2004).
133. Lorna Williams, "Earth Fibres, Weaving Stories: Learning and Teaching in an Indigenous World" (syllabus, EDCI 499, University of Victoria, 2006), 3.
134. Maxine Matilpi, "In Our Collectivity: Teaching, Learning, and Indigenous Voice," *Canadian Journal of Native Education,* 35, No. 1 (2012), 211–220.

I'm deliberate about working toward oneness and do my very best to make it happen, mapping out a thirteen-week semester to build group cohesiveness. But with only five days, CSOP would be a challenge, and we'd need to work quickly.

After Barnga we use a second game, Survivor, where I ask the students to consider for a (silent) moment what special skills they bring to our "community." I ask them to imagine we are marooned together on a tropical island or (since one our course readings is a survival story set there) in the north above the Arctic Circle. I ask them to introduce themselves and tell us about a particular skill they possess that would help our group survive/thrive. I tell them about my midwifery background and also that I'm a laughter yoga instructor. One student admits to being a great cook, another sews, another can sing "to lift our spirits." We have fishers and hunters, plant gatherers, and builders. The students and I have many gifts to share, to notice our complementarity and opportunities for interdependence, to imagine how we fit together. We'll be fine.

Ice-breakers like Survivor and games such as Barnga give us the freedom to be ourselves without the pressure of being articulate or forming smart-sounding questions or comments based on course readings. Similar to theatre games,[135] they encourage sharing, openness, and listening, and are useful for getting to know each other more deeply and building group cohesion. They lead to cooperation and discussion and set a tone of playfulness and creativity, getting us into our hearts and bodies, helping us bring our whole selves into the classroom.

Embodied (or somatic) learning encourages deep thinking. It activates imaginations and helps us think differently. While typical Western education emphasizes cognitive knowledge that can separate us from our bodies and hearts, embodied education connects us to our wholeness and to each other—especially when we create opportunities to work side by side to build community. I've been especially influenced by the ground-breaking work of Dr. Lorna Williams of the Lil'wat First Nation of Mount Currie, British Columbia. In her EDCI 591 classes, *Teaching and Learning in an Indigenous World*, students

---

135. Viola Spolin, *Improvisation for the Theatre* (Evanston, IL: Northwestern University Press, 1974).

work side by side to carve a cedar canoe or a welcoming pole[136] or to create large textiles. Lorna's work is grounded in Indigenous peda-gogical principles and values such as inclusivity, community building, and recognition and celebration of individual uniqueness. For me, this was transformational education at its best. I appreciated how "learning was based on participants' openness to ideas, and on inter-connections made in personal contemplation, but also by [us being] drawn together by a common goal." Context created the conditions for us "to form a collective system, but at the same time, the con-text [challenged] the system to evolve, to exist with an element of uncertainty."[137]

This kind of teaching and—because of its reciprocity—this kind of learning, became my new standard. Hands-on, project-based, ex-periential opportunities are what I strive for. As Dr. Marie Battiste notes, this kind of learning is a first principle of Indigenous peda-gogy: valuing a person's ability to learn independently by observing, listening, and participating with a minimum of intervention or in-struction.[138] While Battiste is primarily concerned with Indigenous learners, in my view, this kind of pedagogy is also beneficial to non-Indigenous students.

At CSOP we would only have five days and no time to carve ca-noes. Still, I needed to design a project that would give students an opportunity to work side by side, something to involve more than just their heads, something that would connect with social justice

---

136. Lorna Williams and Michele Tanaka, "Schalay'nung Sxwey'ga Emerging Cross-cultural Pedagogy in the Academy" *Educational Insights*, 11 no. 3. (Accessed June 13, 2014.) http://www.ccfi.educ.ubc.ca/publication/insights/v11n03/articles/williams/williams.html.

137. Kathy Sanford, Lorna Williams, Tim Hopper, and Catherine McGregor, "Indigenous Principles Decolonizing Teacher Education: What We Have Learned," *in education*, 19, no. 2 (2013). (Accessed June, 13 2014.) http://ineducation.ca/ineducation/article/view/61/547.

138. Marie Battiste, "Indigenous Knowledge and Pedagogy in First Nations Education: A Literature Review with Recommendations," Prepared for the National Working Group on Education and the Minister of Indian and Northern Affairs, Ottawa, ON., October 31, 2002, (Accessed June 13, 2014.) http://www.truworld.ca/__shared/assets/Batiste-Indigenous-Knowledge-and-Pedagogy29331.pdf.

and human rights and that would get them into their hearts. Since we would be learning about missing and murdered Indigenous women, I settled on Christi Belcourt's project, "Walking With Our Sisters."

In 2012, Métis artist Christi Belcourt put out a call on social media, asking for contributions of moccasin vamps (also known as "uppers" or "tongues") for a collaborative art project and memorial ceremony, "Walking With Our Sisters."[139] Each pair of intricately beaded or embroidered moccasin vamps would represent the unfinished life of one of the over six hundred murdered or missing Indigenous women in Canada.[140] Along with my books and papers, my suitcase was stuffed with fabric, scissors, beads, needles, and thread. The students and I would sew together.

On the afternoon of the first day, not knowing how my idea would be received, I introduced the students to Christi's project. Because of an earlier conversation about Mennonites and adornment, I worried that this project of decorating with beads and embroidery might offend the Mennonite students. I let them know of my worry, confessed I didn't know very much about Mennonites—really only what I had learned through literature.[141] I tell them about my discomfort, of not wanting to offend, of feeling embarrassed about not having checked earlier. I opened myself by sharing my feelings of being an outsider, remembering the advice of Tara Brach: "Opening ourselves can be a gift to others ... it invites them to do the same."[142]

I had been teaching about this issue of missing and murdered Indigenous women for the past decade (most notably in my Women's Studies classes), and though I believe in the power of art, I wasn't confident about the art element here. Also, because I hoped the work would involve using our hearts—as opposed to our heads—and because students were still getting to know me and we hadn't quite

---

139. *Walking With Our Sisters.* (Accessed June 14, 2014.) http://walking-withoursisters.ca/.

140. For more information on missing and murdered Indigenous women in Canada, see Amnesty International's "A Human Rights Response to Discrimination and Violence against Indigenous Women in Canada," *Canada Stolen Sisters.*(Accessed June 14, 2014.) http://www.amnesty.ca/sites/default/files/amr200032004enstolensisters.pdf.

141. Miriam Toews, *A Complicated Kindness* (Toronto: Vintage Canada, 2007).

142. Tara Brach, *Radical Acceptance* (New York: Random House, 2003), 292.

developed trust—I worried it might be seen as something trivial or unimportant, or possibly as Heinz Klatt would see it, "poppycock" and "drivel."[143] I'm aware that not everyone recognizes the value of Indigenous pedagogies and that some Western thinkers are challenged by Indigenous knowledge and its respect and appreciation for the metaphysical world.[144]

Perhaps this kind of "spiritual activism," this "coming together of spirituality and activism," would be new to them. I would be encouraging students, as Velcrow Ripper describes, to learn and act "from their hearts, to take their parts in creating change, with a spirit of positivity, compassion, love, and a balance of interdependence and self-determination." My goal was for students to "be the change" they want to see in world within and without, and my hope was to facilitate a course that would be "positive, kind, fierce, and transformative." [145] I also hoped for the kind of "morphic resonance" described by Charles Eisentein, "the ripple effect of changed people changing other people,"[146] or the idea that "once something happens somewhere, it induces the same thing to happen elsewhere."[147] I dream of working the magic of morphogenesis into our classroom with Eisenstein's theory that

> Every act of generosity is an invitation into generosity. Every act of courage is an invitation into courage. Every act of selflessness is an invitation into selflessness. Every act of healing is an invitation into healing.[148]

143. Heinz Klatt, "Embarrassed by 'drivel.'" *CAUT Bulletin: Canada's Voice for Academics 59, no. 2, February 2012.* http://www.cautbulletin.ca/en_article.asp?ArticleID=3401.
144. Wayne Peters, "Indigenous Knowledge Can Enrich Our Campuses," 59, no. 1, (January 2012).
145. Velcrow Ripper, "What is Spiritual Activism," *Fierce Love, There Are No Rules to Follow. No Manual to Read. Only the Open Book of the. Heart.* (Accessed June 14, 2014.) http://fiercelove.wordpress.com/what-is-spiritual-activism/.
146. Charles Eisenstein, *The More Beautiful World Our Hearts Know Is Possible* (Berkeley, California: North Atlantic Books, 2013), 63.
147. Eisenstein, *The More Beautiful*, 62.
148. Eisenstein, *The More Beautiful*, 204.

Still, I fretted that, without student "buy-in," sewing moccasin vamps might be seen as a waste of our precious five days. I worried they might be anxious to get to the meat of the course, the "black letter law" of human rights and Indigenous legal traditions. I decided to expose my vulnerability with this uncertainty but also to tell them about where my confidence comes from.

Years ago I had attended a burning ceremony with Christine Welsh when she was beginning her work on *Finding Dawn*.[149] A burning ceremony is an Indigenous way of showing honour, respect, and remembrance. During the ceremony we were told by one of the ceremonial leaders that our work on this matter of missing and murdered women would be guided by the spirits of the women we were honouring; we should always remember they're watching over us, protecting us.

With only the scantiest bit of information about "Walking with Our Sisters," the students seem to trust me, accepting my idea about sewing beads and adorning vamps, jumping in to sketch designs and select materials. Later I witness them fully engaged, sometimes arriving early to sew before class, helping each other, teaching, learning, listening, reflecting, applying teamwork and synergy[150] to accomplish goals. "Like ripples in a pond, [our physical and] spiritual actions combine and build on each other to magnify an effect beyond what each [of us] could do individually."[151] We're conscious of adding our energy to the collective energy initiated by Christi Belcourt. The whole is greater than the sum of the parts.

Remarkably, prior to this class, some of the students have never learned to sew, even to thread a needle, so the work is slow, requiring much patience and attention, but also it creates opportunities for discussion. A few days into our sewing, we set aside our needles and thread to watch Christine's film, *Finding Dawn*, and students are struck by the significance of the work we're doing. It hits home:

---

149. Christine Welsh, *Finding Dawn* (Montreal, National Film Board of Canada, 2006).

150. Velcrow Ripper, "Spiritual Activism" (Accessed June 14, 2014), http://fiercelove.wordpress.com/what-is-spiritual-activism/.

151. "The Twelve Keys of Spiritual Activism" (Accessed June 14, 2014), http://humanityhealing.net/2011/12/the-12-keys-of-spiritual-activism/

grieving families with no answers about the loss of their mothers, sisters, aunts, daughters. Afterward, we move our chairs into a circle to debrief through tears, anger, and sadness, to speak of motivation and empathy, and of the juxtaposition of the beauty of these extraordinary miniature pieces of art to the ugliness of the story of missing and murdered women. It's apparent in our talking circle that our hearts have become deeply connected to the work of learning about these women, and also to each other through our shared experience.

A talking circle is a powerful tool for building community and working toward peace. I appreciate how talking circles help to develop community through "deep listening" engaging "not just our ears and mind, but our heart and soul."[152] "As in our personal relationships, so also in relationships between communities, races, nations, and religions, listening is also an essential key to harmony."[153] Thich Nhat Hanh, Vietnamese Buddhist teacher and peace activist, points out the fact that our failure to really listen to one another is a great obstacle to global peace:

> America has the potential to listen to the suffering of her own people and to remedy discrimination and injustice within. If you cannot listen to your own people, your fellow citizens, how can you listen to and understand the suffering of others? How can you understand the suffering in Afghanistan, Iraq, Israel, or Palestine?[154]

Listening then, can heal not just individuals but entire communities. Buddhist teacher and clinical psychologist Tara Brach reminds us that listening is important to building trust and developing community.

> When we are listened to, we feel connected. When we're not listened to, we feel separate. So whether it's the communicating between different tribes or religions, ethnicities, racial groups or different generations, we need to listen. The more

152. Jalaja Bonheim, *Evolving Toward Peace: Awakening the Global Heart* (Minneapolis, MN: Two Harbors Press, 2013), 171.
153. Bonheim, *Evolving Toward Peace*, 172.
154. Bonheim, *Evolving Toward Peace*, 172.

we understand, the less we fear; the less we fear, the more we trust and the more we trust, the more love can flow.

She also says,

> When we're fully in that listening presence, when there's that pure quality of receptivity, we become presence itself. And whether you call that God or pure awareness or our true nature, the boundary of inner and outer dissolves and we become a luminous field of awareness. When we're in that open presence we can really respond to the life that's here. We fall in love.[155]

Because there's more listening than talking involved, maybe, as Welsh and Olsen suggest, they should be called "listening circles."[156] In our circles we come to "listening presence" through protocols such as passing a stone, accepting silence, and the simple and powerful act of breathing together. Mindful of the significance of breathing together from my midwifery days, I'm conscious of creating connection through breath-work; and we also create this connection through laughter yoga and movement exercises.

In her book, *Evolving Towards Peace*, Jalalja Bonheim describes how "together, we can move from wounding to healing, from fragmentation to wholeness, from insanity to wisdom, and from violence to peace."[157] Bonheim asserts that if we can muster the courage to communicate authentically, then trust, respect, and friendship can blossom.[158] She observes that consciousness of connection is the antidote to prejudice and hatred, and notes that creating spaces where

---

155. Tara Brach, "The Sacred Art of Listening —Nourishing Loving Relationships," Tara Brach blog, January 8, 2014. (Accessed June 14, 2014). http://blog.tarabrach.com/2014/01/.

156. Christine Welsh and Sylvia Olsen. "Listen with the Ear to Your Heart: A Conversation about Story, Voice, and Bearing Witness," in *Screening Culture: Constructing Image and Identity*, ed. Heather Norris Nicholson (Lanham, MD: Lexington Books, 2003).

157. Bonheim, *Evolving Toward Peace*, 23.

158. Bonheim, *Evolving Toward Peace*, 55.

former enemies can sit face to face, eye to eye, and discover the other really is essential for moving toward peace.[159]

In this high-tech world of universities and other educational institutions competing with webinars, distance education, and MOOCs (massive online open courses), this lively and embodied pedagogy presents opportunities for us to be moved in the moment together, experiencing "the magic of personal connection."[160] Bonheim emphasizes that if we want to bridge cross-cultural barriers, meeting face to face is a crucial first step. "If we want to transform negative relationships, we need to connect face to face and find out who the 'other' really is."[161] Thus, she advocates "relational education" to empower us to create and maintain healthy, harmonious relationships. Relational education she maintains, nurtures values such as kindness, tolerance, and respect, and these are essential to healthy, peaceful communities.[162]

Relational education, heart thinking, and deep listening are all fundamental to the practice of contemplative education, which is now being employed in educational institutions to promote well-being and social justice. Some of my pedagogy would be considered contemplative education because I strive to cultivate deep awareness and knowing, leading to increased concentration, letting students get in touch with themselves through silence or meditation, and through reflexive practices such as writing, art, and poetry.[163] Contemplative education helps us make connections to figure out how we're connected to social problems, encouraging new forms of inquiry and imaginative thinking; and it helps to educate active citizens who will support a more just and compassionate direction for society. The idea is to develop compassion, to become more aware of the world around us, and to restore us so we can address each other's concerns.[164]

---

159. Bonheim, *Evolving Toward Peace*, 95.
160. Bonheim, *Evolving Toward Peace*, 55.
161. Bonheim, *Evolving Toward Peace*, 53.
162. Bonheim, *Evolving Toward Peace*, 71.
163. The Center for Contemplative Mind in Society, "The Association for Contemplative Mind in Higher Education." (Accessed July 26, 2014.) http://www.contemplativemind.org/programs/acmhe.
164. Helen Damon-Moore and others, Webinar: "Fostering Contemplative Life Skills on a College Campus Outside the Classroom," *The Association for*

In our hopes to create a more peaceful world, it's crucial that we look at the inner obstacles that ensnare each of us in destructive ways of thinking and relating. We need to better understand why we behave the way we do and what we can do to reclaim our collective sanity.[165] Deep reflexive practices typical to contemplative pedagogies help us gain that understanding by recasting the "traditional foundations for education into a truly integrative, transformative, and communal enterprise that cultivates the whole person in the fullest possible way."[166]

What happens when we all bring our whole selves to the work we do? I often tell my students the day before a special guest or activity, "Please bring your whole selves." Some of them brush it off as the teacher's quirkiness; however, others have appeared later at my office door thanking me for the invitation: "Never before have I been asked to bring my whole self to school! Usually I have the feeling I need to split myself off, leave who I really am at the door—or maybe leave behind the important parts." Inviting students to bring their wholeness (and even their holiness) encourages and allows them to better serve as agents of peace in the world because they themselves are more at peace.[167] Students are accustomed to leaving major parts of themselves behind, but also, as faculty, we do that to ourselves too because it's expected. Be professional. Be objective. Don't get too involved. Oh—and boundaries—mustn't forget boundaries. In the end, it's about sharing our gifts, about not holding back, about bringing our whole selves to our work.

According to Bonheim, many people in our society view all forms of inner work, including relational education, as "narcissistic hobbies for people determined to ignore life's more pressing problems. Yet when you look at the major problems on our planet, you'll see how many of them can be traced back to relational illiteracy."[168] Furthermore, if we want to create a more peaceful world, relational

---

Contemplative Mind in Higher Education, January 22, 2014. (Accessed June 14, 2014.) http://www.contemplativemind.org/event/webinar-fostering-contemplative-life-skills-on-a-college-campus-outside-the-classroom.

165. Bonheim, *Evolving Toward Peace,* 63.
166. Bonheim, *Evolving Toward Peace,* 53.
167. Bonheim, *Evolving Toward Peace,* 163.
168. Bonheim, *Evolving Toward Peace,* 174.

education (which helps us communicate, co-operate, and co-exist) ought to be seen as an urgent collective imperative.[169]

The five CSOP days are exhausting in the best of ways. Winnipeg is hot and humid and when I arrive back to my plain, university apartment with nothing on the walls and only the most functional of furnishings, it's calm. Clean. Ordered. Spare. Although I recognize that this isn't fully representative of the current Mennonite experience, still I'm grateful for this Mennonite "Feng Shui" and for all I've learned along the way.

By the end of the week, we'd sewn and sung, learned and laughed together. We'd also eaten, cried, prayed, and celebrated. We created synergy by adding our work, our seventeen pairs of tenderly decorated moccasin vamps, to Christi Belcourt's bigger project. On our last day together, before our vamps were bundled up to be sent to Walking With Our Sisters, we transformed our classroom into a sacred space with candles, and music, specifically with Silvia Nakkach's *Medicine Melodies*.[170] Together we created our own ceremony, our vamps lovingly placed along the floor, lined up with care and reverence, and we have invited witnesses to walk alongside our work.[171]

We have created oneness.
We've breathed ("inspired") together.
He'ạm (for now)
Ha-La-Kasla ('til our breath meets again)

---

169. Bonheim, *Evolving Toward Peace*, 173.

170. The Vox Mundi Project. (Accessed July 26, 2014.) http://voxmundiproject.com/02-discography/.

171. To see a short video clip of our project please see the CSOP website: Canadian School of Peacebuilding, and institute of Canadian Mennonite University "CSOP Participates in 'Walking with our Sisters.'" (Accessed June 14, 2014.) http://csop.cmu.ca/index.php/2013/11/walking-with-our-sisters/.

Bibliography

Amnesty International. "A Human Rights Response to Discrimination and Violence against Indigenous Women in Canada," *Canada Stolen Sisters*. (Accessed July 26, 2014.) http://www.amnesty.org/en/library/info/AMR20/003/2004.

Atleo, Umeek/E. Richard. *Tsawalk: A Nuu-chah-nulth Worldview.* Vancouver, UBC Press, 2004.

Battiste, Marie. "Indigenous Knowledge and Pedagogy in First Nations Education: A Literature Review with Recommendations," prepared for the National Working Group on Education and the Minister of Indian and Northern Affairs, Ottawa, ON., October 31, 2002. (Accessed June 13, 2014.) http://www.truworld.ca/__shared/assets/Batiste-Indigenous-Knowledge-and-Pedagogy29331.pdf.

Belcourt, Christi. *Walking With Our Sisters*. (Accessed June 14, 2014.) http://walkingwithoursisters.ca/.

Boal, Augusta. *Theatre of the Oppressed.* New York: Communication Group, 1974.

Bonheim, Jalaja. *Evolving Toward Peace: Awakening the Global Heart.* Two Harbors Press, Minneapolis, MN, 2013.

Brach, Tara. *Radical Acceptance.* New York: Random House, 2003.

Brach, Tara. "The Sacred Art of Listening —Nourishing Loving Relationships," Tara Brach blog, 8 January 2014. (Accessed June 14, 2014.) http://blog.tarabrach.com/2014/01/.

Canadian School of Peacebuilding, and institute of Canadian Mennonite University "CSOP Participates in 'Walking with our Sisters.'" (Accessed June 14, 2014.) http://csop.cmu.ca/index.php/2013/11/walking-with-our-sisters/.

Damon-Moore, Helen and others. Webinar: "Fostering Contemplative Life Skills on a College Campus Outside the Classroom," *The Association for Contemplative Mind in Higher Education,* January 22, 2014. (Accessed June 14, 2014.) http://www.contemplativemind.org/event/webinar-fostering-contemplative-life-skills-on-a-college-campus-outside-the-classroom.

Dansie, Roberto. *Communication and Community*. (Accessed June 13, 2014.) http://www.robertodansie.com/articles/communication.htm.

Eisenstein, Charles. *The More Beautiful World Our Hearts Know Is Possible*. Berkeley, CA: North Atlantic Books, 2013, 63.

Faulkner, Jane. (Accessed June 13, 2014,) http://janefaulkner.net/.

Freire, Paulo. *Pedagogy of the Oppressed*. New York: Continuum Books, 1970.

Idle No More. "The Manifesto." (Accessed June 14, 2014.) http://www.idlenomore.ca/.

Idle No More. "The Vision." (Accessed June 14, 2014.) http://www.idlenomore.ca/.

Klatt, Heinz. "Embarrassed by 'drivel … poppycock.'" *CAUT Bulletin: Canada's Voice for Academics* 59, no. 2, February 2012.

Lennon, John. "Imagine." 1971.

Matilpi, Maxine. "In Our Collectivity: Teaching, Learning, and Indigenous Voice," *Canadian Journal of Native Education*, 35, no. 1 2012: 211–220.

Peters, Wayne. "Indigenous Knowledge Can Enrich Our Campuses." *CAUT Bulletin: Canada's Voice for Academics*, 59, no. 1, January 2012.

Ripper, Velcrow. "What is Spiritual Activism," *Fierce Love, There Are No Rules to Follow. No Manual to Read. Only the Open Book of the. Heart*. (Accessed June 14, 2014.) http://fiercelove.wordpress.com/what-is-spiritual-activism/.

Sanford, Kathy, Lorna Williams, Tim Hopper, and Catherine McGregor, "Indigenous Principles Decolonizing Teacher Education: What We Have Learned." *in education*, 19, no. 2 (2013). (Accessed June 13, 2014.) http://ineducation.ca/ineducation article/view/61/547.

Spolin, Viola. *Improvisation for the Theatre*. Evanston, IL: Northwestern University Press, 1974.

Stadler, Anne. *Doing Open Space, A Two-page Primer*. (Accessed June 13, 2014.) http://www.openspaceworld.org/tmnfiles/2pageos.htm.

The Center for Contemplative Mind in Society. "The Association for Contemplative Mind in Higher Education." (Accessed June 14, 2014.) http://www.contemplativemind.org/programs/acmhe.

The Vox Mundi Project. (Accessed July26, 20 14.) http://
    voxmundiproject.com/02-discography/

Thiagarajan, Sivasailam. "Barnga." 1980. (Accessed June 13, 2014.)
    http://www.google.ca/url?sa=t&rct=j&q=&esrc=s&frm=1&sour
    ce=web&cd=1&ved=0CBwQFjAA&url=http%3A%2F%2Fwww.
    uk.sagepub.com%2Fparker%2FCHAPTER%25207%2FBARN
    GA.doc&ei=CnqcU4jkI9SjyASLzIKwCQ&usg=AFQjCNFz3wA
    Wiv5o3RpKPxgPmNp3DvTHqg.

Toews, Miriam. *A Complicated Kindness.* Toronto: Vintage Canada, 2007

Welsh, Christine. *Finding Dawn.* Montreal: National Film Board of
    Canada, 2006.

Welsh, Christine, and Sylvia Olsen. "Listen with the Ear to Your Heart:
    A Conversation about Story, Voice, and Bearing Witness," in
    Screening Culture: Constructing Image and Identity, ed. Heather
    Norris Nicholson. Lanham, MD: Lexington Books, 2003.

Williams, Lorna. "Earth Fibres, Weaving Stories: Learning and
    Teaching in an Indigenous World," (syllabus, EDCI 499,
    University of Victoria, 2006), 3.

Williams, Lorna, and Michele Tanaka. "Schalay'nung Sxwey'ga
    Emerging Cross-cultural Pedagogy in the Academy"
    Educational Insights, 11 no. 3. (Accessed June 13, 2014.) http://
    www.ccfi.educ.ubc.ca/publication/insights/v11n03/articles/
    williams/williams.html.

Additional Resources

Diamond, David. *Theatre for Living.* Victoria, BC: Trafford
    Publishing, 2007.

Eisenstein, Charles. *Sacred Economics: Money, Gift & Society in the
    Age of Transition.* Berkeley CA: North Atlantic Books, 2011.

hooks, bell. *Teaching to Transgress: Education and the Practice of
    Freedom.* New York: Routledge Press, 1994.

hooks, bell. *Teaching Community: A Pedagogy of Hope.* New York:
    Routledge Press, 2003.

Okada, Lisa. "On the Outside Looking in: Voice, Identity and
    Difference in Women's Studies," in *In Our Own Voices: Learning*

and Teaching Toward Decolonisation. ed. Proma Tagore. Winnipeg: Larkuma, 2006.

Ripper, Velcrow (*Occupy Love*) and Judy Rebick (*Occupy This!*), "On Compassionate Activism" in *Occupy the Economy: Organizer Handbook. 19* April 2013. *Rabble.ca.* (Accessed June 14, 2014.) http://rabble.ca/books/reviews/2013/04/10-key-points-becoming-more-compassionate-activist.

West, Melissa. "Pedagogy and Power Relations" Graduate Programme in Communication and Culture Centre for the Support of Teaching (CST). 10 Num. 2 (York University, February 2001); and Ellen Carillo. "'Feminist teaching/Teaching 'feminism,'" *Feminist Teacher.* 18 no. 1, University of Illinois, 2007.

THREE WOMEN OF PEACE WHO WORKED FOR TRUTH AND RECONCILIATION

—Stan McKay

A S A VERY YOUNG MAN I came to normal school[172] directly from Birtle Indian Residential School, having completed my high school there. Birtle Indian Residential School and the Norway House Indian Residential School were parts of the notorious "government-funded, church-run schools ... set up to eliminate parental involvement in the intellectual, cultural, and spiritual development of Aboriginal children.[173] I came to normal school to take teacher training. And one year after I left Birtle Residential School I found myself teaching in a residential school in Norway House, Manitoba. It is kind of a zombie-like transfer. You don't really assess what is happening around you; and I wound up working in a school that I think had problems for me and for the students. The problems of displacement and marginalization that were parts of the residential school system were overwhelmingly destructive and painful to my people, but that

---

172. The Provincial Normal School was the name of the teacher's training institution in Winnipeg, Manitoba, for several decades in the middle of the twentieth century. The building that housed the normal school is now part of the Canadian Mennonite University and the site of the Canadian School of Peacebuilding.

173. "Residential Schools," Truth and Reconciliation Commission of Canada. (Accessed April 14, 2014.) http://www.trc.ca/websites/trcinstitution/index.php?p=4.

trauma has been overcome by many people who have lived lives of strength and resilience, people who I wish to honour as peacebuilders. As I think of great peacebuilders, I think of the stories of three women.

First I want to tell you my experience of coming to know a woman in Norway House named Florence. Florence is a Cree woman. In 1970, the year before I met her, her eldest son had died while on the trap line. He had gone out in the cold, early in winter and had become wet. He had fallen through the ice, and climbed out, but he was unable to get a fire going, so he perished. He left behind seven children and one soon to be born. His widow lived next door to Florence and Adam, who helped care for these eight young children as part of their extended family. Florence was busy as a grandmother, but she also had a passion for leadership in the community, and she was one of eleven elders in her church.

In the early development of the church, all the elders had all been men, but in Norway House, when I went there in 1971, Florence and two other women had joined the work, and she was a church elder. She also was involved with the women's church group; and one of her major occupations with the women's group was to arrange for layettes. That's an old image, I know. A layette is a bundle of stuff for babies. And in Norway House, there was a small hospital and many, many babies were born in the village. Florence attempted to arrange for every baby to be welcomed with this bundle of clothing and little blankets and stuff that babies need.

Florence communicated only in Cree. She was a Cree woman, and she read the Cree Bible. She had taught herself to read. She was a small, gentle woman. Wherever Florence went there was a sense of peace; and she shared that spirit with all the people she visited. In the summer she walked, because there were no vehicles in the community; and in the winter she walked even further on the ice. At times she travelled by boat.

Sometime before I met her, she had determined that she had a special work. In addition to the other things she was doing, she had a special task. I would describe it as the task of a midwife, but not at the beginning of life. Rather, she was a midwife at the end of life. She would provide a sense of peace and well-being for the person who was going on their spiritual journey. If a person was wondering what they could do to help someone who was near death, they would invite Florence to come to their house. And often they would invite her as soon as the person who was ill would show signs of weakening. Florence would visit, and if she determined that this person was near the end of life, she would stay with them.

Long before any conversation of palliative care was in the network, Florence was a presence. When I would go to visit homes where she was with families, she would be sitting in a chair beside the bed of the ill person, hour upon hour, saying little, only occasionally sharing a prayer. She would sit through the day and through the night. She might stay for two days, or three, because the family needed her to be a comforting, peace-bringing presence in their home. Quietly, she sat as a midwife for the spirit world, bringing comfort and peace as was her ministry.

The second woman I want to tell you about is Jessie Saulteaux, an Assiniboine woman from Saskatchewan. When her family first came to Canada, they had been driven north from Wyoming into Canada as part of the Lakota nation. They were hunted by the Long Knives. In Cree we called the United States cavalry *kihci-mohkomanahk*—the Long Knives. The Long Knives were hunting down Indigenous people in the USA; and Jesse's family fled north and then settled in Cypress Hills in southwestern Saskatchewan, a beautiful, wooded area with hills and water and game to hunt—a good life.

At the time of the treaty signing, the Assiniboine community in the Cypress Hills was required by government decision to move their reserve seventy-five kilometres southeast of Regina, on the bald prairie with few resources. It was a very unfriendly place to spend the winter, so they were moved to a community that was called Carry the Kettle, named after one of their chiefs. The following summer, they packed their belongings and went back to Cypress Hills, only to be arrested later that summer and escorted back to the reserve at Carry the Kettle.

Jessie Saulteaux then was enrolled in a residential school. She succeeded in academics, as she was a very intelligent young woman. When she finished her education she came to Brandon and she dreamed that she would be a nurse. When she went to ask about admission to the school of nursing at the hospital in Brandon, they suggested to her that she was too dark to be acceptable in their program. She returned to Carry the Kettle, married, and raised a family. And then she began to volunteer in the community.

When the community did not have anyone to lead worship in the church, she became a lay minister, leading the community. She was later invited to allow her name to stand as a member on the local council, and she became the first woman in Saskatchewan to serve as an elected leader on a band council.

But, deep in her spirit, Jessie had this notion that there were many, many villages, and reserves that did not have spiritual leadership. And she had dreams of young people from First Nations communities being given theological training and then leading in their own villages in the life of the church there, a dream of spiritual leaders from within the communities. When Jessie was already into her seventies, a group of friends cooperated with her, met with her, and talked. In 1984, the Jessie Saulteaux Centre was developed in Saskatchewan. Two years later, in Saskatoon, she was given an honorary doctorate degree by the university, so the resource centre then became the Dr. Jessie Saulteaux Resource Centre.

She was a small, gentle woman. Does it sound like you've heard it before, that sentence? She was a small, gentle woman with great strength, who encouraged others and supported them so they could find out who they were.

When the Saulteaux Centre was moved to Manitoba in 1988, she travelled to Beausejour. But on the way to Beausejour she had to stop in St. James in Winnipeg for a time because we had negotiated a ten-year lease on a school in St. James, just below the Grace Hospital. For those of you who know Winnipeg, it was near the creek. It was an empty school that was not required by the community anymore.

People in the community heard that we were moving into the community, and they organized. They organized quickly, in large numbers, under the motivation that they would keep us out of that school. They did not want us in their neighbourhood. So when Dr. Jessie came to a meeting in the St. James school division office, it was packed with people. There was standing room only, and the room was filled largely with people from the community who exhibited great anger that we intended to establish our program in their community. The first person who spoke to the school board that night and to the people who gathered was a small, gentle woman named Jessie. She spoke clearly about the intent of her vision for developing leaders from our communities who would be leaders in their own right, having been developed in leadership in the life of the church.

People groaned and complained; and I heard one person sitting beside me say, "Why did they bring her?" They were overcome I think by her gentleness and her peaceful demeanour. The next morning, when the board of the Dr. Jessie Saulteaux Centre met, many of the young students, said "We must go to court. We must challenge this process, because we have a lease and we have every right to be in this facility." Dr. Jessie spoke quietly and said, "We cannot be who we are meant to be in this environment. If we are not welcomed, we cannot develop the kind of spiritual leadership that we are called to be a part of." So we decided that we would not go any further with the process. She advised us that we must be people of peace and move.

We wandered the earth for two years, looking for a place for the Dr. Jessie Saulteaux Centre. There seemed to be none. We were not welcomed in locations that we attempted to use. But Dr. Jessie continued to be a presence, advising us to continue to look for a place, and in a matter of time we found land on the Brokenhead River. And it was a place along the river that we knew had been used for many years as a spiritual gathering place for the people of the Brokenhead Ojibwa Nation. We purchased the land and, in 1992, Dr. Jessie Saulteaux came to the opening of the new location and, with her gentle spirit, again encouraged us to move forward. We had found a place. It is called the Dr. Jessie Saulteaux Centre and it brings many of us peace.

I met Florence in 1971, and I met Dr. Jessie in the early 1980s. But then I met Gladys Cook. Gladys was a Sioux woman whose family, like Dr. Jessie's, had been displaced from South Dakota to Sioux Valley West of Brandon. Gladys was born in Sioux Valley, and she too went to residential school. In the school she experienced horrendous things, but she survived. She married and had a family. They went to live in South Dakota with their young family. But then her husband took ill, and she had to take a job as a housekeeper. Then her husband died, and she was a single mom. So later she moved back to Portage

La Prairie, west of Winnipeg. She bought a small home and found employment at the Indian and Métis Friendship Centre.

There are friendship centres all across Canada. Well, there is one in Portage La Prairie and Gladys went there to work. She was hired as a counsellor because of her gentle spirit and her wisdom. Her primary work in Portage was with people with addictions. She had great patience and helped many, many people. But, even while she worked at the Friendship Centre, she discovered that there was a women's jail in Portage La Prairie, with very little spiritual support for the women who were in that prison. She also learned that in Portage La Prairie was the Agassiz Centre, where many young men were incarcerated. Many of those who were incarcerated were Aboriginal, so she became involved in both organizations.

On a couple of occasions I went with her to those places and saw that she was deeply admired and respected. She was very much a presence to the community. Toward the end of her life, Gladys lived with her daughter, who had advanced-stage cancer, so Gladys thought, "I should be involved with the Canadian Cancer Society. They do not have many programs for First Peoples in the Cancer Society and they do not have much awareness of us as a people." So she volunteered to be an educator and adviser with the Cancer Society. She had input into the Manitoba branch in Winnipeg. She also attended a national meeting for the Cancer Society and made a significant impact on the development of programs within that society.

Her constant involvement in life was with the Anglican Church of Canada. Now, the residential school she went to was an Anglican school, so I find it remarkable that she continued in that church, but she continued to be a member of the church at Portage La Prairie. Out of that church she served on many national church committees and we were very fortunate that, at one point, she agreed to serve on the board of the Dr. Jessie Saulteaux Centre. She advised us as an elder.

She respected traditional spiritual teaching and really, really involved herself in the Christian community, bringing joy and peace wherever she went. Did I tell you she was a small, powerful woman? She demonstrated the capacity to forgive injustice and wrong, and to initiate peaceful relations. Her story has been recorded by the Anglican Church of Canada as an audiovisual resource.

And the last thing she did before she went to the spirit world was to become involved with the building of a new facility for women who are incarcerated. Just west of Winnipeg, toward Headingly, a new building is being completed, and the decrepit, dark dungeon at Portage La Prairie will be closed. So she assisted in this revitalizing, at least of a facility.

Gladys had an amazing capacity. She had been a refugee, with her family fleeing the struggles of South Dakota, but she carried no hatred. Instead she chose to be a healer and a peacemaker.

And so I would like to honour Florence, Jessie, and Gladys.

Bibliography

Archives of Manitoba, "Normal School records regarding teacher training." (Accessed April 14, 2014.) http://pam.minisisinc. com/scripts/mwimain.dll/144/PAM_DESCRIPTION/ DESCRIPTION_DET_REP/REFD+9251?SESSIONSEARCH.

Truth and Reconciliation Commission of Canada, "Residential Schools." (Accessed April 14, 2014.) http://www.trc.ca/websites/ trcinstitution/index.php?p=4.

Rebuilding and Restoring: Challenges and Opportunities for the Churches in South Africa and Canada

—P G J (Piet) Meiring[174]

The South African Truth and Reconciliation Commission (TRC)

I WILL NEVER FORGET THE DAY: May 31, 1994. Images of newly elected President Nelson Mandela on the steps of the Union Buildings in Pretoria—smiling broadly at the hundreds of thousands of South Africans in the gardens below him, embracing foreign dignitaries, royalty, colleagues from the liberation struggle, former opponents—were flashed on television screens across the world. Millions, in six continents, saw jet fighters pass by, trailing the colours of the new South African flag. They heard, many for the first time, the national anthem sung in Afrikaans, English, and in different African languages: *Nkosi sikelele l'Afrika*—"God bless Africa!"

"We are celebrating too soon," a Catholic father observed in the days that followed. We are jumping from a time of struggle and liberation right across to a time of jubilation and celebration, in one gigantic leap. What we now need is a time for remembering, even for

---

174. This chapter is partially based on an article that appeared in *Missionalia* in 2009.

mourning. We have not dealt sufficiently with the past; and it is time that we start doing that. It is impossible simply to close the books, to forgive and forget. "We do indeed have to face the past," Archbishop Desmond Tutu was fond of saying, "for if we do not face the past, it may return!"[175]

How to Deal with the Past

For five years following the watershed announcement of President F. W. de Klerk in February 1990 that the African National Congress (ANC) and other liberation organizations were to be unbanned, that all political prisoners, among them Nelson Mandela, would be freed, and that democratic elections involving the whole South African population were to be held, the issue of the past had been hotly debated. The debate was on the agenda, too, of the multiparty conference, Convention for Democratic South Africa (CODESA). Prior to the 1994 elections CODESA had to struggle with, on the one hand, the plight of the thousands of victims of the apartheid years, and on the other hand, the urgent needs of the many perpetrators of apartheid who were guilty of past gross human rights violations. A blanket amnesty would not work; it would have been a total disregard and dishonouring of the pain and suffering of the victims. On the other end of the scale, Nuremberg-type trials, where the victors take the vanquished to court to be convicted and sentenced, were also not advisable; not if reconciliation was the order of the day. One of the last decisions taken by CODESA was to establish a Truth and Reconciliation Commission.

The South African TRC was established by an Act of Parliament in June 1995 with an important mandate:[176]

- To establish as complete a picture as possible of the Apartheid past (from 1960 to 1994).
- To facilitate the granting of amnesty.

---

175. Piet Meiring, *Chronicle of the Truth Commission: A Journey Through the Past and Present—into the Future of South Africa* (Vanderbijlpark: Carpe Diem Books, 1999), 17.

176. Truth and Reconciliation Commission of South Africa, *TRC Report, Volumes 1–7*, 1998/2002, Vol. 1, 55–57.

- To establish and make known the whereabouts of the victims, restoring their human and civil dignity by granting them the opportunity to relate their own accounts of the violations they suffered, and by recommending reparation measures in this respect.
- To compile a comprehensive report on the activities and findings of the TRC, with recommendations of measures to prevent future violations of human rights in the country.

Seventeen TRC commissioners were appointed by President Mandela, with the charge to add another eleven committee members to their ranks, representing the different cultural, racial, political, and religious communities of South Africa. The TRC was to be subdivided into three committees: the Human Rights Violations Committee, the Amnesty Committee, and the Reparation and Rehabilitation Committee.

Totally unexpectedly, I received a phone call from Archbishop Tutu early in January 1996, informing me that I had been appointed to serve on the TRC. So began my journey, with the other members of the commission, through the history of our country, trying to make sense of what had happened during our apartheid past, and trying to find directions for all of us on the road to reconciliation and nation building.

The Human Rights Violations Committee (HRVC)

During the two and a half years of its existence, the HRVC collected thousands of statements from victims from all over South Africa, many of whom were invited to public hearings. Media coverage was extensive. Night after night the faces of many of the victims appeared on television screens nationwide: tearful faces of parents who lost their children, of husbands and wives who lost their spouses; bewildered faces of old men and women who carried their sorrows over many years; faces of young comrades, of politicians, of farmers who lost their beloved in land mine explosions; faces of innocent passersby when a bomb, hidden in a busy street, exploded.

The definition of "gross human rights violations" was rather restrictive. Not everybody who suffered under apartheid—who was forcefully relocated or humiliated, who experienced discrimination or wrongful arrest—automatically qualified for statement-making. If that were the case millions would have joined the queue! Gross human rights violations were defined as murder, manslaughter, kidnapping, rape, and severe ill treatment that left permanent scars, mentally or physically. Nobody really knew how many victims to expect.

At the end, no less than 140 public hearings were held; 21,400 victims submitted statements; the names of 27, 000 victims were officially recorded. To the majority the experience proved to be worth their while, even if it was difficult to take the stand. Tears flowed freely, but those were tears of catharsis and healing. I vividly remember the words of an old gentleman from Soweto who spoke for many when he remarked at a Johannesburg hearing: "When I was tortured at John Vorster Square my tormentor sneered at me: 'Shout your lungs out! Nobody will ever hear you!' Now, at long last, people do hear me."[177]

Not everybody reacted positively. There were those who returned home disappointed and frustrated. But they constituted a minority. To thousands of victims it was, indeed, a cathartic experience. I reflected on this in my diary (East London Hearing, April 16–19, 1996):[178]

Was everything worth it, I asked myself when after one of the morning sessions I walked outside. What one of the Xhosa women—one of the unknown, practically forgotten witnesses—had to say in the hall just now did not only move the archbishop to tears, but left every one of us with a lump in the throat. With effort she put her tale on the table: of how she sent her fourteen year old son to the local shop to buy bread. There was unrest in the township and somewhere along the way, the boy landed in the crossfire. For some reason the security police arrested the wounded

---

177. Piet Meiring, "The Baruti vs the Lawyers: The Role of Religion in the TRC process," in *Looking Back, Reaching Forward*, ed. Charles Villa-Vicencio (Cape Town: University of Cape Town Press, 2000).
178. Meiring, *Chronicle*, 371.

child and subjected him to brutal torture. Two days later the mother who, panic stricken, was trying to find out what had happened to her son, saw on their neighbour's television set how the boy was being pulled down from a pickup truck by his ankles, how he was dragged across the tarmac. The mother told the hushed audience how the police eventually gave her an address where she could find her son. When she arrived there, it was the mortuary. With her own hands she had to prepare her son's body—with the gaping wound at the back of the head, with the burn marks where he was tortured—for the funeral. Remembering this, she broke down in tears. Many in the hall followed suit. Tutu called for a lunch break.

My meal in my hand, I encountered the woman in the midst of a small group of victims. "Madam", I asked, "you have come such a long way, over so many years, with your story…. You had to travel such a distance to come here. All of us saw how difficult it was for you to tell the story of your son. Please tell me, was it worth it?" The marks of her tears were still on her cheeks. But when she raised her head and smiled, it was like the dawn breaking. "Oh yes, Sir, absolutely! It was difficult to talk about these things. But tonight, for the first time in sixteen years, I think I will fall asleep immediately. Maybe tonight I will sleep soundly without having nightmares!"

Apart from the victims' hearings a number of special events hearings had been organized to look into specific events, to try and establish as complete a picture as we could from past events: Sharpeville 1960, Soweto 1976, the Boipatong massacres of the early 1990s. Special-interest groups, prison officials, security police, women, youth and children, the media, the health sector, business and labour, the legal community, political parties, as well as the faith communities, were all asked to explain their role in the history of South Africa. From time to time individuals were subpoenaed to provide information. Bit by bit, piece by piece, the jigsaw puzzle of South Africa's recent history was fitted together.

The Amnesty Committee (AC)

The Amnesty Committee had an equally arduous task: to receive applications from perpetrators from all sides of the struggle. The offer was extremely generous—to some critics, far too generous—enabling perpetrators of gross violations, by making a full disclosure of the acts under consideration, and by persuading the committee of the political and military nature of those acts, to walk out of the amnesty court with a clean slate. No legal actions or civil claims would be brought against a successful applicant.

As was the case with the Human Rights Violations hearings, nobody really foresaw how many perpetrators would come to ask for amnesty. The AC had a rather slow start; but when, by the middle of 1996, General Johann van der Merwe, chief of police during the last years of the National Party government, agreed to appear before the AC, a number of policemen and security police officers followed suit. A smaller number of military officers, as well as politicians representing many parties, joined their ranks, even though some high-profile politicians and senior military officers, to the disappointment of many, refused to do so. All in all 7,112 amnesty applications were lodged before the TRC, of which 849 were granted. A total of 5,392 applications were refused, because of non-compliance with the prerequisites for amnesty.

The first rounds of amnesty hearings involved testimony from perpetrators from the ranks of the previous regime, followed by perpetrators from the liberation movements. Day after day the media carried reports on the criminal acts of police and security police, of people employed by the previous government. These reports fuelled the growing perception among some whites that the TRC was little more than a witch hunt, a one-sided action of blacks (the ANC) against whites, with the single purpose to embarrass the National Party government. Tutu did his level best to allay these perceptions, pointing out that the TRC was mandated to work in an even-handed, unbiased manner, that perpetrators from all sides of the struggle were treated in the same way. Not everybody was persuaded.

Ironically, half way through the course of the TRC, the National Party (NP) and the ANC went to court together. Both groups sought an interdict against the publication of the findings: Former President F. W. de Klerk of the NP, because he objected to some of the findings concerning his own role in the past, and Vice President Thabo Mbeki from the ANC, who was angered because the report, in his view, "criminalized" the ANC's role in the struggle. Perpetrators from the ranks of the liberation movement fighting against apartheid, the ANC argued, operated on a higher moral level than perpetrators from the previous regime who fought to uphold apartheid; thus they should be treated more leniently.

The Reparation and Rehabilitation Committee (RRC)

While I was often called to work with the Human Rights Violations Committee, most of my time was spent with the Reparation and Rehabilitation Committee. The committee received a twofold responsibility. Our first task was to put support systems in place, to guide victims who appeared at the hearings through the often-traumatic process of reliving and dealing with the past. Our second task was to assess the harm suffered by the victims, and to make proper recommendations on reparation and rehabilitation. In order to do this we had to keep proper records of the victims' circumstances, carefully listing their most urgent needs.

Members of the TRC felt strongly about reparations: the victims of gross human rights violations had a moral and a legal right to proper reparation. If the amnesty process seemed to indicate that the TRC process was "perpetrator friendly," the reparations proposals were to show that the process was, indeed, a "victim friendly" process. The generous offer of amnesty was to be counterbalanced by an equally generous reparation program to the victims. Taking into account the needs of the victims, five categories of reparation were decided upon: 1) urgent interim reparation for victims who were old, sick, or in dire need, 2) individual reparation grants, 3) the improvement of community services, 4) symbolic reparation, and 5) institutional reparation. While the need for monetary reparation for the victims was accepted by all, the need for symbolic as well as institutional reparations was equally urgent. *Symbolic* reparation asked for a number of symbolic acts: the renaming of streets and towns, the erection of monuments and memorials, the calling for special reconciliation and healing ceremonies on local and national levels, as well as the expunging of criminal records of men and women who, in the past, had been convicted on apartheid charges. To bring about *institutional* reparation, the TRC called for a number of hearings where representatives from various institutions—the media, academia, business, the judiciary, correctional services, the faith communities, et cetera—were invited to discuss their role in the past as well as their future commitments to change.

Faith Community Hearings

For almost two years, thousands of victims of apartheid had made statements to the Human Rights Violations Committee, sharing the pain of living in South Africa during the apartheid years. After the victims' hearings, the institutional hearings followed. The last of these hearings belonged to the Christian churches and the other faith communities in the country (East London, November 17–19, 1997). Careful consideration was given by the TRC to the hearing. Should it indeed take place? Did the faith communities have much to confess? None of them—not even the Afrikaans churches that openly favoured apartheid—were guilty of *gross* human rights violations. On the other hand, it was felt, the churches and the other communities were so closely involved with everything that happened in South Africa —on both sides of the struggle—that it was inconceivable to exclude them from the process of truth telling and reconciliation. Having been appointed coordinator of the hearing, I had my work cut out to ensure that the proper invitations were distributed and to encourage representatives of the different faiths to attend.

For three days the leaders of the faith communities addressed the TRC and the nation, explaining their histories, admitting their guilt, asking for forgiveness, committing themselves to justice and restitution, to reconciliation and healing. I will report in the following paragraphs on what transpired at these meetings. Suffice to say that Archbishop Tutu, who chaired the event, was more than satisfied. "Probably the best of all the TRC hearings," he said to me when he sat down to address the press at the conclusion of the hearings.[179]

---

179. Meiring, *Chronicle*, 266.

The Canadian Truth and Reconciliation Commission

In recent years no less than twenty-one truth commissions were established in many countries: in Argentina, Chile, El Salvador, Fiji, Germany, Guatemala, Liberia, Sierra Leone, Korea, and East Timor, to name but a few. However, it came as something of an eye opener to the rest of the world when the news broke that a Canadian Truth and Reconciliation Commission was established.[180] Was such a process really asked for in Canada of all countries? And the Canadian churches—were they really responsible for human rights violations? The answer to both questions came as an unequivocal *Yes*.

Indian Residential School System

In the nineteenth century the Canadian government, accepting its responsibility for the care and education of the country's Aboriginal people, decided that their best chance of success was to teach the First Nation (Indian), Inuit (Eskimo,) and Métis ("mixed blood") children the English language, and to have them adopt Christianity as well as European customs. The aim was, as it was said quite bluntly at the time, "to take the Indian out of the Indian." The Canadian government developed a policy called "aggressive assimilation" to be taught at church-run, government-funded industrial schools, later called residential schools. Removing the children from their communities and taking them to boarding schools was the best way to prepare them for life in the main stream of Canadian society. The schools were under the supervision of the federal Department of Indian Affairs. Attendance was mandatory, and government agents were employed to ensure that all Aboriginal children attended.[181]

---

180. David MacDonald, "A Call to the Churches: You Shall be Called the Repairer of the Breach," in *From Truth to Reconciliation. Transforming the Legacy of Residential Schools,* Marlene Brant Castellano, Linda Archibald, and Mike DeGagne, eds. (Ottawa: Aboriginal Healing Foundation, 2008), 353.
181. *CBC News Canada,* Truth and Reconciliation Commission of Canada, *Home Page.* (Accessed April 29, 2009.) http://www.trc.ca/websites/trcinstitution/index.php?p=3.

Initially about 1,100 students were taken to sixty-nine schools across the country. More followed, and in 1931, at the peak of the system, eighty residential schools were operating in Canada. This program continued for 150 years, from the early nineteenth century to 1996, when the doors of the last school were closed. There were a total of about 130 schools, operating in every territory and province except Newfoundland, Prince Edward Island, and New Brunswick. It is estimated that, during these years, about 150,000 First Nation, Inuit, and Métis children were removed, sometimes forcibly, from their communities. In 2009, there were an estimated eighty thousand living—mostly aged—residential school survivors in Canada.[182] Throughout the years the children suffered severely. They were often forbidden to use their own language and, if caught doing so, experienced harsh punishment. A recent report describes their plight as follows:[183]

> Throughout the years, students lived in substandard conditions and endured physical and emotional abuse. There have also been convictions of sexual abuse. Students at residential schools rarely had opportunities to see examples of normal family life. Most were in school 10 months a year, away from their parents; some stayed all year round. All correspondence from the children was written in English, which many parents couldn't read. Brothers and sisters at the same school rarely saw each other, as all activities were segregated by gender....
>
> When students returned to the reserve, they often found they did not belong. They didn't have the skills to help their parents, and became ashamed of their native heritage. The skills taught at the schools were generally substandard; many

182. Wilton Littlechild, "Truth and Reconciliation Canada Commissioner, Wilton Littlechild" *Remarks at Witnessing the Future Ceremony, Rideau Hall* (Thursday, October 15, 2009) (Accessed July 14, 2014.) http://www.trc.ca/websites/trcinstitution/File/pdfs/Commissioner_Littlechild_speech.pdf.
183. *CBC News Canada,* "A history of residential schools in Canada," May 16, 2008. (Accessed April 29, 2009.) http://www.cbc.ca/news/canada/a-history-of-residential-schools-in-canada-1.702280,

found it hard to function in an urban setting. The aims of assimilation meant devastation for those who were subjected to years of abuse.

The Canadian churches were deeply involved. The residential schools were, after all, *church* schools. The Roman Catholic, Anglican, and Presbyterian churches, as well as the United Church of Canada cooperated with the government, erecting and running these institutions for one and a half centuries. When stories of atrocities, of misconduct, and of sexual abuse started to surface, fingers were often pointed at church officials. In recent years a large number of legal challenges have been raised, accusing the churches of colluding with the government in violating the rights of First Nations families and children.

In 1990 Phil Fontaine, then leader of the Association of Manitoba Chiefs, himself a survivor of the residential school system, called for the churches to acknowledge the physical, emotional and sexual abuse inflicted upon the students over the years. In 1991 the Canadian government convened a Royal Commission on Aboriginal Peoples. One of the recommendations of the commission, that a public enquiry into the running of the residential schools be held was, sadly, never followed. The churches, however, *did* work with government to design plans to compensate the former students, many of whom had already turned to the courts of law in search of justice and compensation, and in 2008 no less than 1.19 billion Canadian dollars had been paid to survivors in 61,473 cases. The churches involved in the system pledged up to one million Canadian dollars, in cash and services, toward healing initiatives. A solemn promise by government to appoint a Truth and Reconciliation Commission, was made to the victims and their families. In Parliament on June 11, 2008, Prime Minister Stephen Harper delivered an official apology to residential school students.[184]

---

184. This paragraph draws on CBC, "A History of Residential Schools."

The Establishment of the Canadian TRC

The Canadian TRC was formally established on June 1, 2008 as part of a court-approved Indian Residential School Settlement Agreement that was negotiated by former students at the residential church schools, legal counsel for the churches, the Government of Canada, the Assembly of First Nations, and other Aboriginal organizations. The TRC was an independent body that had to provide former students, and anyone who has been affected by the Indian residential school legacy, with an opportunity to share their individual experiences in a safe and culturally appropriate manner. "It will be an opportunity for people to tell their stories about a significant part of Canadian history that is still unknown to most Canadians. The purpose of the TRC is not to determine guilt or innocence, but to create a historical account of the residential schools, help people to heal and encourage reconciliation between Aboriginal and non-Aboriginal Canadians."[185] With a budget of sixty million Canadian dollars, the TRC had to complete its work within five years. Over the course of its mandate the commission was required to, inter alia,

- Prepare a comprehensive historical record on the policies and operations of the schools
- Complete a publicly accessible report that will include recommendations to the Government of Canada concerning the Indian residential school system and its legacy
- Establish a research centre that will be a permanent resource for all Canadians
- Host seven national events and support local events, to promote awareness and public education about the residential school system and its impacts

The TRC had a slow start. Justice Harry LaForme, a member of the Mississaugas of the New Credit First Nation in Southern Ontario,

---

185. *CBC News Canada,* "What Is the Residential Schools Truth and Reconciliation Commission?" May 16, 2008. (Accessed June 10, 2014.) http://www.cbc.ca/news/canada/faqs-truth-and-reconciliation-commission-1.699883.

was appointed the first commission chair, but he resigned in October 2008 citing political interferences and conflict among the commissioners.[186] The co-commissioners Claudette Dumont-Smith and Jane Brewin-Morley resigned in January 2009.

On June 10, 2009 Justice Murray Sinclair, an Aboriginal judge in Manitoba, was appointed as the new chief commissioner, with Marie Wilson and Wilton Littlechild at his side. In a public statement on June 22, 2009, Justice Sinclair and his colleagues announced that the TRC had commenced with its work. He made an urgent appeal to all victims to support the process and to approach the TRC with their stories:

> ... We will ensure that the whole world hears their truths and the truth about residential schools, so that future generations of Aboriginal and non-Aboriginal Canadians will be able to hold to the statement that resonates with all of us: This must never happen again.[187]

According to its mandate, the TRC was required to stage seven national events, together with numerous local events, inviting victims from all over the country to tell their stories and to bring their plight to the nation's attention. The seven national events were Winnipeg (June 2010), Inuvik (July 2011), the Atlantic National Event (October 2011), Saskatoon (June 2012), Montréal (April 2013), Vancouver (September 2013), and Edmonton (April 2014).

---

186. *Truth and Reconciliation Commission of Canada: Interim Report*, 2012:2. (Accessed June 10, 2014) http://www.attendancemarketing.com/~attmk/TRC_jd/Interim_report_English_electronic_copy.pdf.
187. Truth and Reconciliation, *Home Page*; *CBC News Canada*, April 29, 2009.

Rebuilding the Walls, Restoring the Ruined Houses: Will South African and Canadian Churches Rise to the Challenge?

Will the churches in the two countries rise to the twofold challenge of searching for the truth and of contributing to the process of healing and reconciliation? The circumstances surrounding the South African and Canadian TRCs are not the same. In South Africa, as was the case in most other countries, the truth and reconciliation process followed major social upheaval or a dramatic political change. This was not the case in Canada, and the chances for it to happen in the near future are very slim.[188] The question, however, remains: Will the churches on both sides of the Atlantic join in the venture? Will the *South African churches* continue on the road to reconciliation? Will the faith communities, at a time when the country seems to be torn apart again by poverty and despair, by violence and corruption, by racism and xenophobia, help heal the land? In the same vein: Will the *Canadian churches* that were so deeply involved in the injustices of the residential school system, contribute to the healing of their community? "Overall, the churches have been given a tremendous gift and opportunity," a senior Canadian cabinet minister commented at the establishment of the TRC. "(It) represents an opening to initiate many actions toward right relations."[189]

The interest in the work of the two TRCs proved to be sincere and mutual. During the South African truth and reconciliation process a number of visitors from Canada received a warm welcome at the TRC offices. The senior politician Michael Ignatieff, at the time a professor at the University of Toronto, contributed much to our process through his presence and his writings.[190] A second visitor was David MacDonald, an ordained United Church of Canada pastor who, after joining Parliament, held various cabinet positions in the federal government. MacDonald travelled to Cape Town in 2006 to review

---

188. MacDonald, *A Call*, 353.
189. MacDonald, *A Call*, 349.
190. Piet Meiring, "Leadership for Reconciliation," *Verbum et Ecclesia* 23, no. 3 (2002): 724.

the South African TRC in the light of the experiences of other TRCs from across the globe. In their turn, numerous South Africans have shown a keen interest in the work of the Canadian TRC. Alex Boraine, former minister in the Methodist Church and vice-chair of the South African TRC, visited Toronto to lecture on the subject. Archbishop Tutu, who was unable to attend the First National Event in Winnipeg (June 2010), sent a special message. It was my privilege to read the message at the event on his behalf.

The question now is, Will the Canadian churches and their South African counterparts join forces as well? Will they be willing to co-operate, to share experiences, and to learn from one another? David MacDonald held high expectations for the Canadian truth and reconciliation process:[191]

> On a late Sunday in August 2007, I sat in a downtown church in Halifax where the minister read from Isaiah 58:12: "you shall be called repairers of the breach." The words spoke of authentic compassion and justice. In an instant I could see what true reconciliation is all about. It is recognizing and responding to the hurt and the need. Years of alienation and oppression resulting from Indian residential schools require a concrete response. Without that, reconciliation is nothing more than hollow words without meaning. The challenge of reconciliation is both to know and to do the truth. These are not separate functions, but part of the same reality.

Can the South African Christians, with their experience of success, and sometimes failure, accompany their Canadian colleagues on the road of truth, reconciliation, and healing? Can we, together, help "to rebuild the walls and to restore the ruined houses" (*Good News Translation*) in our two countries? To do this, a number of things are required: asking for forgiveness, searching for truth, campaigning for justice, and developing a ministry of healing and reconciliation.

---

191. MacDonald, *A Call*, 343.

Asking for Forgiveness

For the South African faith communities the TRC offered an ideal opportunity to look one another, as well as the nation, in the face. The Faith Community Hearing (East London, November 17–19, 1997) created a space for the churches and other communities to stand before the mirror of history, to analyze and explain their own past, coming to grips with their errors, and confessing the pain that they have caused to many apartheid victims. Reports were tabled of churches that opposed apartheid, and suffered; as well as of churches that supported apartheid. It was a time of asking for—and extending—forgiveness. Leaders of the Christian churches joined Desmond Tutu in a sincere apology to the other faith communities in South Africa:[192]

> I am certain that all my fellow Christians in South Africa will agree with me if I express our deep apologies to you, the members of the other faith communities in the country, for the arrogant way in which we as Christians acted—as though ours was the only religion in South Africa —while we have been a multi-religious community from day one.

In Canada the churches' season of "rebuilding the walls and restoring the ruined houses," initiating the process of acknowledgement of guilt, of healing and of reparation, arrived even before Prime Minister Harper's apology in Parliament (June 11, 2008). For many years, leaders in the Catholic, Anglican, Presbyterian, and United churches agonized about the residential school system and their involvement in the process. It culminated in 2007, when the leaders of these churches proclaimed a covenant, issued on the fifth anniversary of the adoption of the new Canadian Constitution and the *Charter of Rights and Freedoms*, calling for the recognition and protection of Aboriginal self-government in Canada. The covenant was reaffirmed in March 2007. David McDonald captured the mood at the time:[193]

---

192. Meiring, *Chronicle*, 272.
193. MacDonald, *A Call*, 345.

Behind the covenant lie many challenging and difficult years as the churches struggled to come to terms with their colonialist past. In particular, the last decade has been an agonizing one for the churches in discovering the degree to which they had participated in a ruthless program of assimilation of Aboriginal children. Stories have been told of acts of cruelty and disrespect, which are totally at odds with the stated attitude and practices of these very same faith communities. Increasingly, church members are recognizing that attitudes and acts, which were not just a part of these schools but also deeply resident in all aspects of Canadian society, run counter to what the churches themselves believe and declare.

The Anglican Church was involved in the system from the very beginning. At various times between 1820 and 1969 the church administered about three dozen Indian and Inuit residential schools and hostels. Already after World War II the Anglican Church started to question the prevailing practice of church-run schools. By 1969 all the church-run schools had been given over to the government under a plan to close them down as soon as possible or to turn them over to First Nation groups. Many initiatives were taken by the church to redress the injustices of the past. In 1991 the church established an Anglican Healing Fund to support the healing initiatives undertaken by local Aboriginal communities and institutions. In 1993 the Anglican Primate, Archbishop Michael Peers, in an address to the National Native Convocation, offered a full apology for the church's role in being part of the system and for the wrongs committed. In 1998, the Aboriginal Healing Foundation was established to manage the church's healing strategy and to complement initiatives undertaken by government and by the churches, as well as First Nations programs.[194]

In 1986, and again in 1998, the United Church of Canada issued apologies to Canada's Aboriginal communities. This was followed, in 2003,

---

194. The Anglican Church of Canada, "Historical Sketch for Anglican Residential Schools," in *Remembering the Children, in an Aboriginal and Church Leaders' Tour to Prepare for the Truth and Reconciliation Commission. Anglican Church of Canada News*, February 21, 2008. (Accessed June 11, 2014.) http://www.rememberingthechildren.ca/history/index.htm.

by a commitment by the General Council of the United Church of Canada to healing and to the building of new relationships in the country. "In all that we do in relation to our responsibility for the residential school system, the goal of working toward right relations between Aboriginal and non-Aboriginal peoples should be uppermost in our thoughts, words, and actions," the Council's statement reads. According to David MacDonald, himself an ordained minister of the church, the statement affirmed the council's belief that the United Church and its members are to act to overcome and, indeed, reverse the decades and centuries of discrimination and exploitation.[195]

Four leaders of the Presbyterian Church in Canada signed a statement of apology in 1994: "It is with deep humility and in great sorrow that we come before God and our Aboriginal brothers and sisters with our confession."[196] The General Assembly of the Presbyterian Church, in 2006, made a similar statement to accept the church's role in the past and its responsibility toward the Aboriginal community in the country. Plans for creating a healing and reconciliation ministry were approved. A call was made to local church members and groups—also to the youth—to reach out and get to know their Aboriginal neighbours.

The Roman Catholic Church oversaw three-quarters of the 130 residential schools. Yet it was the last church to have its leadership officially address the issue. Eventually, on April 29, 2009, Pope Benedict XVI, at a meeting with Catholic leaders and representatives of the Canadian Aboriginal community, apologized to victims of the church-run schools, expressing his "sorrow" for the abuse and "deplorable treatment" that students suffered at the schools. He offered his sympathy and prayerful solidarity." Phil Fontaine, National Chief of the Assembly of First Nations, was a member of the delegation. "What we wanted the pope to say to us was that he was sorry and ... that he deeply felt for us," Fontaine commented. "We heard that very clearly today."[197]

---

195. MacDonald, *A Call*, 344.
196. *CBC*, "A History of Residential Schools."
197. Nicole Winfield, "Pope sorry for school abuse," thestar.com. (Accessed July 15, 2014). http://www.thestar.com/news/world/2009/04/29/pope_sorry_for_school_abuse.html.

The other churches in Canada were not directly involved in the residential school system, though they were involved in other parts of the assimilation policy. These churches, too, accepted responsibility for reconciliation and healing in the country. On June 21, 2007, on National Aboriginal Day, Lutherans as well as delegates from the Christian Reformed and Mennonite Church es joined with the Anglican, Catholic, Presbyterian, and United Churches —as well as a number of ecumenical organizations—to renew the churches' covenant with the First Nations Peoples, committing themselves again to human rights and justice initiatives.

Standing for Truth

Central to the business of reconciliation and peacemaking is the quest for truth. The South African TRC, therefore, was mandated "to establish the truth in relation to past events as well as the motives for and circumstances in which gross violations of human rights have occurred, and to make the findings known in order to prevent repetition of such acts in future."[198] When the Minister of Justice, Dullah Omar, introduced the TRC legislation to Parliament he exhorted all South Africans to join in the search for truth, without which there can be no genuine reconciliation. When political change came to South Africa, the issue and the wisdom of truth-finding was widely debated. There were those who, with the best intentions, said, "Let us close the books, let us forgive and forget!" The response of many—Archbishop Tutu included—was, "No! We can never do that! We need to open the books; we need to deal with our past—horrible as it may be—before we close the books." Searching for truth can be painful and difficult, even hazardous. It can disrupt the journey toward reconciliation. But in the long run, it is the only way to go. Reconciliation is about uncovering the truth, not about amnesia.

How does one determine "the truth"? After listening to so many victims, after working through stacks of paper, how does one determine what *really* happened, what the motives of the people involved *really* were? Modesty, it seemed, becomes everyone in search for truth. The TRC, at the time, was encouraged by our Canadian guest Michael Ignatieff, who said that although we will never be able to present a perfect picture to establish the final truth, the very least we should be

---

198. TRC *Report,* vol. 1, 55.

able to do was "to curtail the number of lies that up to now had free rein in society."[199]

Finding truth goes beyond establishing historical and legal facts. It has to do with understanding, accepting responsibility, exercising justice, and restoring and maintaining the fragile relationship between human beings. It has to be handled with the greatest sensitivity. Had that not been the case during the TRC years, the nation could have bled to death. But if the TRC succeeded in its quest it would — we hoped— lead to a national catharsis, to peace and reconciliation, to the point where the truth sets one free.

This, indeed, is what happened. Many *victims* of gross human rights violations, 22,400 in total, approached the TRC. For many, telling their stories and reliving the agonies of the past was difficult. Emotions sometimes ran high and tears flowed freely, but in the vast majority of cases, testifying before the commission proved to be a cathartic and a healing experience. The victims were edified and honoured by the process. Many *perpetrators* who appeared before the TRC had similar experiences. When they, after much anguish and embarrassment, unburdened themselves to the Amnesty Committee, and when they made a full submission of all the relevant facts of their misdeeds—after the questioning and cross-questioning came to an end—it was as if a cloud lifted.

But it was not only the victims and the perpetrators who needed the truth telling, *the nation* needed it as well—to listen to the truth, to be confronted by the truth, to be shamed by the truth, to struggle with the truth, and finally to be liberated by the truth. The South African TRC was a public process. All the hearings were open to the nation, and large audiences attended the events. The media had free access to all sessions of the commission. Every day the newspapers carried TRC reports. Every night, in a special TRC program after the eight o'clock news, the highlights of the day were shown. The nation had to know![200]

---

199. Meiring, "Leadership," 724.

200. For video material of the TRC hearings as well as television newscasts at the time, contact the Institute for Justice and Reconciliation (IJR), Cape Town. Their publications and DVDs are readily available via Internet. Probably the most interesting video on their list is *Justice, Truth, Memory*, with fifteen clips of twenty minutes each, covering the most important aspects of the TRC's work.

The majority of South Africans entered into the spirit of the truth and reconciliation process. They wanted to come to grips with the past. Sadly, there were also those who did not want to know. Up till the end of the process, the TRC was dogged by some people—especially from the white community—who were unwilling or unable to accept the truth, and who described the TRC's work as a one-sided witch hunt, designed to shame and embarrass one section of the community.

The process, however, was not intended to stop when the TRC closed its doors. Truth telling had to go on. There are still millions of South Africans, from all the communities in the land, who did not qualify to appear before the TRC but who also are in need of healing, who also need to be recognized and edified by having people listen to their stories. They need people to share their pain. In its final report the TRC urged the South African faith communities to continue with this process, to invite members of all walks of life—black and white, perpetrators and victims alike—to meet one another and to talk to each other. Ellen Kuzwayo, a celebrated South African author, wrote:

> Africa is a place of storytelling. We need more stories, never mind how painful the exercise may be. This is how we will learn to love one another. Stories help us to understand, to forgive, and to see things through someone else's eyes.[201]

In *Canada* the same high premium is placed on truth telling. The preamble to the TRC Mandate made it very clear:

> There is an emerging and compelling desire to put the events of the past behind us so that we can work towards a stronger and healthier future. The truth telling and reconciliation process as part of an overall holistic and comprehensive response to the Indian Residential School legacy is a sincere indication and acknowledgment of the injustices and harms experienced by Aboriginal people and the need for continued

---

201. Ellen Kuzwayo, quoted in Van Vught, W. and Cloete, D., eds., *Race and Reconciliation in South Africa* (Lanham: Lexington Books, 2002).

healing…. The truth of our common experiences will help set our spirits free and pave the way to reconciliation.[202]

Immediately after his appointment as chair of the TRC, Judge Murray Sinclair and his co-commissioners made an urgent plea to victims from the First Nation, Inuit, and Métis communities to come to the fore:

> I promise you that we will seek out the stories of all those connected to the schools who are still alive, from the students to the teachers, to the managers and the janitors, as well as the officials who planned and carried the whole thing. If you have a story to tell about the schools, we will hear it. If you cannot come to us, we will come to you. If you cannot speak, we will find someone to speak for you.[203]

For the victims and their families the process may prove to be difficult, having to relive the past and having to report on it. But in the end, as was the case in South Africa, it will prove to be worthwhile. This is the process Phil Fontaine and his colleagues asked for, and this is what they deserve to get: acknowledgement of the injustices and the suffering of the past. The churches may be able to contribute to the process, not only by accepting their own complicity but by standing behind their congregants, guiding them with love and care and understanding through the months and years of the TRC process.

But not only victims are in need of the truth-telling process. As in South Africa, the *nation* needs it. In years to come all Canadians will be forced to ask, How did this happen? What was in the mind of government officials and church leaders?[204] Moreover, what was, and is, in the minds of the majority of Canadians? Are they willing to face the truth? Aaron Janzen, a senior student at Canadian Mennonite

202. Truth and Reconciliation Commission of Canada, "Our Mandate." (Accessed July 15, 2014.) *http://www.trc.ca/websites/trcinstitution/index.php?p=7.*
203. Denise Titian, "Truth and Reconciliation Commission Meets with ha'wiih at Tin Wis Resort," *Ha-Shilth-Sa* 37, no. 2 (January 28, 2010):2. (Accessed July 15, 2014.) nuuchahnulth.org.
204. MacDonald, *A Call*, 345.

University (CMU), described the difficulty young people have in questioning the "Conventional Canadian Narrative":

> While most Canadians are aware, at least to some extent, that personal and cultural abuses occurred ...most do not know (and do not want to know).... Canadians are often guilty of underestimating the impact of these abuses. The prevailing attitude among many non-indigenous Canadians is that the abuses ... are largely exaggerated. It is difficult for Euro-Canadians to believe that their government and people ... were responsible.... Euro-Canadians have been raised to believe that they are the morally upright demographic in Canada. This is a belief that can be traced back to the colonization of Canada, when the "civilized" Europeans first interacted with the "savages" of North America. [205]

Canadians will have to prepare themselves for the adventure of speaking and of listening to each other. They will have to re-examine their *real* history. They will have to question stereotypes and assumptions, the dubious truths of the past. "How can we learn from one another?" David MacDonald asked. Echoing Ellen Kuzwayo's sentiments, he continues: "Can we begin the journey of walking in each other's shoes or moccasins?"[206] There are many opportunities for the Canadian churches to help guide the process. From their own checkered past, with humility and understanding, they can reach out to all Canadians, helping them to open the books in order, eventually, to close them again.

A serious obstacle in the process of truth telling—in the minds of many—is that the Canadian TRC is mandated to hold all hearings in camera. In order not to "jeopardize any legal proceeding" that may be undertaken in the present or in the near future, the TRC is required not to identify persons alleged to have been involved in wrongdoing, unless the person has been convicted already by the court. No names of persons involved in atrocities may be recorded. Other information

---

205. Aaron Janzen, "Truth Telling and Peace" (course assignment, Canadian School of Peacebuilding, Winnipeg, 2009), 2.
206. MacDonald, *A Call*, 351f.

that may be used to identify such individuals shall be anonymized (*Mandate* 2.i). In a Submission to Justice Sinclair, a class of CMU's Canadian School of Peacebuilding (CSOP) students, participating in "Truth-telling and Peace: An Insider's Perspective on South Africa's Truth and Reconciliation Commission" (2009), voiced the concern of many who fear that the TRC hearings may lose some of their integrity, at worst be seen by some as a cover-up:[207]

> It is of utmost importance that the [Indian Residential School (IRS)] survivors be afforded the freedom to publicly name their perpetrators and for the Commission to make public records of the alleged perpetrators' names. Without naming, there will exist no full disclosure and thus there will exist no real truth. We believe that amnesty would enable the Commission to seek full disclosure.

Another obstacle was the Canadian government's reluctance to make sensitive information available to the TRC. In December 2012 Justice Sinclair approached an Ontario court, seeking an interpretation of the TRC Act regarding the power to subpoena government documents." It came as a great relief when the Court decided in favour of the TRC, ordering the government to hand the relevant files over for perusal by the TRC. Justice Sinclair's statement, that in the end the whole world will hear the truth, gives some assurance that the TRC will find a way to publish its findings in the public domain. It has to happen, because public reconciliation is not even a remote possibility without public understanding and insight.

Campaigning for Justice

Justice and reconciliation are two sides of the same coin. For reconciliation there has to be a sense of justice being part and parcel of the process. Lasting reconciliation can flourish only in a society where justice is seen to be done. In *South Africa*, during and after the TRC process, this brought a number of issues to the fore: not only proper

---

207. Robert Walker, "Remembering Rightly. Does Canada Need a TRC?" (course assignment, Canadian School of Peacebuilding, Winnipeg, 2009), 5.

reparation for the victims of gross human rights violations to balance the gift of amnesty that was given to perpetrators of these abuses, but also the wider issues involving every citizen in post-apartheid South Africa (unemployment, poverty, affirmative action, equal education, restitution, redistribution of land, HIV/AIDS, etc.).

Desmond Tutu described the vital link between justice and reconciliation in his book *No Future without Forgiveness* [208] After visiting some of the horrendous genocide sites where up to one million Rwandese died at the hands of their compatriots in 1994, the archbishop addressed a rally at Amahoro Stadium in Kigali. He made a passionate plea for forgiveness and reconciliation because without that the future was bleak. Neither the audience nor the Rwandese government was persuaded. Forgiveness, amnesty for perpetrators in a society where for years there was no sense of justice and no rule of law, was unimaginable. Tutu's plea that they move from a position of retributive justice to restorative justice fell on deaf ears.

In South Africa, with the granting of amnesty to perpetrators of apartheid, a choice was made between *retributive* justice and *restorative* justice. The latter, Tutu contended, was characteristic of traditional African jurisprudence:

> Here the central concern is not retribution or punishment, but in the spirit of *ubuntu,* the healing of breaches, the redressing of imbalances, the restoration of broken relationships. This kind of justice seeks to rehabilitate both the victim and the perpetrator, who should be given the opportunity to be reintegrated into the community he or she has injured by his or her offence.[209]

In Canada too, the call for justice is loud and clear. The preamble of *Mandate for the Truth and Reconciliation Commission* states unequivocally that "the injustices and harms experienced by Aboriginal people and the need for continued healing" need to be addressed.[210] Without that, there is little chance of success.

---

208. Desmond Tutu, *No Future Without Forgiveness* (London: Rider Books, 1999).
209. Tutu, *Forgiveness.* 51f.
210. Truth and Reconciliation Commission of Canada, "Mandate."

Over the years many examples of injustice perpetrated against the Aboriginal population have been chronicled. In his book *A National Crime,* John S. Milloy described the failure of the policy of "aggressive civilization" to meld the different cultures in the land. He presented a catalogue of the suffering the students at the residential schools had to endure. As early as 1907, medical inspectors were discovering unsanitary conditions in the schools. Between 1888 and 1905, 24 percent of 1,537 children had died. In 1918, the Spanish flu pandemic killed more Aboriginal than non-Aboriginal people, and the numbers were high in the schools due to "poor living conditions, poor nutrition, and lack of access to medical care. Doctors, commissioned to visit the schools in the early twentieth century, presented shocking reports. In one school 60 percent of the students had scabies; in another 70 percent had contracted tuberculosis.[211]

A century later, First Nation, Inuit, and Métis students and communities are still suffering. The marks of the past are still on them. Nancy Wallace reports:[212]

> ...[They] are still suffering. Many act out with violence or self-destructive behaviors. These survivors, relatives of survivors or victims of survivors, are still hurting and are in need of closure. Whole communities have been devastated from the consequences of abuse at the schools. Disrupted lives and social ills that resulted as a consequence of the family and cultural destruction are seen in the overrepresentation of Aboriginals in jail populations, poverty statistics, unacceptably high infant mortality rates, poor health, city gang life (which had its genesis in the residential schools), sexual confusion, the high rates of substance abuse, and the high rates of suicide. Parents cannot parent and other victims are not able to lead or guide the community back to health.

---

211. John S. Milroy, *A National Crime* (Winnipeg: University of Manitoba Press, 1999), 98f.
212. Nancy Wallace, "An Argument for a Truth and Reconciliation Commission in Canada" (course assignment, Canadian School of Peacebuilding, Winnipeg, 2009), 2.

It is not only the victims and their immediate relatives who need justice; the wider community is suffering as well. The CSOP students reminded Judge Sinclair that the work of the TRC should include "[t]he full range of issues that attend the colonial manner in which the dominant society has treated the Aboriginal peoples, including isolation, loss of access to land, loss of culture and language, and the resultant diminution of life quality in matters of health, cultural fitness to live within their historical culture, and environmental and industrial encroachment on First Nation territories."[213]

The issue of reparation is tied to that of justice. The Canadian churches, as well as the government, have realized their responsibility in this regard. In 2007, while the churches committed themselves to a substantial amount to be paid to victims, (1.19 million Canadian dollars) the federal government formalized a 1.9 billion Canadian dollar compensation package for all residential school students who were still alive as of May 30, 2005. The compensation, called Common Experience Payment, amounts to $10,000 for the first year or part of a year a student attended school, plus $3, 000 for each subsequent year. By the end of March 2008 $1.19 billion had already been paid out, representing 61,473 cases. The question is, Is monetary reparation sufficient? The CSOP participants also touched on the matter, recommending that the TRC should, where its discretionary powers permit, model its final recommendations on the South African TRC's reparation proposals to include not only the above payments to be made but to also attend to symbolic reparation, as well as community and institutional reparation.[214]

Finally, in most discussions on the Canadian TRC, the matter of amnesty is brought to the table. The mandate of the TRC does not allow for amnesty for perpetrators, which impacts heavily on the work of the commission and on the long-term outcomes of the truth and reconciliation process. Again, the CSOP group expressed their fervent hope that the TRC in some way may be allowed to broaden its scope

213. "Submission to Honorable Justice Murray Sinclair" (prepared by students at the Canadian School of Peacebuilding, Canadian Mennonite University: Winnipeg, 2009), Par. 1 (c).
214. *Submission,* Par. 2(a).

to include amnesty to perpetrators, who meet established criteria. Two reasons were offered:

> *First*, amnesty is a moral necessity. Without the potential for qualified perpetrators to be released from legal culpability, reconciliation will be unattainable and the moral responsibility to one party in the abuse of Aboriginal peoples will be unfulfilled. *Second*, providing amnesty will enable the Commissioners to access truthful confessions from alleged perpetrators.[215]

It remains an open question whether the TRC commissioners will find a way to acquiesce to the request. In the meantime the churches will be wise to introduce the concept of restorative, instead of retributive, justice to their congregants. During the TRC years—and after, when the results of their work will be made known—the Canadian community will need healing and forgiveness. Justice will be asked for and, if the Christian dhurches are able to lead the people on the road of restorative justice, true and lasting reconciliation may be reached.

A Healing Ministry

Reconciliation requires a deep, honest confession, and a willingness to forgive. The South African TRC Act did not require of perpetrators to make an open confession of their crimes, to publicly ask for forgiveness before amnesty was granted. Yet it has to be stated clearly that lasting reconciliation rests firmly upon the capacity of perpetrators—individuals as well as perpetrator communities—to honestly and deeply recognize and confess their guilt toward God and their fellow human beings, toward individual victims as well as victim communities, and to humbly ask for forgiveness. And it equally rests upon the magnanimity and the grace of the victims to reach out to them, to extend forgiveness. A prime example of the latter was provided by Nelson Mandela, who after suffering much at the hands of the apartheid government returned from twenty-seven years in captivity with

---

215. *Submission*, Par. 1(b).

one goal in mind: to liberate all South Africans, white and black alike, the oppressor and the oppressed.[216]

Tutu, against the background of his TRC experience, reflected on the many aspects of forgiveness and healing, things the churches in Canada and South Africa in developing their healing ministries, will do well to take note of.

Forgiveness is a *risky business*. In asking for— and extending— forgiveness, you are making yourself vulnerable. Either party may be spurned. The process may be derailed by the inability of victims to forgive, or by the insensitivity or arrogance of perpetrators who do not want to be forgiven. A common misunderstanding is that reconciliation requires national amnesia. This is totally wrong.[217]

> Forgiving and being reconciled are not about pretending that things are other than they are. It is not patting one another on the back and turning a blind eye to the wrong. True reconciliation exposes the awfulness, the abuse, the pain, the degradation, the truth. It is a risky undertaking, but in the end it is worthwhile because in the end there will be real healing from having dealt with a real situation. Spurious reconciliation can bring only spurious healing.

Forgiveness, however, does mean *abandoning your right to retribution*, your right to pay back the perpetrator in his own coin. But it is a loss that liberates the victim. Tutu explains:[218]

A recent issue of the journal *Spirituality and Health* had on its front cover a picture of three US ex-servicemen standing in front of the Vietnam memorial in Washington DC. One asks: "Have you forgiven those that held you prisoner of war?" "I will never forgive them," replies the other. His mate says: "Then it seems they still have you in prison, don't they?"

Reconciliation, I came to realize, *requires a firm commitment*. It is a costly undertaking. Building bridges between opposing individuals

---

216. Nelson Mandela, *Long Walk to Freedom* (London: Macdonald Purnell, 1995), 614.
217. Tutu, *Forgiveness*, 218.
218. Tutu, *Forgiveness*, 219.

or groups is often a hard and thankless task. Jesus Christ, the ultimate Reconciler put his life on the line, and he expects us to follow his example. During the 1930s the German theologian Dietrich Bonhoeffer repeatedly warned his fellow Christians against the temptation of *cheap grace,* which is a mortal enemy of the gospel. In our times we are called to warn against the temptation of *cheap reconciliation* which, too, is a mortal enemy of the gospel of our Lord.

Another lesson that I have learned is this: on the road to reconciliation, expect the unexpected! The road to reconciliation is indeed rocky, full of dangers and disappointments. But it is also full of surprises. "It never ceases to astonish me," Tutu said, "the magnanimity of many victims who suffered the most heinous of violations, who reach out to embrace their tormentors with joy, willing to forgive and wanting to reconcile." As I wrote in my diary (April 21, 1997):[219]

> One can see God's influence in what is happening tonight", Mcibisi Xundu, pastor and TRC committee member said, looking at Eric Taylor, former security police officer who had applied for amnesty for his part in the killing of the "Cradock Four." "It is God who has led you to take this step towards reconciliation." A few weeks earlier a young DRC [Dutch Reformed Church] pastor Charl Coetzee approached me. One of his parishioners, Eric Taylor, wanted to meet the family of Matthew Goniwe, the activist he had tortured and murdered.
>
> Mrs. Goniwe, a strong critic of the TRC process, refused to come, but the rest of the family as well as the families of the rest of the Cradock Four travelled from Cradock to Port Elizabeth for the occasion. Suspicion and anger were in the air. The families of the victims had many questions, needed many answers. Taylor answered as best he could. At the end of a long evening he turned to the Goniwe family and to their colleagues: "I came to ask you to forgive me, if the Lord can give you the strength to do that."
>
> The response was moving. One after another the family members came to the fore to shake Eric Taylor's hand and to

---

219. Meiring, *Chronicle*, 123–127.

assure him of their forgiveness. Many a cheek was wet with tears. The son of Goniwe walked up to the policeman. His right arm was in plaster, but with his left arm he embraced Eric Taylor. "It is true," he said, "you murdered my father. But we forgive you...."

When Charl Coetzee reported to me about the meeting, I immediately phoned Desmond Tutu in Cape Town. "I have heard the news," he commented. "Mrs. Goniwe told me this morning that the next time she would be there!" When we concluded our conversation Tutu wanted us to pray: "O Lord, we thank You for being the God of surprises, for surprising us every day, for the miracles of reconciliation in our country...."

A very poignant episode in the Canadian healing process arose with the canonization of Kateri Tekakwitha as the first Native American saint in history. The decision from the Vatican was widely welcomed, especially by Indigenous Canadians. Together with Commissioner Littlechild, hundreds of Indigenous people from across Canada and the United States travelled to the Vatican to witness the occasion (October 2012). Many wore traditional regalia. Scanning the crowd, Wab Kinew (the University of Winnipeg's director of Indigenous inclusion) reported:

> I saw Anishinaabe jingle dresses, beautiful turquoise jewelry from the Pueblos of the southwestern United States and many, many outfits with the purple and white colours of the Haudenashonee, Kateri's people (also known as Mohawk) .... The rite itself featured a prayer in the Mohawk language. The night before, at a special vigil for Saint Kateri, the cardinals, bishops and worshippers present smudged with sage and sweetgrass—this in the San Giovanni in Laterano Basilica, the "mother of all churches"![220]

---

220. Wab Kinew, "'It's the same great spirit,' Canonization of Kateri is a big step toward true reconciliation, but the embrace could go further," *Winnipeg Free Press*, October 22, 2012, A3. (Accessed June 11, 2014.) http://www.winnipegfreepress.com/local/its-the-same--great-spirit-175193351.html.

For Willie Littlechild it was a momentous occasion. "It's unbelievable, just amazing" he remarked. Kinew added, "He should know. This is the latest step on a journey for Littlechild that has taken him from a residential school as a boy to an appointment as commissioner for the Truth and Reconciliation Commission of Canada. Indeed, reconciliation between the church and First Nations people was on the minds of many here."

For the Indigenous Canadians the occasion spoke of new beginnings, of healing and moving on. In a quiet courtyard in Vatican City at a post-canonization reception, Littlechild said, "I've forgiven, even more now, I think. For myself, the experiences that I've had, but also for my family." Wab Kinew was equally touched: "For me … the example set by Chief Littlechild and countless other residential school survivors in Rome this week is a miracle of at least equal significance: that people treated so poorly by the church as children grew up to not only forgive but embrace it."[221]

Conclusion: Building and Restoring—An Awesome Responsibility

At the end on the South African process the TRC, in its final report, made a number of recommendations to the faith communities, urging them to continue with the process of truth, justice and reconciliation: organizing healing ceremonies, creating special liturgies, making available the skills of its members, and identifying the land in their possession that can be made available to landless people or to return it to its rightful owners. Trauma centres need to be erected. In terms of reconciliation there were as many requests: that marginalized groups be welcomed, that interfaith dialogue be promoted, and that theologies to promote reconciliation and a true sense of community be designed. Above all, that the faith communities promote a culture of tolerance and peaceful coexistence in the country.[222]

In a similar vein, the Canadian TRC has numerous expectations of the churches and other religious organizations, stating the important of working hand in hand with government and church officials.

---

221. Kinew, "It's the same great spirit," A3.
222. *TRC Report, vol. 5*, 316ff.

MacDonald mentioned support to be given to victims who want to testify, the organizing of special events, building programs, offering their facilities to people in need, preparing how-to and resource manuals, identifying and empowering leadership, and creating networks of organizations and individuals working in the field of justice and reconciliation.[223] Building walls and restoring ruined houses have many faces!

It is gratifying to know that, in spite of the failures of the past, government and civil society are still looking to the churches in our two countries to do their bit, to help guide the nation on the road to healing and reconciliation. What David MacDonald wrote about Canada applies to South Africa as well:

> The churches have been given a tremendous gift and opportunity.... We now have the opportunity to learn our true history, to repent, to apologize, to heal, to reconcile and to restore right relations....
>
> It is of critical importance that future generations see our generation as one that has responded positively and bravely to this call to be active "repairers of the breach."[224]

Building, restoring, is an awesome responsibility. We, on both sides of the Atlantic Ocean, have to contend with the realities of our situations. In South Africa we still live in a fractured society, with seemingly insurmountable problems. In spite of all of this, at the conclusion of the South African TRC process, the chairperson, Archbishop Tutu, could not but rejoice. His words may serve as an exhortation to Canadians, embarking on *their* journey of truth and reconciliation:

> We have been wounded but we are being healed. It is possible even with our past of suffering, anguish, alienation, and violence to become one people, reconciled, healed, caring, compassionate, and ready to share as we put our past behind

---

223. MacDonald, *A Call*, 350ff.
224. MacDonald, *A Call*, 350 and 357.

us to stride into the glorious future God holds before us as the Rainbow people of God.[225]

In similar vein Bob Watts, former CEO of the Assembly of First Nations, after lamenting the fact that so many public institutions are not doing as much as they should to promote the cause of the Truth and Reconciliation Commission in Canada, ended on a hopeful note:

We need to expose the beauty of its work to all of us.... We have to figure out how to coordinate ourselves as a better country. And it's not too late. In spite of a lot of things that are going on in the country that could make people wring their hands or give up, I am very hopeful.... I am hopeful that things are going to get better. [226]

Bibliography

The Anglican Church of Canada. "Historical Sketch for Anglican Residential Schools," in *Remembering the Children, in An Aboriginal and Church Leaders' Tour to Prepare for the Truth and Reconciliation Commission.* Anglican *Church of Canada News*, February 21, 2008. (Accessed June 11, 2014.) http://www.rememberingthechildren.ca/history/index.htm.

CBC News Canada. Truth and Reconciliation Commission of Canada, *Home Page.* (Accessed April 29, 2009.) http://www.trc.ca/websites/trcinstitution/index.php?p=3.

CBC News Canada. "A history of residential schools in Canada," May 16, 2008. (Accessed April 29, 200.9) http://www.cbc.ca/news/canada/a-history-of-residential-schools-in-canada-1.702280.

CBC News Canada. "What is the residential schools truth and reconciliation commission?" May 16, 2008. (Accessed June 10, 2014.) http://www.cbc.ca/news/canada/faqs-truth-and-reconciliation-commission-1.699883.

---

225. Quoted in Meiring, *Chronicle*, 379.

226. Bob Watts, quoted by Charlie Smith in "Native academic Bob Watts aims for a true reconciliation," *Straight.com*, 31 October 2012. (Accessed June 11, 2014.) http://www.straight.com/news/native-academic-bob-watts-aims-true-reconciliation.

Institute for Justice and Reconciliation (IJR). *Justice, Truth, Memory.* Publications and DVDs, Cape Town.

Janzen, Aaron. "Truth Telling and Peace" (course assignment, Canadian School of Peacebuilding). Winnipeg, 2009.

Kinew, Wab. "'It's the same great spirit,' Canonization of Kateri is a big step toward true reconciliation, but the embrace could go further." *Winnipeg Free Press*, October 22, 2012. (Accessed June 11, 2014.) http://www.winnipegfreepress.com/local/its-the-same--great-spirit-175193351.html.

Littlechild, Wilton. "Truth and Reconciliation Canada Commissioner, Wilton Littlechild." Remarks at Witnessing the Future Ceremony, Rideau Hall (Thursday, October 15, 2009). (Accessed July 14, 2014.) http://www.trc.ca/websites/trcinstitution/File/pdfs/Commissioner_Littlechild_speech.pd.

MacDonald, David. "A Call to the Churches: You Shall be Called the Repairer of the Breach," in *From Truth to Reconciliation. Transforming the Legacy of Residential Schools.* Marlene Brant Castellano, Linda Archibald, and Mike DeGagne eds. Ottawa: Aboriginal Healing Foundation 2008.

Mandela, Nelson. *Long Walk to Freedom.* London: Macdonald Purnell, 1995.

Meiring, Piet. *Chronicle of the Truth Commission: A Journey through the Past and Present—into the Future of South Africa.* Vanderbijlpark: Carpe Diem Books, 1999.

Meiring, Piet. "The Baruti vs the Lawyers: The Role of Religion in the TRC process," in *Looking Back, Reaching Forward.* Charles Villa-Vicencio, ed. Cape Town: University of Cape Town Press, 2000.

Meiring, Piet. "Leadership for Reconciliation." *Verbum et Ecclesia* 23, no. 3(2002): 724.

Meiring, Piet. "'You will be known as the people who rebuilt the walls, who restored the ruined houses.' Challenges and opportunities for the churches in South Africa and Canada." *Missionalia,* 37, no. 3 (Nov 2009): 51–68.

Milroy, John S. *A National Crime.* Winnipeg: University of Manitoba Press, 1999.

"Submission to Honorable Justice Murray Sinclair," prepared by students at the Canadian School of Peacebuilding, Canadian Mennonite University, Winnipeg, 2009.

Titian, Denise. "Truth and Reconciliation Commission meets with ha'wiih at Tin Wis resort." Ha-Shilth-Sa 37, no. 2 (January 28, 2010):2. (Accessed July 15, 2014.) nuuchahnulth.org.

Tutu, Desmond. *No Future Without Forgiveness.* London: Rider Books, 1999.

Truth and Reconciliation Commission of Canada. Interim Report. 2012. http://www.attendancemarketing.com/~attmk/TRC_jd/ Interim_report_English_electronic_copy.pdf.

Truth and Reconciliation Commission of Canada. "Our Mandate." (Accessed July 15, 2014.) http://www.trc.ca/websites/ trcinstitution/index.php?p=7.

Truth and Reconciliation Commission of South Africa. *TRC Report, Volumes 1–7,* 1998/2002, Vol. 1, 55–57.

Van Vught, W. and Cloete, D., eds. *Race and Reconciliation in South Africa.* Lanham: Lexington Books, 2002.

Walker, Robert. "Remembering Rightly. Does Canada Need a TRC?" (Course assignment, Canadian School of Peacebuilding). Winnipeg, 2009.

Watts, Bob. quoted by Charlie Smith in "Native academic Bob Watts aims for a true reconciliation." *Straight.com*, October 31, 2012. (Accessed June 11, 2014.) http://www.straight.com/news/native-academic-bob-watts-aims-true-reconciliation.

Wallace, Nancy. "An Argument for a Truth and Reconciliation Commission in Canada." (Course assignment, Canadian School of Peacebuilding). Winnipeg, 2009.

Winfield, Nicole. "Pope sorry for school abuse," thestar.com. (Accessed July 15, 2014.) http://www.thestar.com/news/ world/2009/04/29/pope_sorry_for_school_abuse.html.

Additional Resources

On the South African TRC:

Publications

Numerous books, articles, and theses on the TRC have been published in recent years. Apart from the publications in the footnotes of this chapter, the following books are of prime importance:

Boraine, Alex A. *Country Unmasked. Inside South Africa's Truth and Reconciliation Commission.* Oxford: Oxford University Press, 2000.

Krog, Antjie. *Country of my Skull.* Johannesburg: Random House, 1998.

Villa-Vicencio, Charles, and Fanie Du Toit. *Truth and Reconciliation in South Africa: 10 years on.* Cape Town: David Philip, 2006.

Websites:

The final report of the TRC, together with a vast amount of additional information, may be found on the official website of the *South African Government*, under the Department of Justice.

Of all the NGOs dedicated to reconciliation, healing, and justice, the Cape Town-based Institute for Justice and Reconciliation arguably has the best array of publications and video material. The annual *Reconciliation Barometer* published by the IJR is widely used. *The Institute for the Healing of Memories* (also based in Cape Town) provides hands-on information on current reconciliation initiatives in South Africa. The *Restitution Foundation* runs programs, especially for religious communities, who want to involve themselves in reconciliation and peacebuilding. All of these institutions may easily be visited on the web, via *Google*.

On the Canadian TRC:

Henderson, Jennifer, and Pauline Wakeham. *Reconciling Canada: Critical Perspectives on the Culture of Redress.* Toronto: University of Toronto Press, 2013.

Niezen, Ronald. *Truth and Indignation: Canada's Truth and Reconciliation Commission on Indian Residential Schools.* Toronto: University of Toronto Press, 2013.

Regan, Paulette, and Talaiake Alfred. *Unsettling the Settler Within: Indian Residential Schools, Truth Telling, and Reconciliation in Canada.* Vancouver, UBC Press, 2011.

Wallace, Rick. *Merging Fires: Grassroots Peace-building Between Indigenous and Non-indigenous Peoples.* Winnipeg: Fernwood Publishing, 2013.

LESSONS FROM DRIFTWOOD

—Kay Pranis

EDITORS' NOTE: THE PEACEMAKING CIRCLE PROCESS has its origins in many cultures around the world. In Canada, there is a growing awareness that North American Aboriginal culture has used circles to build a peaceful people. Fundamentally the circle process is an instrument of communication, involving verbal and non-verbal activities. In its most simple form the circle process consists of a group of people seated in a circle, using a talking piece (a small object that is passed from participant to participant) to control the pattern of activity within the circle, and with participants engaging in patterns of behaviour that differ markedly from traditional Western Caucasian means of communication. The keeper of the circle process, while holding the talking piece, introduces the topic(s) to be addressed by the circle participants and then passes the talking piece to the next person in the circle. The person holding the talking piece is free to speak, to sit in silence, or to pass the talking piece to the next person. Only the person holding the talking piece may speak. This process—speaking or not speaking while holding the talking piece—continues until the talking piece is passed around the circle without anyone speaking.

The circle process may involve non-verbal communication, undertaken in a manner similar to that of verbal communication within the circle process. The circle process, like all disciplines, incorporates the use of some specific terminology. The reader may find it useful to understand four terms prior to reading this chapter.

Circle: the general circle process described above; it can refer to a particular group that is participating in the circle process. It is a universal term, not requiring an article ("a" or "the"). Context provides clarity in the use of the term "circle."

Keeper: the person who is responsible for initiating the activities and for ensuring collective agreement regarding the termination of the circle process. As noted above, a keeper is not a leader. The term is often used in verbal form: "keep" and "keeping."

Talking piece: a small physical object that is used in the circle process to designate the person who, at any particular time, has the privilege of being active (speaking or manipulating physical objects).

Training: the teaching and learning of the circle process, particularly to the learning of the role of keeper. It is commonly used as a universal term that requires neither an article ("a" or "the") nor a noun ("session" for example).

Driftwood exercise: a non-verbal form of the circle process described in detail in the chapter. It serves as the foil for this chapter. And, usually, in this chapter the term "driftwood" will refer to the driftwood exercise; its occasional use in reference to the physical object will be clear from the context.

A rich understanding of the circle process includes an emphasis upon "process." The process is undertaken entirely devoid of intentions regarding the outcome; the process (the communication that occurs) is the essence of this work. Communication occurs between participants, and it occurs deeply within each participant; it involves much self-reflection.

Ironically, the circle process involves the use of a large measure of power: power to disable hierarchy, power to shift the possession of ideas and authority from individuals of influence to the common possession of a group, power to discipline the patterns of human interaction, power to command personal reflection, power to enable individual and group movement in relation to strongly-held beliefs, and power to transcend the constraints of a single culture.

Connected to the power that is resident in the circle process is the matter of the circle keeper. A portal to understanding the role of the keeper is the concept of "leader." The keeper is patently not a leader; the keeper has the responsibility of initiating the circle process and of

*enabling the participants to conclude the process or to experience a hia-
tus that can allow the process to continue at a later time; but the keeper
does not lead the circle process. The keeper remains consciously and per-
sistently aware of avoiding any acts of leadership, allowing the process to
proceed by way of the dynamic of communication resident in the group.*

*An uninitiated observer might conclude that the process is passive,
weak, slow, and directionless. Each of these descriptors is antithetical
to the circle process. The circle process involves great intellectual, emotional, and interpersonal energy. As noted above, the circle process is
exceedingly powerful. Though the circle process demands pacing that
is attendant to each individual sequentially controlling the activities of
the circle as the talking piece is passed from participant, the work of the
circle moves participants rather rapidly through reflection upon, evaluation of, and understanding of the collective wisdom of the group.*

*The circle process has direction; the direction however is curvilinear
rather than rectilinear. This is to say that the circle process moves the
group in an important direction, but that direction is not the shortest
distance between two preselected points. Rather it is the tortuous line
that is determined by the collective insights of all participants, often ter-
minating in an unforeseen destination. That is, the discussion shifts in
direction as each participant speaks. By intent, no leader is present to
ensure that each speaker is kept on topic (the topic chosen by an individual leader). Contrarily, the conversation is kept in the flux of
each individual's insights, perceptions, goals, and vocabulary until the
group—collectively—determines that an appropriate end point, or resting point, has been reached. This chapter, though written by a single
individual is written to model the interconnectedness, and the nonlinear
intellectual and emotional activity, that is expressed in the opening
paragraph of the chapter.*

*In summary the circle process consists of a group of people seated
in a circle, using a talking piece. The people—working within a system
that is sufficiently powerful to elicit the wisdom of each member of the
group— interact in disciplined, mutual respect. The work of the circle
results in intellectual, emotional, and interpersonal interchange that liberates a collective wisdom.*[227]

---

227. With thanks to Denny Smith for this brief overview that provides
context for the discussion that follows.

Because I think that the nature of the universe is interconnectedness I will begin by acknowledging that these reflections are connected to other people, to life experiences, to my beliefs. They do not exist independently of those influences.

I am a freelance trainer of the peacemaking circle process. I learned the process initially from Barry Stuart, a former judge in Yukon, Canada, and from Harold Gatensby and Mark Wedge, First Nations people of Yukon, Canada. In the 1990s I was introduced to the peacemaking circle process as way to determine sentences in criminal proceedings within the framework of restorative justice when I worked for the Minnesota Department of Corrections.

The peacemaking circle process became my primary focus within the field of restorative justice, and it became for me more than a way to respond to harm. It became a way for me to see how humans can live more successfully with each other and the natural world, balancing group needs and gifts with individual needs and gifts. The circle became a way to move toward the kind of world I want to live in. I am grateful to my original teachers and the many people who have continued to teach me every time I sit in circle.

My work in circles now spans nearly twenty years and has involved sharing circle face to face with many people and through writing. Barry Stuart, Mark Wedge, and I co-authored the first book about circles in the context of restorative justice. [228] I have since worked with other authors on books about circles and democracy, and about the use of circles with young people to promote emotional literacy and healthy relationships.[229] Circle trainings have taken me coast to coast in Canada and the United States, and to half a dozen cities in Brazil. Everywhere I go I find that participants exhibit an eagerness for this way of coming together that honours the uniqueness of each while

---

228. Kay Pranis, Barry Stuart, and Mark Wedge, *Peacemaking Circles: From Crime to Community*, 1st ed. (St. Paul, MN: Living Justice Press, 2003).

229. Jennifer Ball, Wayne Joseph Caldwell, and Kay Pranis, *Doing Democracy with Circles: Engaging Communities in Public Planning* (St. Paul, MN: Living Justice Press, 2010); Carolyn Boyes-Watson and Kay Pranis, *Heart of Hope Resource Guide: Using Peacemaking Circles to Develop Emotional Literacy, Promote Healing and Build Healthy Relationships* (Boston: Center for Restorative Justice at Suffolk University, 2010).

holding us strongly together.[230] My journey to circles was accidental—not of conscious intention on my part. My journey *with* circles has also been one of unexpected challenges and blessings.

One of the most intriguing accidental gifts of this journey is the driftwood exercise. The driftwood exercise is the first exercise I do in circle training. For many participants it is the most memorable part of circle training. A colleague who participated in a circle training many years ago once suggested making T-shirts that say "I survived driftwood!" as a fund raiser for restorative justice.

Over the years driftwood became a profound teacher for me about circle and about how to be a circle keeper/facilitator. I have participated in this exercise more than two hundred times, and still I learn as I sit through it again and again. Unknowingly I embarked on this grand experiment: watching over and over—with a wide variety of people—the ebb and flow and the similarities and differences in how people reacted to the same set of instructions in an interactive group process. I have done this exercise with men in prison, youth on the South Side of Chicago, students at the Canadian School of Peacebuilding at Canadian Mennonite University, teachers, prison staff, social workers, church groups, First Nations communities in Canada, groups in several cities in Brazil, mediators, farmers, and others. What emerged for me were profound lessons about human nature that inform the circle process and profound lessons that reveal who I am.

What Is the Driftwood Exercise?

I lead this exercise as the first activity of a training session, immediately after a welcome and an opening ceremony. Members of the group have not yet introduced themselves; no agenda has been presented; and no teaching about the circle process has occurred. The training group is seated in a circle of chairs without desks or tables. There is a small table (card table size or smaller) in the centre of the circle. I am holding a bag of driftwood.

---

230. Kay Pranis, *The Little Book of Circle Process es: A New/Old Approach to Peacemaking* (Intercourse, PA: Good Books, 2005).

I introduce the exercise as follows: "We have a bag of driftwood and a table. This activity will be done without talking. We will go clockwise around the circle taking turns. When your turn comes you may take pieces out of the bag and arrange them; you may put pieces back in the bag; you may rearrange the pieces already out. Basically, when it is your turn, you may do what you wish, arranging the driftwood. Or, you may choose to leave it without making any change. If you decide to leave the driftwood as it is without making any changes, signal non-verbally to the next person that you are passing. We will continue going around the circle multiple times, manipulating the driftwood until it comes to a natural ending. We will know we are finished when everyone passes all the way around the circle."

The exercise is deliberately ambiguous. There is no clear goal or stated purpose for the activity. The ambiguity facilitates the lessons that can be drawn from the process because it creates so much space for individual meaning-making. As the trainer I am also a participant, and I generally am active in making some move with the driftwood for the first three times around the circle; then I usually pass and observe what is happening. Sometimes the activity is done in fifteen minutes. Sometimes it takes an hour and a half or two hours.

When everyone passes in their turn around the circle without changing the driftwood arrangement, the first stage of the activity is complete. We then verbally debrief the experience using a talking piece. The talking piece is an essential tool in the peacemaking circle process. It is an object with meaning to the group or the facilitator that is passed from person to person around the circle to regulate the dialogue. When you have the talking piece you may speak without interruption. When you do not have the talking piece you must wait until it comes to you to speak. The talking piece ensures that every voice is heard and encourages thoughtful reflection and attentive listening. It is always okay to pass the talking piece without speaking. There is never an obligation to speak.

In the debriefing session I ask participants to respond to two questions when they get the talking piece:

- What meaning did the activity have to you in your turns to alter the arrangement of the driftwood? Or, what were you trying to do in your turns?
- What did you notice about your reaction to the process?

After each person (including me) has shared his/her answers to those two questions, I pass the talking piece again to give participants the opportunity to offer additional thoughts or to respond to what they heard from others in the first round.

Accidental Discovery

I was introduced to the driftwood exercise as an aesthetic opening ceremony for a circle. It was done with wooden blocks. My friend Don Johnson was co-facilitating a training session with me in Oregon and wanted to share a new opening ceremony he had just learned on his recent trip to Roca Inc., an organization in Chelsea, Massachusetts, that works with street-involved and gang-involved youth.[231] When Don led the exercise, the activity proceeded sweetly to a peaceful consensus. It was a lovely, meditative opening. Inspired by the beauty of it, I decided to start my next training session using the same opening ceremony. While in Oregon I walked the beach with a colleague and started picking up driftwood, thinking the opening would be so lovely with driftwood instead of blocks.

My next training session came soon after and, on the first day of the training, I tried the new opening ceremony using driftwood. There were two people who had different ideas about how the driftwood should be arranged. After a few rounds all other participants were passing but these two kept changing it to their preferred arrangement. Everyone else was not only ready to be done but impatient to be done, but it just kept going around and around to these two who changed the driftwood each time. The activity is not done until everyone passes.

I cannot remember now how it finally ended. I only remember thinking, "This is no aesthetic opening ceremony! This is the real

---

231. Carolyn Boyes-Watson, *Peacemaking Circles and Urban Youth* (St. Paul, MN: Living Justice Press, 2008).

thing—sitting with conflict!" For me the activity became an exercise of sitting with differences. When it finally ended and we verbally processed what we had just experienced together, many of the core teachings of the circle process emerged in the participants' reflections. I had stumbled onto an exercise that brought out core ideas of circle from the participants before I had taught the group anything about the process! That was glorious—an elicitive trainer's dream![232]

The Challenge to Me

The exercise sounds simple enough, but in reality it can be a very challenging experience. I can now sit comfortably with intense conflict because of sitting through this exercise so many times. Over and over and over again the driftwood exercise forced me to sit with my own discomfort about others being unhappy, frustrated, or annoyed—and not try to fix it.

I struggled greatly during that first experience with the driftwood. I was terrified that the participants who were impatient would get up and walk out of the training. I am a middle child. I want people to be happy. People were not happy, and I would be seen as responsible for the situation. Over and over I asked myself whether I should just end the activity by taking control. I wanted so much for it to be over, for everyone to be happy. I agonized and I repeated over and over in my head, "It's not for me to fix it for the group. The group has to find its way through. It's not for me to fix it for the group." It was a deep lesson about keeping circle.

In the years since that first experience, the original lesson has been reinforced for me tens of times. Whenever the exercise has lasted more than forty-five minutes there has been tension in the room, along with palpable impatience and frustration. Each time I feared that someone would be so annoyed or angry or disconnected, they would leave mentally, if not physically. I was afraid I would lose credibility with the participants before we even introduced ourselves to each other. Each time I had to practise not intervening by reminding myself, "It's not for me to fix it for the group." Struggling with my

---

232. John Paul Lederach, *Preparing for Peace: Conflict Transformation across Cultures* (New York: Syracuse University Press, 1995).

desires to intervene forced me to confront my discomfort with people being unhappy with me, and it forced me to realize that it was my need that was driving my anxiety. It forced me to sit in intense conscious awareness of my anxiety while staying fully present with the group. Unwittingly I had found an exercise, used in nearly every training session, that made me practise over and over the stretching of my own edge of conflict avoidance. I was uncomfortable; not only with my own conflicts, but with conflict among others as well.

Impatience, a wish by some for the exercise to be over, is a source of conflict in the exercise. I have had times when I was certain I should never do this exercise again because I was afraid someone was being hurt in the process. I have watched, astounded, as someone else in the circle offered a creative solution to the tension that had developed without a word being spoken. Consequently, I have always let the exercise run its course and in the end the group has always resolved the apparent issues. The participants' reflections that follow those particular experiences are usually profound.

I love this exercise. It is one of my favourite parts of circle training, though it still challenges me. Sitting through the discomfort and the moments of panic, and holding still through my own uneasiness, have given me great confidence in the capacity of a group to find its way through thorny places if there is a structure that honours each participant and gives each a turn (voice.) Learning the ability to sit still, not trying to exert some type of control when I feel panicky, made me grow as a keeper.

I had an opportunity to use that ability to sit still through a panicky moment in a circle in Costa Rica. Sara Castillo asked me to facilitate a circle to deal with a land dispute on an Indigenous reserve near the Panama border in Costa Rica. I do not speak Spanish so Sara translated for me. In the second half of the circle, as the group discussed the contentious issue, they began to speak in their native language which neither Sara nor I spoke. There was a moment of panic as we did not know what was being expressed; then we let our breath out, realizing that they needed to talk to each other, not to us. After a bit of conversation in their native language the conversation returned to Spanish and some participants filled us in on the key communications. We had successfully let go of control and allowed the process to unfold.

Early Lessons

I noticed from the very first time I did the exercise that the physicality of manipulating the wood made visible several core concepts of the circle process. The exercise made apparent the fact that we each have something to offer and that we each have a unique perspective on what is in the centre. The circle process expresses the value of each participant. It reveals how differently people respond to a situation and it stimulates in participants a creativity that bubbles up.

The pieces of wood are symbolic of ideas; when you put an idea in the circle it is no longer yours. Others get to pick up your idea, to move it around, and to change it, just as they can rearrange the wood in the exercise. When you contribute an idea to the circle process, individual ownership of the idea is relinquished. What is in the centre belongs to everyone, to work with and modify.

Another relatively early lesson for me in watching this exercise was the realization that, in a process where everyone has a voice, the group will not allow any one person to take over. I see a very clear pattern played out again and again when some participants become impatient and want the exercise to end. It often begins with a participant putting all the sticks in the bag and then placing the bag beside me (the trainer). It is a clear non-verbal message that it is time to be done. But the exercise is not over until everyone passes. Someone always comes, takes the bag and begins again with the driftwood. Then the attempt to end the activity becomes more assertive. Sometimes a participant puts all the sticks in the bag and sits on the bag hoping that will be the end of it. Another participant comes and gently gets the bag from underneath the one sitting on it and it continues. Then a participant might put all the sticks in the bag and take it out of the room to hide the wood. Generally another participant in turn will go looking and find the bag and bring it back.

I observed an interesting phenomenon when someone removed the bag from the room. I noticed that other participants who had been passing and were clearly ready to be done got back in and tried to find the bag. It seems that even when people want the circle process to be over they resist it being ended by someone taking control. On one occasion a participant put all the sticks in the bag and walked out the door of the training room to the parking lot outside. He returned without the bag and dangled his truck keys to signal to us that he had locked the wood in this truck. He then put the keys in his pocket. No one felt they could retrieve the keys from his pocket so the first few people passed thinking, "The wood is gone. We must be done." However, it is not over until everyone passes.

As the opportunity to take a turn went around the group one individual got up, wandered around the room, found a stack of slips of paper, and brought the paper into the centre of the circle. The group proceeded to manipulate the pieces of paper! So even without the wood the exercise continued. The group would not allow one person to unilaterally control how it ended. That pattern of resisting a unilateral move to end the exercise occurred over and over again with many different types of groups.

This resistance to having someone take control—even when they are acting in the direction you want (for instance, to end the exercise)—explains a lot of behaviour that otherwise does not make sense. People often act against a decision in their own best interest if they feel they had no voice in the decision. Often social service providers are stymied by a lack of cooperation. They have the client's best interest at heart, but the client often perceives the provider as exercising control and therefore resists the provider's decisions. The driftwood exercise physically demonstrates that resistance in a powerful, non-analytic way.

This natural resistance by the circle to someone taking over the process makes it possible to incorporate participants who might otherwise be excluded because those who attempt to dominate are seen as "bullies" or "bad influences," as tending to dominate open air space. People who are seen as manipulators can be welcomed in circle and become part of the solution instead of part of the problem because they cannot take over the circle. Everyone having a turn, having a voice, is a core characteristic of the circle process. In a circle the group will not allow any one person to take over. I think that is a profound idea.

A corollary lesson from the driftwood activity is that it takes time for everyone to have voice and that takes patience. A very large number of participants have identified a challenge to their patience in the exercise. A student from Lebanon described her experience: "At the very beginning, the process seemed fun and engaging. Nevertheless, after some time, it became unbearable." Many have acknowledged that the exercise changed their understanding of why patience is so important. There are no short cuts. It takes time for everyone to have voice. The student stated further, "Reflecting back on this circle, I have learned more than I thought I could. I realized that no one person can take control in a circle process since everyone has an equal voice." We often express a desire for all voices to be heard but we rarely allow the time it takes for a full expression of all perspectives, not just once, but in an iterative process that allows for perspectives to be influenced by what they hear from others.

There was another "Aha" moment derived from the circle in which the bag of driftwood was locked in the truck. I had the following realization: It is not about the wood; just as most conflicts are not about the visible surface issue. The exercise is not about the wood. It is about our relationships and it is about power. In conflicts, very often the core issues are relationships and power rather than the issues initially identified by the parties. Concern with distribution of power and the importance of relationships are central to the circle process. The circle process shifts the interpersonal activities toward equality of power and focuses on relationships before delving into difficult issues.

Around 2001 the Minnesota Department of Corrections developed an infrastructure for using restorative processes, including workplace circles to address staff conflicts.[233] One of the requests for a circle process named, as the core issue, conflict about the manner in which mop heads were being cleaned, going from one shift to the next. In the circle a participant brought up an incident of disrespectful treatment of one corrections officer by another corrections officer. As the circle continued participants spoke only about their treatment of one another and dropped any discussion of the mop heads. The time limit for the circle arrived and they closed the circle, but there was no resolution of the mop head problem. The following morning two corrections officers got together and took care of the mop head problem.

---

233. Kay Pranis, "Restorative Justice in Minnesota and the USA: Development and Current Practice" (Tokyo: United Nations Asia and Far East Institute for the Prevention of Crime and the Treatment of Offenders, 2004), 111–123.

Clearly the mop heads were not the core problem. Their relationships were the problem. It's not about the wood!

In one training session the driftwood exercise went on for a very long time. There was great frustration. At one point a garbage can was brought into the circle and one participant in her turn got into the garbage can. Later she was out of the garbage can and it was removed from the circle. Finally it seemed the exercise was about to end. The participant who had been in the garbage can made a move; every participant after her passed until it came back to her. We only needed for her to pass for the exercise to be done. She made another move in her turn, so we had to go all the way around again.

I was very surprised. Usually once turns to act pass all the way around and come back to the person who made the last move, that person passes. That person has had the last word and is usually satisfied. In that moment it seemed a selfish and irresponsible action to continue. The group needed to be done and needed her cooperation. When we debriefed the experience that participant explained that she came in late, got instructions from someone next to her, and did not know that it needed to pass all around the group in order to be finished. She was being playful and outrageous and waiting for the facilitators to rein her in. This participant was a middle-aged woman who worked in a juvenile correctional facility. She was a very responsible person. I was struck by the realization that when we think someone else will put limits on us we can allow ourselves to be irresponsible. The more we use authority, the less people self-regulate. The use of authority undermines the development of responsibility and self-regulation. The structure of the circle process shifts responsibility to all participants for the quality of the process and the quality of the decisions or outcomes. The talking piece is a powerful equalizer, not just of the participants but of the keeper as well.

Later Lessons

Over time I noticed a pattern to the ebb and flow of the exercise across many different groups. The early rounds are usually tentative, focused on the driftwood itself, and they form a process of individual action, each participant acting independently in his/her turn. The action is on the top of the table. As it continues participants become more confident and definite in their arrangements with the driftwood. Once it gets past the third round the area of play has usually expanded to include the floor and I see the emergence of a sense of collectivity. Participants are still acting in individual turns, but there is a greater awareness of the collective, what others may want, attempts to meet the collective needs of the group. Sometimes the participants become part of the action. Someone may distribute a piece of the wood to each participant or participants may put themselves or others in the centre. It is no longer about the wood but about the group.

Consistently I have observed that the most interesting, creative, and "out of the box" arrangements occur after the point in the process where some people have become very impatient. When some participants become impatient the action becomes far broader; often the table is removed completely. There is a sense of freedom when the table is removed and the creativity takes a big jump. The driftwood taught me that if we want innovation or new ideas we may have to sit through a space of impatience. The impatience prods us to break through surface conformations to unexpected possibilities.

Gradually I realized that this pattern has implications for consensus building. My inclination as a peacemaker is to start looking for consensus right away in a process. The driftwood taught me that there is great benefit in not looking for consensus too soon. On the occasions when the driftwood exercise went around only a few times, quickly, and peacefully the groups came to consensuses about arrangements that were much less interesting and less creative and involved reflections were less insightful than the experiences that went much longer, where there was tension and impatience. It was uncomfortable to sit through that space of tension and impatience, but the result was much richer. I also found that participants had greater self-awareness about their internal state when the exercise went long enough to trigger annoyance in some participants.

I began to finally feel in my body the wisdom about the potential gift in conflict. In the early years I had great anxiety about the exercise going too long and people being upset. As the years went by I found myself anxious that it would not go long enough to experience the impatience and the creativity that accompanies conflict and its rich offspring.

Paul Mickelson is the coordinator for a juvenile circle sentencing program in Carlton County, Minnesota. In an interview with him about details of his program I asked, "What do you do if a kid in your program messes up and commits another crime?" He responded with a chuckle, "That's when we really get the work done!" The deeper work happens when we stay with the challenge through frustration and impatience.

Somewhere in my second hundred experiences sitting through the ups and downs of the exercise it occurred to me that what I was seeing was the deep human drive to make meaning out of whatever is happening. I came to see that humans are incredibly meaning-making creatures. Out of a bunch of sticks and a structured group process, participants will often make profound meanings. However, we make meaning uniquely. This became very important to my understanding of conflict. We are incredibly meaning-making creatures, but we make meaning uniquely. In the circle no two relationships to the wood are exactly the same. Meaning matters very much to us and is also the source of a great deal of conflict.

I saw over and over again that some participants would interpret what others were doing in a certain way, but when a participant explained the meaning of what he/she had done it often did not match the assumption. This meaning-making process is fraught with possibilities for conflict because meaning comes from and expresses core values and beliefs; thus the meaning is deeply held. In addition, even when we use language to try to communicate meaning, our language is not very precise. We never know completely what is in another person's view, no matter how articulate they are or how attentive we are.

We are constantly making meaning out of what we do, and we are also assigning meaning to what others do. The meaning that we assign to the situation or to the action of a person may or may not be the actual meaning the situation or action has to others. Again and again in the driftwood exercise I saw the gap between the meaning that an arrangement of the wood had to an individual and the interpretation others had of that arrangement. I watched apparent conflict: some wanting all pieces to touch versus some wanting pieces spread out with space between; some wanting to build high versus some wanting all the pieces at the same level; some wanting everything orderly or symmetrical versus some wanting a degree of randomness. Then, when participants explained the meaning of their arrangement, the apparent conflict disappeared. There was a difference in meaning for participants but not a conflict.

This insight has taught me to be more conscious of asking about meaning; to be curious about what the meaning of a situation is to someone else. Mary Clark in her book, *In Search of Human Nature*, suggests that meaning is the most fundamental human need. She writes, "A central need of human beings is for meaning. Our need for meaning is our greatest need, superseding all others."[234] That insight has helped me understand the power of circles. Conversation in circle creates space for each participant to share meaning, and the conversation in circle moves easily to that which has deepest meaning for the participants.[235] To be human is to make meaning out of every experience, every thought, every interaction, every feeling. The meaning-making process both connects and disconnects us; we all care about meaning yet we never fully know the meaning for another person.

Lessons in Humility

From the beginning of my experience as a participant I have been aware of my own reluctance to dismantle what others have done. In my turns to take action in a circle I tend to make small moves or do something outside the main structure that others have created. Observing this in myself more than two hundred times, I became aware of how deeply this need is embedded in me. I deeply appreciate those who can sweep the wood all off and start over; the ones who can change what others have done. I am aware that life would be quite dull and limited if we could only make small changes on the edges like the moves I make in the exercise. And yet I cannot bring

---

234. Mary E. Clark, *In Search of Human Nature* (New York: Routledge, 2002), 50.
235. Christina Baldwin, *Calling the Circle: The First and Future Culture* (New York: Random House Publishing Group, 2009); Jean Shinoda Bolen, *The Millionth Circle: How to Change Ourselves and the World: The Essential Guide to Women's Circles* (Newburyport: Conari Press, 1999); Charles Garfield and Cindy Spring, *Wisdom Circles: A Guide to Self Discovery and Community Building in Small Groups* (New York: Hyperion, 1999).

that gift to a group, at least under normal circumstances. Now I am much more conscious that, in group process, it is important to make sure that there is someone else present who has that ability. Difference is essential!

In the driftwood exercise I have repeatedly tripped over my assumptions about others. One time I was conducting a training session inside a prison. The participants were primarily inmates but included a couple of staff and a couple of community volunteers in addition to me and my co-trainer. In the first round of the driftwood exercise, an inmate took one of the pieces of driftwood and gave it to a man who is a volunteer in the prison. I was surprised by that move. It is not unusual for pieces to be given to others but it is unusual for that to happen in the first round of the exercise. The exercise went on with lots of different arrangements and interactions. At some point my co-trainer decided that all the wood should be gathered together, so he took the bag around and collected all the pieces of driftwood, except that the volunteer refused to put his piece in the bag. The exercise continued, and sometime later, another participant decided it was time to gather all the pieces. She collected all of the pieces except the one held by the volunteer. She stood in front of him and non-verbally begged him to put his piece in the bag. He refused. I was very upset with him and thought, "What's the matter with him? What kind of power trip is he on?" I felt embarrassed for her because she failed in her mission in front of us all. And I thought he was a very difficult person. I was worried that she would be hurt by his behaviour. I became anxious that the exercise was causing harm. However, I did not intervene. A little later an inmate facilitated a peacemaking gesture between the woman and the volunteer, and I was relieved about the process but still thought the volunteer was on a power trip. When we debriefed, the inmate who gave the volunteer the piece of driftwood explained that he felt this man had saved his life in a spiritual sense and giving the piece of driftwood was a symbol of his gratitude to the volunteer. When I heard that explanation I was so glad the volunteer had not given up his piece. And I was internally horrified at the judgment I had made about him. I was so wrong about what was going on with him.

Because the exercise is conducted without talking, there is ample opportunity to notice my own thoughts, to become more aware of assumptions and judgments that are flowing through my head. Then, when we talk about meaning, I often discover that my assumptions about meaning were entirely wrong. The driftwood has taught me to try to stay curious as an antidote to judgment or, at the very least, to stay open to changing my assumptions. Speaking about the impact of the driftwood exercise, a student from Lebanon wrote, "I learned about myself and the importance of self-awareness. I learned about my behavior, attitude, and emotions through silence."

In the early years I thought those who were impatient or who thought the exercise was a waste of time were just "not getting it." I thought they were "wrong." As I sat through circle again and again I recognized that conclusion as a judgment that did not allow those participants their own relationship to the exercise. I began to see the driftwood exercise as a situation in which there is no right or wrong. It is whatever it means to each person. It is not wrong to want it over and feel impatient. It is not wrong to conclude at the end that it was a waste of time. The experience is not one characterized by "right" and "wrong" answers. Every action with the wood, every reaction to the process has its own legitimacy as long as no one is being hurt and no property is being damaged. The legitimacy of difference, too, is the nature of the circle process. Each gets to speak his or her truth into the circle and to be listened to with respect. It is not about "right" and "wrong"; it is about heart truth for each participant. In a circle you get to speak your truth; you just do not get to assume that is the truth for anyone else. Reframing away from right/wrong dichotomies is an ongoing struggle.

Stepping away from right/wrong framing has been very helpful to me in facilitating workplace conflicts. It is an enormous relief to me that I do not have to determine who is "right" or who is "telling the truth." The driftwood has helped me feel, in a visceral way, that at times we each may have a different truth. The goal is not to get everyone to agree on a truth; it is to understand how others see and feel their truth. From the place of understanding the truth of another we can often find a way to move forward without seeing things in exactly the same way.

Other Ways of Knowing

The driftwood exercise has become one of the most powerful tools for my own growth, turning each participant in my trainings into a teacher for me. It is a metaphor for the journey of my work. I never planned it; I did not understand in the moment what was happening, but in repeated experiences I saw patterns that moved me to new levels of understanding what I was seeing. The lessons I've learned from driftwood are not original. Many others have carried those teachings for thousands of years. What seems important to me is that we each need to learn those things for ourselves, in addition to being taught by the wise ones among us. For me there has been something very powerful about learning those lessons through a wordless collective experience, using objects from the natural world. I suspect that the exercise accesses other ways of knowing, ways other than the cognitive, verbal, analytical way of exploring meaning. We use words to process the experience, so we supplement the non-verbal experience with our verbal ability, but we begin our exploration stripped of our reliance on words. The silence opens space for participants to notice their own internal processing—thoughts, ideas, feelings, and metaphors of meaning—at a deeper level than they ordinarily do in a group and in a more holistic way.

In this adventure with driftwood another gift has come my way. Very recently Ted Lumley, a participant in a training in Vancouver in 2012, shared his reflections on the exercise. He identifies the exercise as an experience in a relational space that is more reflective of the nature of the universe than is our usual verbal space.[236] He suggests that this is because our language architecture disconnects us from the fundamental relational nature of the universe. Consequently, in the driftwood exercise we are more in touch with the relational reality of our lives that is normally masked by our way of communicating. Understanding the relational nature of the universe is key to the transformation sought by movements such as restorative justice. Lumley believes that the pre-eminence of relational space over analytical/intellectual space is the deep power of the circle process. The driftwood

---

236. See Ted Lumley, *A Fluid-Dynamical World View* (Victoria, BC: Printorium Bookworks, 2008).

exercise immerses participants in the relational space that is the foundation of the circle process, even when we are using words in a circle. In that relational understanding of life, we are never the independent author of our own acts. Our acts are the result of the confluence of many forces, including our own thoughts and intentions but not only our thoughts and intentions.

Every move in the exercise is relational. Our innate relational understanding of the universe comes to the forefront. That is the source of wisdom, insight, and transformative possibility in a circle.

In Lumley's analysis I find resonance with how the exercise feels to me and how circles feel to me. Something is happening at a level that I cannot capture in words and that I do not understand but I know (for me) is important and powerful. I was taught recently by a First Nations elder that, "a teaching is the rekindling of a truth we were born with." The driftwood exercise continues to help me uncover "truth I was born with," and I would like to place this truth—my learning—into the centre of the circle formed by readers and writer. Like all ideas placed put into the circle, I invite you to pick it up, move it around, change it, and use it to rekindle the "truth that you were born with."

Bibliography

Baldwin, Christina. *Calling the Circle: The First and Future Culture.* New York: Random House Publishing Group, 2009.

Ball, Jennifer, Wayne Joseph Caldwell, and Kay Pranis. *Doing Democracy with Circles: Engaging Communities in Public Planning.* St. Paul: Living Justice Press, 2010. (Accessed June 03, 2014.) http://books.google.com/books?id=BC5Wz55ssGMC&pgis=1.

Bolen, Jean Shinoda. *The Millionth Circle: How to Change Ourselves and the World: The Essential Guide to Women's Circles.* Newburyport: Conari Press, 1999.

Boyes-Watson, Carolyn. *Peacemaking Circles and Urban Youth.* St. Paul, MN: Living Justice Press, 2008.

Boyes-Watson, Carolyn, and Kay Pranis. *Heart of Hope Resource Guide: Using Peacemaking Circles to Develop Emotional Literacy, Promote Healing and Build Healthy Relationships.* Boston, MA: Center for Restorative Justice at Suffolk University, 2010.

Clark, Mary E. *In Search of Human Nature.* New York: Routledge, 2002.

Garfield, Charles, Charlotte Milholland, Cindy Spring, and Sedonia Cahill. *Wisdom Circles: A Guide to Self Discovery and Community Building in Small Groups.* New York: Hyperion, 1999.

Lederach, John Paul. *Preparing for Peace: Conflict Transformation across Cultures.* New York: Syracuse University Press, 1995.

Lumley, Ted. *A Fluid-Dynamical World View.* Victoria, BC: Printorium Bookworks, 2008.

Nassif, Cynthia. "Power of Circles: Reflection on Circle Process." unpublished page, Harrisonburg, VA 2012.

Pranis, Kay. "Restorative Justice in Minnesota and the USA: Development and Current Practice." 111–123. Tokyo: United Nations Asia and Far East Institute for the Prevention of Crime and the Treatment of Offenders, 2004.

——. *The Little Book of Circle Process es: A New/Old Approach to Peacemaking.* Intercourse, PA: Good Books, 2005.

Pranis, Kay, Barry Stuart, and Mark Wedge. *Peacemaking Circles: From Crime to Community.* 1st ed. St. Paul, MN: Living Justice Press, 2003.

Additional Resources

Block, Peter. *Community: The Structure of Belonging.* San Francisco: Berrett-Koehler, 2008.

Horton, Myles, and Paulo Freire. *We Make the Road by Walking: Conversations on Education and Social Change.* Edited by Brenda Bell, John Gaventa and John Peters. Philadelphia: Temple University Press, 1990.

Lederach, John Paul. *The Little Book of Conflict Transformation.* Intercourse, PA: Good Books, 2003.

Vogt, Eric E., Juanita Brown, and David Isaacs. *The Art of Powerful Questions: Catalyzing Insight, Innovation and Action.* Mill Valley, CA: Whole Systems Associates, 2003.

Westerhoff, Caroline A. "Conflict: The Birthing of the New," in *Conflict Management in Congregations,* ed. David B. Lott. Bethesda: The Alban Institute, 2001.

Wheatley, Margaret J. *Turning to One Another: Simple Conversations to Restore Hope to the Future.* San Francisco: Berrett-Koehler, 2002.

TEACHING PEACE, BEING PEACE

─Karen Ridd

> We teach who we are.
> —Parker Palmer[237]

Peacebuilding, Teaching, and Finding One's Voice

IN THE MID-1980S I MADE my first trip to Latin America, travelling with a human rights delegation of Witness for Peace (WFP) to Nicaragua. Deeply disturbed and moved by what I experienced there, particularly the suffering caused by the USA-backed Contras, I organized and embarked on a speaking tour through the Canadian Prairie provinces. Looking back, I suspect I was a profoundly boring speaker. The problem was that I was trying to imitate those I had heard speak; I was trying to adopt an academic "lecturer" voice, believing at some subterranean level that such a voice would give me credibility with my audience. I thought that there was a "right voice" and that my lecturer voice was it.

Of course it didn't work. I am not sure that voice works all that well even for those for whom it is natural. Certainly it didn't work for me. I even bored myself. The "credible voice," palpable in its falseness, instead, added to the lack of credibility and underscored my insecurity as a speaker. I could feel this happening, but had no idea what to do. Sad as it is to acknowledge, I was a bright twenty-five-year-old who had absolutely no idea what my own true voice might sound like.

---

237. Parker Palmer, *The Courage to Teach* (San Francisco: Jossey-Bass, 1998), 1.

No idea, that is, until a few years later. On this occasion I was returning to North America after a brief imprisonment in El Salvador, where I had been working as a volunteer with Peace Brigades International (PBI). Traumatized by that experience, I was raw with the awareness that I was home, and safe, while the Salvadoran church workers who I'd most recently been accompanying were still in prison, perhaps were being tortured, and surely were faced with the possibility of death or long-term incarceration. I could not muster the energy to put on an academic voice. I simply opened my heart, and the words flowed from me. The first press conference I gave on my return opened with me listing the names of the twenty-eight church workers still in prison: I remember the mainstream media turning off their cameras in frustration. I expect they were thinking, "When will she get to the 'real thing'?" I enjoyed that moment, feeling so profoundly that what I was engaged in was, in fact, the real thing, for me. I had, for the first time, a sense that, not only was I where I was meant to be in that moment, but that I was speaking with a voice that was deeply mine, that I was being who I was meant to be.

Now I teach at Menno Simons College (MSC), and I continue to face this question. Who is it that I am meant to be as a teacher, as a peacebuilder? The Canadian School of Peacebuilding (CSOP) has offered an unparalleled opportunity for me to reflect on how to *be peace* while teaching peace. This is an absolutely crucial concept with which to struggle. Teaching peacebuilding comes with the requirement that we live as peacebuilders, or at least that we be seen to be trying to live our lives in concordance with what we teach. If we don't, then what we do (and do not do) will undercut anything that we try to teach. Grace Kyoon describes it this way: "Practitioners are invited to think of themselves as being the 'mothers of peace' and, in that position, to strive toward being the best they can be."[238]

If we accept that teaching peacebuilding requires being a peacebuilder, then questions need to be asked, including the questions What does that mean? and Who is a teacher of peace? I do not presume to answer for others: that is taking a trip back down the path of the "right

---

238. Grace Kyoon, "Story-Telling and the Moral Imagination: Mothering Peace," *Peace and Conflict Monitor* (University for Peace).(Accessed 29 May 2014.) http://www.monitor.upeace.org/printer.cfm?id_article=583.

voice," which was profoundly unhelpful to me on my own journey. What I am required to do, though, is to find that answer for myself.

Those Who Go Before: Mentors and Guides

> I am not a teacher but an awakener.
> —Robert Frost[239]

Who teaches us how to teach if the moral imperative is to teach who we are? This is not simply what we will learn in education classes or skills workshops. This is the journey of our lives; and those who guide and mentor us on that path may not be recognized as teachers by mainstream society. One such guide and mentor is Chico.

Chico's Story or "Those Who Teach, Care"

Our older son passionately loved to play soccer, but as a twelve-year-old boy he found himself on a team where he was being bullied by the kids and also by the coach. It was an unbearable situation to be in, and impossible to watch. As his mother, I wanted nothing more than to pull him away but, lest we were to further disempower him, we had to respect his own process of leaving.

After one particularly tough game, he and I went to watch another team play. In a painful incident, his abusive coach came by, looked straight at my son, ignored his greeting and stood a few yards away, back turned. I could feel my son's heart sinking; I could feel him holding in his tears. Then, into this abyss bounced Victor "Chico" Vargas, a coach with an opposing soccer club. Chico was a stubby older guy—a Chilean refugee, truck driver, soccer coach—whose English was so thickly accented that his assistant coaches would translate from "Chico English" for the kids. Chico immediately engulfed my son Daniel in a bear hug, put a headlock on him, pounded him on the back. With the abusive coach right there it was an awkward moment, but oh, so healing.

---

239. The epigraph to this chapter is widely attributed to Robert Frost. We have not been able to locate the source and thus welcome any information about the source.

Chico was an anomaly in the world of competitive sport. He had been a top player himself but, while some coaches focused on the best players or on winning, Chico managed to care about all the kids. He just wanted everyone to love soccer as much as he did, even if they were lousy at it. He was delighted when anyone improved, not just the superstars; and he rooted for the opposing players not just "his" players. Some people read and understand others by learning how to do it or by using their heads. But Chico did it with his heart; he just cared about people so much that he could connect with how they would feel. He loved them.

Chico died suddenly, from cancer. His brother told story after story at his funeral, describing the ways in which Chico had always loved people; as a child he had found a family living on the street and brought them home with him. I don't think I have ever met anyone with such a combination of humour, passion, and compassion. It was the power of his love, and his belief in my son that finally pulled Daniel out of the abusive situation, to a new team, and back to loving sport. Five years later, Daniel still plays soccer and loves the game.

Chico was not "my" teacher. Officially, he was not a teacher at all. When I met him he was driving a garbage truck. He liked the hours because the early start to the day meant that he would be home for his family and for coaching in the evenings. Though he knew that he taught, I am not sure that Chico would have thought of himself as a teacher. He taught me, though, and I am profoundly grateful to have known him. Here, in a soccer coach, was the embodiment of a teacher of peace: he demonstrated the transformative power of an open heart; he radiated joy and exuberance; he understood the need for creativity and risk-taking. And he knew that part of being a mentor or guide is to allow people to be fully who they are.

Peacebuilding, Teaching, and the Compassionate Self

> Non-violence: a way of being, a philosophy that is committed to living non-violently. May include a commitment to activism: if so, the commitment is to non-violent action. Well-known practitioners include Gandhi, Cesar Chavez Aung San Suu Kyi.

> Non-violent Action: Behavioural term. Act of commis-
> sion or omission, without threat or use of injurious force,
> which has a 'political' intent: social change, social defense or
> third party accompaniment.[240]

Definitions bore me. But, inexplicably, I routinely start the university
courses that I teach in non-violent action (NVA) with these definitions. Perhaps I am trying to get the boring stuff out the way, so that
we—the students and I—can grapple together with what these ideas
mean in the real world. Perhaps I am just being thoughtless. What I
hope I am doing is giving the students a bit of grounding, enough of
an idea of what this course is about so that they can tentatively begin
to engage with the material.

In a feminist spirit of transparency I then disclose my social and
philosophical location; I often share the story of my own journey
to become a passionate student of NVA. I describe my early university years, raising funds and support for armed struggles in Central
America. In those years of my life I would say things like "NVA
worked for Gandhi because the Brits were so civilized" (Anyone
want to hazard a guess about my cultural heritage?) or "Proponents
of NVA are naïve," or "Real revolutionary change can only come
through armed revolution." It took working in Central American
war zones, among hardened Latin American activists, and watching
them effectively use NVA, to convert me to believe in NVA. It has
taken a much longer journey to convert me into a fledgling follower
of non-violence.

I hesitate even to write the phrase "follower of non-violence."
Notice the "fledgling" qualifier in the previous paragraph. My inner
critic immediately points out that I do too much violence to the natural world and to myself: my carbon footprint is too big, and I am
drinking a soft drink as I write this paragraph. I spend too much time
on the computer and, recently, on Facebook, and not enough time
hiking in the bush. Currently I am not enough of an activist, and I

---

240. George Lakey, "Training for Social Action Trainers" (lecture, Training
for Change, Philadelphia, PA, December 27, 1990). The definition of non-violent action presented here is similar to the one given by Gene Sharp, *Power
and Struggle* (Boston: Porter Sargent, 1973), 64.

do not have enough time to give to all the people whose paths have crossed mine and who have a right to my attention.

But I am consciously, and self-consciously, on a journey, one about which I rarely, if ever, talk. I know, of course, that most practitioners of NVA are committed to NVA as a tactic. That is well and good. They see how effective NVA can be, and they carry it out in numerous creative and amazing ways. If there are any doubts about the efficacy of NVA, the work of Erica Chenoweth in her book, *Why Civil Resistance Works: The Strategic Logic of Nonviolent Conflict,* should lay them to rest. Chenoweth and co-author Maria Stephan's research and analysis show that NVA has a significant strategic advantage over violence. NVA has a success rate of 57 percent compared to approximately 25 percent for violence. NVA exhibits an additional partial success rate of approximately 23 percent versus approximately 12 percent for violence, and a failure rate of only approximately 20 percent whereas violence fails more than 60 percent of the time.[241] What makes these numbers so impressive is that Chenoweth and Stephan are looking at the most difficult cases: regime change, secession, or defence from an occupying force.[242]

It is clear to me, then, that one does not need to be committed to non-violence to carry out effective NVA. And I do not, in the least, want to suggest that it is somehow morally wrong to be committed to NVA without a commitment to non-violence. Not only do I not think that; in my experience all that kind of judgment does is divide and discourage. This world hardly needs more division and discouragement.

So, why then, would I be actively choosing to pursue non-violence? I have two reasons. My first reason was acquired many years ago when an anti-war activist in Toronto, Len Desroches, told me that he was committed to non-violence because, if he was committed to NVA and he ran out of ideas, then he would only have violence to turn to. On the other hand, if he was committed to non-violence, he would be bound to keep trying to come up with more options. That argument made sense to the pragmatic side of my personality and

---

241. Erica Chenoweth and Maria Stephan, *Why Civil Resistance Works: The Strategic Logic of Nonviolent Conflict* (New York: Columbia University Press, 2011), 9.

242. Chenoweth and Stephan, *Why Civil Resistance Works,* 7–10.

to the part of me that knows my own tendency to be intellectually lazy. My second reason for embracing non-violence runs deeper than this; it is a sense of rightness—what is, simply, the right path for me. Non-violent is what I am called to be if I am to be living in fullest connection to my deepest self. You see, my understanding of non-violence is that it means, among other things, to walk through the world with love, with passion, and with compassion. And that is the way I want to be in the world.

My journey is to be a "Chico," walking open-heartedly, joyously, creatively in the world. In this chapter I will explore that journey and my, sometimes covert, invitations to students, such as the students at CSOP, to join me as co-conspirators and co-learners on that journey.

Compassion Story 1: Stan

I was sitting in a Protestant church in Winnipeg. We were in a circle, and an Aboriginal elder was leading us. It was the mid-1980s and the man leading us was Stan McKay. Later he would become well-known throughout Canada as the first Indigenous moderator of the United Church of Canada (UCC), the "Right Reverend Dr. Stanley McKay." For now, though, he was just "Stan": humble, kind, warm, and brilliant.

I don't remember what the circle was about, although I do remember that there was a mix of Indigenous people and settler allies.[243] Toward the end of the circle one of the young Indigenous men spoke up to thank Stan and to describe the warmth and compassion that he could feel all around Stan. I sat, stunned, thinking, "That's it!" That was exactly what I too felt from Stan, but unlike the speaker, I could not articulate it as being a presence around Stan, something that all of us felt in his company, something emanating from him. The illuminating comment started me on a life journey: a longing to become a

---

243. "Settler Ally" is a term used to refer to non-Indigenous people who live on what was once Indigenous land (for example, North America), and who seek to be allies to Indigenous people in undoing the impact of colonialism. A Solidarity Committee of the Canadian Union of Public Employees has produced a useful article on this topic: The Political Action Committee, "Practicing Relations of Solidarity," *The Ally* 2, no. 1(2011). (Accessed 29 May 2014.) http://pac3906.files.wordpress.com/2011/08/settlerally-practicing-relations-of-solidarity1.pdf.

person from whom love and warmth might flow out onto all who were around me.

For two decades after that event I rarely thought of it. When I did, its apparent unattainability hurt. It was like looking through a window at posters for voyages that one cannot take. I knew that I wanted to be like that; I even felt that perhaps, maybe—possibly—it might be something that, someday, I might be able to do in a small way. But the evident gap between where I wanted to be and where I was felt like a chasm. All I could really feel was the longing, the absolute depth of heartfelt longing, a physical aching to be open-hearted.

As I look back, I am not sure where the shift began. Perhaps the longing itself was part of the shift. But while I cannot identify its beginning, I can identify moments along the way.

Compassion Story 2: The Treasury Policeman

The noise in the post-midnight pitch darkness sounded to my unaccustomed ears like a massive concrete wall falling over. It was not, of course. It was a gunshot, very near, in front of the small hotel where I was staying. Shortly after the noise, there were a woman's cry and dogs barking. We slid from our beds and ventured to the street, where a young man lay bleeding. The elderly woman was now keening, wailing over the body. One of my colleagues, a nurse, tried to resuscitate him. I ran through the darkened streets to the nearest telephone to use my fractured Spanish to call for an ambulance.

It was 1987 and I was an anxious young woman, studying Spanish in Antigua Guatemala. With a few new acquaintances I had headed off to Panajachel for the weekend. It was a safe tourist destination, and none of us were prepared for murder.

When I returned from the payphone, the resuscitation attempt had been stopped. The young man was gone. Now all that remained was to wait by the body. It was a long vigil—first the ambulance came. And then the Policia de la Hacienda, the notorious Treasury Police, came to examine the crime scene and the body. As we waited, I spent time holding the grieving mother, trying with my arms to contain her grief, my tears mixing with hers. I didn't have the Spanish words to say much, but really what would there be to say? The young man was barely twenty; I thought of my own brother, my own mother. The other task I had that long, sleepless night was to chase the dogs away from the body. Their interest in it repulsed me. I could not imagine how much more traumatic it must have been for the mother.

At the time I did not understand what had happened. I still don't. The boy/man held a small knife, like a small steak knife. He was killed late at night by a single gunshot to the body. He was a member of the Treasury Police. There was a military raid that night on a community across the lake. There were rebels in town.

Was this a political killing? A reprisal for government acts of repression? Or was he simply killed in a late-night brawl? It didn't matter. A life was lost. A mother grieved and, to the best of my limited ability, I held that grief. It didn't matter; except that it does—obviously—to him, to his mother, to their friends and family. It also mattered to me: it was a moment that shaped my life.

The Treasury Police, I later came to learn, were a repressive force deeply involved in the torture and assassination that scarred the histories of Guatemala and El Salvador and their people. The Treasury Police, ironically, were the ones who would imprison me, years later, in El Salvador. The Treasury Police were the ones who are easy for me to hate, for me to "other." But how can I hate them, when my memory holds the story of a mother mourning, when my body held the weight of a lifeless body, when my feet remember chasing dogs away. This experience has bonded me with the "other"; it is a bond that can never be undone.

As a mediator, I know that mediation requires a series of skills, knowledge of a model or plan, intuition. More importantly, mediators require the ability to care about both parties, to hold both parties in their hearts. A colleague, Jan P. Schmidt, and I once posed the question to each other: If conflict resolution could be distilled to just two things what would they be? Independently, we both realized that we believed the two things would be transparency and compassion.

Transparency is easy enough to enact; it is, more than anything, an intellectual willingness to be honest. It requires discipline, but is a rational action. But, compassion? How do we get there? It is not, at least for me, simply a matter of choice. I can choose to do things that will support my heart to be open, and I do. One way is with the

"Gates" (often attributed, perhaps incorrectly, to Sufism). The "Gates" constitute a relatively simple concept that we talk about in our home.

Okay, I offer an admission: I talk about them and freely remind my children of them, but still need work on them myself. The Gates invite us to think before we speak, and then only speak if what we say can pass through the three Gates.

1. Is this true?
2. Is this kind?
3. Is this necessary?

The Gates remind us to be conscious of what we say, and to remember to try to speak with compassion.

Another deeply important and, for me, even more difficult compassion practice is the metta meditation which I first learned in 2007, during a workshop on the inner life of the mediation practitioner, led by mediation practitioner Daniel Bowling in Winnipeg, at Mediation Services.[244] I don't remember much from that workshop, but what I remember is still vividly with me. At the time I was feeling intense anger (hatred?) toward the soccer coach who was hurting Daniel so much. Bowling introduced a compassion meditation, in which he asked us to think of three people: a person who is a beloved mentor toward whom we can readily feel love; a person toward whom we feel neutral (perhaps a neighbour whom we see but do not know well); and a person toward whom we feel negativity (perhaps well-deserved negativity). For each of these people, and toward ourselves, Bowling suggested saying the following statements out loud or silently. We were to say the first statement five times, inserting the name of the beloved mentor; then to say the second statement five times for the mentor, followed by the third, and then the last statement, each said five times.

We were to begin a second series of statements, this time with our own names, still repeating each sentence five times before moving on to the next. We were to make a third series of statements, inserting

---

244. Daniel Bowling, "The Inner Life of the Mediator" (lecture, workshop at Mediation Services, Winnipeg, MB, September 25, 2009).

the name of the neutral person. Finally we were to insert the name of the "other" person in each of the statements which were spoken five times.

May _____ be peaceful and happy.
May _____ be safe and protected from harm.
May _____ be free from mental and physical disease.
May _____ take care of him/herself with ease.

I think I must have looked horrified when Bowling described this sequence. I know that inside my head I was thinking some version of "Wish _____ to be safe and protected from harm? Are you kidding me? I *want* to harm him!" Perhaps Bowling read my face. Whatever the case, he realized he needed to explain a bit more, and he offered these thoughts: the meditation is intended to build compassion for the "other," for those with whom we struggle. That of course, frees them. But as Bowling pointed out, our hostility toward someone else ultimately hurts us, as we carry, embodied, our anger and pain. Our lack of compassion may hurt them; certainly it hurts us. We started the meditation, and almost immediately I began to weep: for Daniel, for myself and, yes, unbelievably, for the unkind soccer coach too.

My anger toward the coach did not end that day. Indeed, years later, as I sit here writing this I still feel some anger. Still, the end began that day. And compassion seems to be something that is indeed more journey than destination.

So I journey on this path, working, hoping, and willing to be more heart open. What does it mean for my students? What does it mean for my teaching?

In 2005 I made one of the smarter decisions of my life, supported by my hugely patient thesis advisers, Dr. Arthur Walker-Jones and Dr. Loraine MacKenzie Shepherd. I decided to switch to a course-based master's degree instead of doing a thesis. I had run aground on the thesis. I simply could not shake the feeling that by doing the research for it I had already gained what I had hoped to learn, and that writing the thesis was simply an act of willpower—and anyone who saw my earlier incarnation as an elite athlete will testify that I am doing fine on the willpower front. What was welling up in me, instead, was the decades-old desire for greater openness of my heart, a desire that was being beckoned to by the opportunity to take two courses on compassionate listening as part of the replacement for my thesis. The courses were a great experience, but more importantly, for one of those courses I was tasked with creating an annotated bibliography.

I read and read and read like one who has been wandering in a desert. I read books on listening, books on communication, but most of all, I read books on compassion. It seems that with intention, practice, reading, and support one can indeed become more open-hearted. It is a journey that I personally find supported by laughing, by loving, by playing, and by listening to music. I am not, by the stretch of anyone's imagination, a musician, but I have created, in the quiet of my office, a playlist of pieces that open my heart. I don't know that they will work for others; I expect that we all have playlists that meet the rhythms of our own hearts. I have, however, included my list here in case it works for others.[245]

From my perspective, the compassionate heart is central to being peaceful. Certainly it was a fundamental part of my experience of Chico. One way that Chico put compassion into practice was by his endorsement of mistakes. Chico would say to me about my son: "He tries it and he makes a mistake. He tries again, and makes a mistake again. But that is how he learns to do it." It is not just in soccer, of course, that we need to embrace risk and creativity. The "trickster" is crucial to the journey of building peace.

---

245. Resources for Opening the Heart: Tomaso Abinoni, *Adagio in G Minor*, http://www.youtube.com/watch?v=IWGPNG-Hgdc; Johann Sebastian Bach, *Air on the G String*, http://www.youtube.com/watch?v=FUPx42UmSng; Samuel Barber, *Adagio for Strings*, http://www.youtube.com/watch?v=lV3SHBFyDZM; Anton Dvorak, "Going Home," Symphony No. 9, from the New World, http://www.youtube.com/watch?v=mVERlJgghOY; Eleanor Daley, *Requiem*, http://www.youtube.com/watch?v=e551OImCURw; Johann Pachelbel, *Canon in D*, http://www.youtube.com/watch?v=JvNQLJ1_HQ0; Louie Schwartzberg, *Nature. Beauty. Gratitude*, Ted Talk. http://www.ted.com/talks/louie_schwartzberg_nature_beauty_gratitude.html; Secret Garden Duo, *You Raise Me Up*, Josh Groban version: http://www.youtube.com/watch?v =aJxrX42WcjQ; Jill Bolte Taylor, *My Stroke of Insight*, Ted Talk. http://www.ted.com/talks/jill_bolte_taylor_s _powerful_stroke_of_insight.html.

Peacebuilding, Teaching, and the Trickster

> In a manner that is analogous to the "Holy Fool"
> tradition in the Greek and Russian Orthodox
> churches, in which the monk assumed the role of
> the fool, or engaged in bizarre or impious behav-
> ior, in order to reveal the folly of the people and
> awaken piety, the Zen master becomes a clown
> and behaves or instructs in unorthodox ways in
> order to reveal the comedy in a false view of self,
> and to awaken a new perspective on existence.
> —M. Conrad Hyers[246]

Compassion and the trickster walk hand in hand, as Shakespeare well knew. Shakespeare's Falstaff is recognized as one of the great clowns of the stage. W.H. Auden points out that Falstaff radiates happiness, and "this happiness without apparent cause, this untiring devotion to making others laugh becomes a comic image for a love which is absolutely self-giving."[247] As teachers of peace, and as peacebuilders, we need to remember that we are continually inviting people into haz-ardous spaces: spaces that not only challenge their ways of seeing and being in the world, but that challenge the fundamental tenets of their worldviews. This is, ultimately, the role of the trickster, to envision an alternate reality and to bring people to that reality, with joy and compassion. The trickster inspires and provokes those around to take risks, to see things anew. With this role comes another moral impera-tive. If we are asking others to take risks, then surely—morally and ethically—we must be willing to take risks ourselves. In practice, for me as an instructor in conflict resolution studies, this means trying new things every time I teach. It means being willing, myself, to make mistakes and to fail. It means walking out of my own comfort zone if I am requiring students to walk out of theirs.

---

246. M. Conrad Hyers "The Ancient Zen Master as Clown-figure and Comic Midwife," *Philosophy East and West* 20, (1970): 10, in a master's thesis: Sue Proctor, *The Archetypal Role of the Clown as a Catalyst for Individual and Social Transformation* (Montreal, Concordia University (2013), 27.
247 W. H. Auden *An Anatomy of Laughter* (London: William Collins Sons Company, 1974), 239.

I can push others to take risks, and I can push myself. But it is far more effective to invite, to make the risk-taking and new steps attractive, intriguing, delightful, and joyful. Joy, laughter, delight resonate much more deeply in us than do fear, guilt, or duty. The former are states of mind that encourage us forward and give us the strength and motivation to try new things.

University classrooms are all too often static and sterile environments. Elementary school teachers spend time and energy on the creation of a physical space that will welcome students. In the university, we create that welcome, not through the physical space over which we often have precious little control but through the space that we create among the people of the class.

There are, of course, specific things that we can do: the "how" of building a learning community in the classroom. On the first day of class I am in the room ahead of everyone else. I greet everyone, learn their names, and shake their hands as they walk in the door or settle into their seats. It's messy and awkward and takes a while, but right from the start it sends the message that we are going to create something different here. I lead a lengthy "University Welcome" that I am grateful to have learned from Judith Jones of Training for Change.

"Diversity Welcome," as I utilize the method, involves highly intentional interactions between the leader and the participants at the beginning of a course. I take the time to offer an explicit welcome to participants from each of the commonly used social categories, as the participants might see themselves: learning styles, religious beliefs, sexual orientation, desire to participate in the course, social and family history, age, ability, linguistic diversity, and geographic origin. Then I explicitly welcome the spirits of ancestors and of those whose land we occupy to be present during the gathering. I attempt to provide a social and spiritual setting that is open, and I seek to stimulate participants to interact with each other and with me in ways that make diversity an asset to the learning and growing endeavour. Details of this process may be found both on the Training for Change website and also in George Lakey's book, *Facilitating Group Learning.*[248]

---

248. Access to Diversity Welcome resources include "Training for Change" (http://www.trainingforchange.org/) and George Lakey, *Facilitating Group Learning: Strategies for Success with Diverse Adult Learners* (San Francisco: Jossey-Bass, 2010).

At CSOP I very much appreciate that all of these efforts to create an open-hearted space for learning are intentionally supported by CSOP structure. There are student liaisons in the classrooms, a welcome on the first day, mutual break times, sharing of classrooms and lectures, and evening activities. Most important, there is food: food at snacks, food at Peacebuilder Banquets, and food at the closing gathering.

If I were to give a new teacher of peace, or a peacebuilder, one bit of advice, it might be "Share food." My father, a well-loved professor of religious studies, had the students in his classes—all his classes—come to our house, and there would be copious amounts of food. As an undergraduate student I still remember fondly those occasions when professors would take a class out for a drink or to the faculty club. Now that I am an instructor I live out of town, and I have young children and classes of more than thirty-five people. Much as I would love to do it, I cannot afford to take them all out for food; nor can I invite them home. But I can, and I do, organize potlucks and I bring snacks. In the course *Conflict and Culture* I have learned from my colleagues that the best assignment, early in the course, is to have each student bring a food from their cultural tradition, to share it, and to talk about it. Food is central to our human interactions and to our rituals; classrooms are an oddity in that they are places where we rarely share food. The immediate result of eating together is a sense of closeness and collegiality, of breaking bread together.

The trickster's job, then, is to break the rules, to bring in the unexpected, and to do it with compassion. Often the best peacebuilding actions are creative, rule-breaking, and funny! For years I have been collecting examples of creative NVAs around the world. Examples include the Thai woman in the tree with her water buffalo that was dressed in a suit of men's clothing and named after the premier; the "Sick-In" staged by Swedish Lesbian, Gay, Bisexual, Queer/Questioning and Transgender/Transexual (LGBQT) folks and their allies, where people conspired to remove the "Homosexuality as Illness" designation from the Swedish Medical Association handbook of diseases, by calling in to work to say "'Sorry, can't come in, I'm feeling too gay today"; Russian soldiers on the border with China, "mooning" a portrait of Chairman Mao; along with sex strikes, swim-ins, and sheep-ins. The list is endless, and endlessly inspiring. Humour, with its undercurrent of delight, invites and intrigues us, even in the most unlikely of places.

The Trickster Meets Compassion

> Hurt people hurt people. Abusive patterns get
> passed on, generation after generation, but we can
> break the chain with our choices. Meet anger with
> sympathy. Meet contempt with compassion. Meet
> cruelty with kindness. Meet grimaces with smiles.
> When you forget about the fault, there is nothing
> to forgive. Love is the weapon of the future.
> —Yehuda Berg[249]

For the North American members of the 1989 PBI team in El Salvador, staying in the country meant repeatedly having to get our short-term visas extended. Often we worked with only fifteen- to thirty-day visas. Getting them extended often got us tangled up with lawyers, border officials, and the bureaucrats at Migracion at the cost of scarce time, energy, and money.

As a newcomer to the team, I had heard horror stories about visits to Migracion, in the Ministry of the Interior. People had been deported, detained, and had even disappeared directly from their offices. So, prior to my first visit to Migracion I had spent hours preparing: arranging papers, translating documents, copying and typing letters, considering how to discreetly explain myself.

When I arrived at Migracion I was nervous—and justifiably so. First visits are more likely to be routine, but mine seemed quickly headed for disaster. The officials immediately zeroed in on the Nicaragua stamps in my passport. They ignored my explanation that I had spent six months travelling throughout Central America the previous year. Instead, they

---

249. Yehuda Berg, "Forgive and Forget," *Kabbalah for Everyone*. (Accessed May 6, 2014.) http://www.yehudaberg.com/content/forgive-and-forget.

called me a communist and a drug trafficker, and demanded to know in what neighbourhood of San Salvador I was living. When I told them where I was staying—really, it was just a middle-class neighbourhood abutting, unfortunately for me, the rather radical National University—they pounced on the information. Everyone living in that area, they shouted, was "subversive"!

At this point they began to interrogate me angrily about my activities and those of my friends. More men were called over: there were now five or six men standing over me yelling at me as I sat in a chair. Excited, outraged, they grabbed my bag and began to search it. They scrutinized the books I was carrying and tried to read letters that I had brought from my Member of Parliament and from my church in Winnipeg. In one of those letters they found the words "human rights," ominous words from their perspective.

By now I was not so much concerned about getting my visa extended: I was, simply, scared and on the verge of tears. But I had been living with, and being inspired by, Salvadorans and Guatemalans who found ways to act creatively and non-violently while under pressure. I had to try something. So, tentatively, afraid, I firmly said, "No. I'm not a terrorist, subversive, drug trafficking, communist guerrilla. I'm a clown." Perhaps you can imagine that that did not go over well. The men reacted with more taunts. "Can you believe these foreigners, what liars they are! This one says she's a *clown*." Politely, and as calmly as I could, I replied, truthfully, "Sirs, I know that I don't look like a clown. But I am, and I'll prove it to you." I pushed a photo of myself in whiteface across the table to a chorus of scoffing "Prove it!" And I pulled out an animal modelling balloon from my bag. Even as I began inflating it, I could feel the tension in the room subside. The shouts and jeers died away. By the time the rubber was twisted into a dog, the atmosphere had completely changed. Suddenly, it was like being at a children's party. "Can I have a green one?" "Do you make birdies? Rabbits?"

I had, fortunately, brought a gross of balloons, and I made all 144 that day, as the office and desks flowered with multi-colour balloon animals of all shapes and sizes. But the high point was when the most antagonistic of the men came over to me and pounded me on the back, eager to show me the cute face he had drawn on his orange bunny, and the tiny cardboard spectacles he had fashioned for it. I was stunned. The turnabout was so rapid and so absolute. Not only were we now partying but the officials were admiring my pictures, advising me where I might buy balloons in El Salvador, en-quiring solicitously after the state of my health.

And my visa? They gave me a fifty-seven-day extension and waved goodbye to me from the door, their arms filled with balloons.[250]

The experience with the balloons was only possible, I think, be-cause of the young Treasury Policeman who had died. I could not have reached to the humanity within the men in the Department of the Interior if the young Guatemalan man and his mother had not shown me the heart of the "other." Chico's brother told story after story at his funeral. We are, of course, the sum total of the stories of our lives.

Peacebuilding, Teaching and the Power Of Story

> There isn't anyone you couldn't love, once you
> heard their story.
> Stories affirm who we are.
> —Andrew Stanton[251]

---

250. This is an adaptation of an article that I wrote that was originally published in a newsletter, *Quaker Concerns*, then reprinted in Jack Ross, *Nonviolence for Elvin Spirits* (Argenta, BC: Jack Ross Publishing, 1992), 58–60.

251. Andrew Stanton, "The Clues to a Great Story" TED Talk. (Accessed May 6, 2014.) http://www.ted.com/playlists/62/how_to_tell_a_story.html.

Artem Dolya

the young man
before
me
has a wide smile
to match the quick sense of humour that I later come to know
a warmth that flows like water around him
clear
a sharp mind.
i remember our first handshake,
my awkwardness.

In a picture he shows us on the fourth day
he's standing in a river,
proud, powerful, a young woman laughing as he carries her in his arms.
One day later, the diving accident
paralysis
a wheelchair for life

i didn't know
the streets in Kyiv do not have curb cutaways for wheelchairs
he plans his routes
not by what is shortest, most direct, most scenic
but by where the curbs are broken and a wheelchair can bump cross

2010 was my first year teaching at CSOP. I was teaching *Peace Skills* and it looked like such an easy gig. I was teaching very familiar material; the hours were short, the setting idyllic; it would be a cinch. Then the class arrived—thirty extraordinarily differing people, some having travelled half a globe to get there. My mentor, George Lakey, has often said that if there are thirty people in a workshop, in fact, there are thirty different workshops happening concurrently. Each student arrives with her/his own lenses, goals, stuff; and so each one experiences the class differently, and takes from it different things according to their interests and their needs. In the class I faced that first day, I found this diversity dazzlingly evident, and daunting. How was

I to balance the desire of the middle-aged American man, eager to get at the material, the older Canadian woman's need to tell me what she knows, and others' need simply to "arrive"?

Gato Munyamasoko

The older Rwandan man sits
dignified, upright
quiet
listening, listening, listening.
On Day Four he finally tells a story:
breaking his traditions he ate food in a rival tribe's home
with the "enemy"
risking life, risking ostracism
but
breaking barriers by
breaking bread

Day Four. We heard Gato's and Artem's stories on day four. There are only five days of classes. We came so close to *not* hearing those awe inspiring stories all because I, the professor, misjudged. I should have known better. I had learned this lesson before, from rice farmers and activists in the Esaan region of northeast Thailand.

George Lakey and I were leading a multi-day residential training program for Thai environmental activists who wanted to hone their use of non-violent direct action. But the workshop was moving slowly for the first days. In fact, it did not begin to "pop" until several days in. The turning point occurred when people began telling each other their own stories, stories that I still remember. There were the rice farmers whose paddies were being devastated by massive changes to the water table, changes caused by the development of huge eucalyptus plantations. Eucalyptus trees are much in demand for lumber, as they grow very quickly and very straight. But they can do that only because they draw unusually heavily from the water table. These corporate plantations were sucking the water away from the land of the subsistence rice farmers. But the farmers were creative, persistent, and resilient; among other things, they held mock funerals for their rice. They would fill actual coffins with the stalks of the rice that had withered from lack of water, and parade the coffins through their communities before laying the rice on the doorsteps of the corporate lumber farm or the government authorities.

After the farmers told stories of their resistance, a group of students spoke up. They were working on issues of water quality. In their rural community, effluent from a fish sauce factory was polluting the local river on which the community depended for drinking water. So the students, together with community activists, called a press conference at which they offered a glass of the polluted water to the fish sauce factory owner and invited him to drink. The activists told us that, to really drive home their point, they lit the water on fire, blew it out, and then handed it to the owner.

Their story was followed by the community leader who told us how her community was resisting the construction of a new corporate strip mall in their small town. She led her community, every night, to take down the unwanted hydro poles that the developers were erecting in the midst of the community. Every night the poles came down and were delivered to the developer's office with the note "Excuse us, it looks like you've left something behind."

It was not until these stories surfaced that the workshop participants could come alive. It was not until they told their own stories that people could listen to, and learn from, the stories of others. It was not until people *felt* heard that they could also feel "known." This is especially true, I believe, when people are coming from contexts where they are confronting injustice. Faced with a new group of people, one thing that they see is a new group of potential allies for their cause. They arrive carrying not just their own interest in learning, but an implicit commitment to their community back home that they will educate others about their struggle, and bring new allies into the fold. And how can they do that unless there is time, space and attention for them to tell their stories?

So I learned, years ago, that participants, especially in cross-cultural settings, need to tell their stories to be able to be fully present, to be able to "arrive." What I learned is, of course, backed up by the work of others, one of whom is Dr. Gordon Neufeld. Neufeld is a Canadian developmental psychologist who promotes an attachment-based development model, the idea that children need to feel a warm emotional connection to a caring adult in order to thrive and grow. Neufeld and his associates know the power of telling stories as a mode of teaching. My personal favourite Neufeld anecdote is the story of early stimulation. As Neufeld Institute Faculty member Pamela Whyte tells it, children who were being read to were studied to examine the impact of early reading on children. Not surprisingly, when activity in the language centres of the brain was measured it was clear that reading to the children caused a significant increase in brain activity. From this, the researchers concluded that reading to children from an early age would stimulate brain development. But then subsequent studies failed to show the same surge in brain activity. What was the difference? In the first study, the children were sitting on their mothers' laps, whereas in the later studies they were being read to by research assistants. Researchers came to realize that it was not that the children were being read to at a young age that made the difference. It was that the children were being read to by someone who loved them, and whom they loved. It was the children's attachment to the reader that opened the child to learning.[252]

This attachment, according to Neufeld, happens in a variety of ways. At a surface level, attachment happens through "sameness." I work this angle very consciously on the first day of every class, when I take pains to greet and shake hands with each student as they enter the room or settle into a desk. With each one, I look for some point of connection, some sameness. I say things such as "I love that shirt; that shade of blue is one of my favourite colours, too!"; "Oh, you are reading a book by Kenneth Oppel. Have you read *Silverwing*?"; "Jets jersey, eh? What did you think about the draft picks this summer?" But "sames-ies" is really a superficial way of connecting, which is why it is easy!

Much more profound, Neufeld suggests, is attachment through being known. Bruce Tuckman's work on the stages of group development says much the same thing; a group becomes a high functioning team only when it has moved past the stage of polite sameness—"Oh, look how alike we are!"—to a stage where we allow our real selves to show. At this point the profound question for the group is, Will these people still like me if they know how I really am? One of the most

---

252. Gordon Neufeld, "Hold Onto Your Kids" (lecture, Winnipeg Art Gallery, November 7, 2005).

important ways to come to know people, and to support people to feel known, is to give space for the stories of their lives.

So why would I get neglectful? Why would I fail to give enough time for people to tell each other about their lives, their work, their stories? At CSOP 2010 I definitely did not get it right. I did notice, slowly, that people were a bit quiet, reserved, buttoned up. But it took me until day four of the course to realize that this was happening because people were not yet real to each other. It took me until day four to realize that the overseas students were being stifled by their own overwhelming need to share something of their lives with their classmates. And it took that long because I fell into a typical North American trap. I got enslaved to my agenda, to all the things that I felt I needed to cover when, all along, the real work of the class was waiting in front of my eyes, just needing me to get out of the way long enough for it to happen.

Parker Palmer, in his inspiring book *The Courage to Teach,* writes about this enslavement to agenda:

> When I remind myself that to teach is to create a space in which the community of truth is practiced—that I need to spend less time filling the space with data and my own thoughts and more time opening a space where students can have a conversation with the subject and with each other—I often hear an inner voice of dissent "But my field is full of factual information that students must possess before they can continue in the field."[253]

But at least I got it on day four! So on day four I set aside time for sharing photos and Facebook pages, struggles and tears. I jettisoned the agenda (which, after all, was to be culture and conflict; how appropriate is that!) and followed the group. And I learned the lesson, again, that people will need to tell their stories in order to "arrive."

All this learning made CSOP 2012 better because we told stories from the very start, using four important pedagogical elements. Students were asked to participate in activities that stimulated

---

253. Palmer, *The Courage to Teach* (San Francisco, CA: Jossey-Bass, 1998), 123.

movement so that they were brought into close physical approximation of each other and so that they were led to engage in conversations involving the expressions of personal beliefs about issues of substance. Each student was paired with a "buddy" in order to stimulate mutual accountability and mutual emotional support. These activities were set in the context of circles of comfort: three concentric circles that represented "Comfort" "Discomfort" and "Danger," with students being encouraged to move into the intellectual and emotional discomfort zone in order to stretch their senses of understanding, their systems of belief, and their embrace of otherness. Finally, in each day there was time set aside for hearing from each other.[254] That it was better is evidenced in the words of Rebekah Grisim, a student in the class who wrote in her final reflection paper:

> I really enjoyed engaging with the other classmates in order to learn from them and their experiences. One thing that I most appreciated about the course was the diverse group of people who took the course. I was able to learn the material while keeping in mind the many different outlooks that people had. I felt inspired from hearing about all the amazing work done by people in the class. I was encouraged by knowing that there are peacemakers from all over the world who have a common goal for peace. The participation in the class was so beneficial for me because it challenged me to come out of my comfort zone and I am really glad I did. I made sure that I engaged with the people in the class in order to get the most out of my experience.[255]

Rebekah "got it" that the most important learning resource in CSOP is not the readings or—Heaven forbid!—the professor. The most important resource is the other students in the class, the Artem Dolyas and the Gato Munyamasokos, but they cannot serve as full resources unless those of us holding the chalk at the front of the room make space for them, lots and lots of space. And that means being willing to

---

254. Further insights into these teaching methods can be acquired from trainingforchange.org.
255. Used with permission.

change the way we teach. It means being ready to toss our curriculum overboard; it means setting the needs of those who want to "get to the material" aside for a while, so that what will be the real material can surface.

I am grateful that I keep getting invited back to the Canadian School of Peacebuilding. I have not got it right yet, and I know that. It helps to tell stories on day four, but that is not nearly soon enough. It helps, but it is not enough, to begin with sharing from our lives, and to hold time open each day for people to tell the class about their lives.

Why is story so profoundly important? Jessica Senehi notes that story is a key vehicle for coming to know the other but also for knowing ourselves: "Stories create and give expression to personal and group identity. The very process of storytelling and narration fosters empathy as listeners identify with the characters in a story."[256] The stories of our lives both express and create who we are. They are, also, certainly about connecting with and understanding another perspective; they "[a]llow us to experience the similarities between ourselves and to others, real and imagined."[257] From the perspective of someone teaching peacebuilding, perhaps the best thing about stories is that they "translate well across culture, mutual recognition is fostered when people listen to each other's stories even across cultural divides and in the context of social conflicts."[258]

Closing Words

> Our strategy should be not only to confront em-
> pire, but to lay siege to it. To deprive it of oxygen.
> To shame it. To mock it. With our art, our music,
> our literature, our stubbornness, our joy, our bril-
> liance, our sheer relentlessness—and our ability
> to tell our own stories. Stories that are different
> from the ones we're being brainwashed to believe.

---

256. Jessica Senehi, "Constructive Storytelling: a Peace Process," *Peace and Conflict Studies* 9, no. 2, December 2002. (Accessed November 9, 2014.) http://shss.nova.edu/pcs/journalsPDF/V9N2.pdf
257. Stanton, *The Clues to a Great Story*, TED talk.
258. Senehi, "Constructive Storytelling," 49.

The corporate revolution will collapse if we refuse
to buy what they are selling—their ideas, their
version of history, their wars, their weapons, their
notion of inevitability. Remember this: We be
many and they be few. They need us more than
we need them. Another world is not only possible,
she is on her way. On a quiet day, I can hear her
breathing.
                                    —Arundhati Roy[259]

When academic papers come to an end, they customarily conclude
with a synopsis of the preceding pages, with, perhaps, a few recommendations thrown in. This paper will conclude, instead, with a
benediction.

If you are reading this, perhaps you are on your own journey of
discernment about what it means to you to be a peacebuilder or a
teacher of peacebuilding. For you, I wish

- Mentors on your journey. May you have "Chicos," "Stans"
  and "students" in your life.
- An encounter with your own authentic voice. It is the right
  one. Keep it.
- Engagement with your heart. This world will batter at your
  open heart: keep it open. This world will only be healed by
  open, and active, hearts.
- Free your inner trickster.
- Connect with your passion: it will fuel your life.
- Find, and tell, your story. In the last accounting, it is all we
  have.

Go well.

---

259. Arundhati Roy, "Confronting Empire," Closing Talk, World Social
Forum, Porto Alegre, 2003. (Accessed May 06, 2014.) http://www.wildness-
within.com/landandk.html.

Bibliography

Auden, W. H. *An Anatomy of Laughter.* London: William Collins Sons Company, 1974.

Berg, Yehuda. "Forgive and Forget" in *Kabbalah for Everyone.* (Accessed November 9, 2014.) http://sevenintentions.wordpress.com/tag/earthing/.

Bowling, Daniel. "The Inner Life of the Mediator" (lecture, workshop at Mediation Services, Winnipeg, MB, 25 September 2009).

Chenoweth, Erica, and Maria Stephan. *Why Civil Resistance Works: The Strategic Logic of Nonviolent Conflict.* New York: Columbia University Press, 2011.

Hyers, M. Conrad. "The Ancient Zen Master as Clown-figure and Comic Midwife." *Philosophy East and West* 20, (1970): 10.

Kyoon, Grace. "Story-Telling and the Moral Imagination: Mothering Peace," *Peace and Conflict Monitor.* (Accessed: 29 May 2014.) http://www.monitor.upeace.org/printer.cfm?id _article=583.

Lakey, George. *Facilitating Group Learning: Strategies for Success with Diverse Adult Learners.* San Francisco: Jossey-Bass, 2010.

—— "Training for Social Action Trainers" (lecture, Training for Change, Philadelphia, PA, December 27, 1990).

Neufeld, Gordon. "Hold Onto Your Kids" (lecture, Winnipeg Art Gallery, November 7, 2005).

Palmer, Parker. *The Courage to Teach.* San Francisco, CA: Jossey-Bass, 1998.

Proctor, Sue. *"The Archetypal Role of the Clown as a Catalyst for Individual and Social Transformation."* Master's thesis, Concordia University, 2013.

Ross, Jack. *Nonviolence for Elvin Spirits.* Argenta, BC: Jack Ross Publishing, 1992.

Roy, Arundhati. "Confronting Empire" (lecture, World Social Forum, Porto Alegre, Brazil, 27 January, 2003).

Senehi, Jessica. "Constructive Storytelling: a Peace Process" in *Peace and Conflict Studies.* (Accessed December 2002.) http://image.lifeservant.com/siteuploadfiles/VSYM/7AF4374C-961E-4F5F-A526A9C0A749C054/DC0FF9A4-C29A-8FCE-B888FC062C0A1E7.pdf#page=48p.

Stanton, Andrew. "The Clues to a Great Story." TED Talk. (Accessed November 9, 2014.) http://www.ted.com/talks/andrew_stanton_the_clues_to_a_great_story?language=en

The Political Action Committee. "Practicing Relations of Solidarity." *The Ally* 2, no. 1(2011). (Accessed May 29, 2014.) http://pac3906.files.wordpress.com/2011/08/settlerally-practicing-relations-of-solidarity1.pdf.

Training for Change. Accessed November 9, 2014.

Additional Resources

Barasch, Marc Ian. *Field Notes on the Compassionate Life: A Search for the Soul of Kindness.* Emmaus, PA: Rodale Press Inc., 2005.

Boston, Richard. *An Anatomy of Laughter.* London: William Collins Sons Co. Ltd., 1974.

Braden, Gregg. *Walking Between the Worlds: The Science of Compassion.* Bellevue, WA: Radio Bookstore Press, 1997.

Compassionate Listening Project. (Accessed May 29, 2014.)

Fulwiler, Toby. "Staffroom Interchange: Looking and Listening for My Voice" in *College Composition and Communication.* Vol. 41, no. 2, (1980). (Accessed May 29, 2014.) http://www.jstor.org/stable/358161?seq=1.

Gatto, John Taylor. *Dumbing Us Down.* Gabriola Island BC: New Society Publishers, 1992, 2005.

Gobodo-Madikizela, Pumla. *A Human Being Died That Night: A South African Woman Confronts the Legacy of Apartheid.* Boston: Houghton Mifflin Co., 2004; Hopkins, Jeffrey. *Cultivating Compassion: A Buddhist Perspective.* N.Y.: Broadway Books, 2001.

Lederach, John Paul. *The Moral Imagination: The Art and Soul of Building Peace.* New York: Oxford University Press, 2005.

McCraty, Rollin, and Doc Childre. *The Appreciative Heart.* Boulder Creek, CO: Institute of HeartMath, 2002.

Neufeld, Gordon. *Hold on to Your Kids: Why Parents Need to Matter More than Peers.* New York: Ballantine Books, 2004.

Ridd, Karen. There Ought to Be Clowns: Child Life Therapy Through the Medium of a Clown. Winnipeg: Canadian Association of Therapeutic Clowns, 1987, 2009. (Accessed May 29, 2014.) http://www.therapeuticclowns.ca/docs/ThereOughtToBeClowns.pdf.

Ross, Jack. *Non-violence for Elvin Spirits*. Argenta, BC: Jack Ross Publishing, 1992.

Sharp, Gene. *Power and Struggle*. Boston: Porter Sargent, 1973.

SoulPancake. "The Science of Happiness: An Experiment in Gratitude." (Accessed May 29, 2014.) http://www.youtube.com/watch?v=oHv6vTKD6lg&feature=c4-overview-vl&list=PLzvRx_johoA8PC6S5k5S2SszRQOR8oSEa.

Tuckman, Bruce, and Mary Ann C. Jensen. "Stages of Small Group Development Revisited." (Accessed May 29, 2014.) http://www.freewebs.com/group-management/BruceTuckman%281%29.pdf.

Vanzant, Iyanla. *One Day My Soul Just Opened Up: 40 Days and 40 Nights Towards Spiritual Growth and Personal Strength*. NY: Fireside, 1998.

Whyte, Pamela. (Accessed May 29, 2014.) https://www.facebook.com/PamelaWhyteConsulting?ref=stream.

AUTHOR BIOGRAPHIES

Editors

RICHARD MCCUTCHEON
Founding CSOP Advisory Council member

Richard McCutcheon is Associate Professor of Law and Politics and Academic Dean at Algoma University in Sault Ste. Marie, Ontario (http://www.algomau.ca/). He holds a PhD in Anthropology and an MA in Religious Studies from McMaster University; his honours BA is in Religious Studies and Sociology from Brandon University. Prior to starting his work at Algoma University in 2014, Rick taught conflict-resolution studies for twelve years at Menno Simons College, a College of Canadian Mennonite University, located on the campus of and affiliated with the University of Winnipeg. Since its inception Rick has supported the Canadian School of Peacebuilding and believes deeply that the work done by CSOP is foundational for creating more just and peaceful communities.

Rick has blended service work and activist organizing with his university work for over thirty years, working as coordinator of Canadian Quaker service work, as a Mennonite Central Committee field representative to the Middle East, and as a board member of Mediation Services, a non-profit organization committed to alternative forms of conflict resolution and restorative justice. Rick is passionate about the teaching and practice of peace and conflict studies. He currently lives with his wife Tamara and son Declan in Sault Ste. Marie.

JAREM SAWATSKY
Founding CSOP Co-Director

Jarem Sawatsky is a Christian peacebuilder. He lectures and consults and is published on topics relating to restorative justice and peacebuilding. He has fifteen years of experience in field of peace and conflict. His research into healing justice has taken him to communities in Sri Lanka, Papua New Guinea, Israel, Scotland, England, Canada, United States, France, and Fiji.

Jarem was born in Richmond, British Columbia. His degrees include a PhD (Law) from the University of Hull (UK); a MA in Conflict Transformation, Peacebuilding and Restorative Justice from the Center for Justice and Peacebuilding, Eastern Mennonite University (2001); a BA in Religious Studies and Conflict Resolution Studies from the University of Winnipeg and Menno Simons College (1998); a BTh from Canadian Mennonite Bible College (1996). He has spent much of the past twenty-five years in Winnipeg as a member of an intentional church community, Grain of Wheat Church Community.

Jarem enjoys canoe camping and spending time with his wife, Rhona, and their two daughters.

VALERIE SMITH
Founding CSOP Co-Director

Valerie Smith is Co-Director of the Canadian School of Peacebuilding (csop.cmu.ca). She has worked with the CSOP since its beginning in 2009, and prior to that she worked with Mennonite Central Committee for three years in Bosnia and Herzegovina, working with a local relief and development agency and teaching peace studies and theology at the Novi Sad Theological College. She has taught writing and served as an editor in a variety of settings. She has a BTh from Canadian Mennonite Bible College, a BA in philosophy from the University of Manitoba and a MDiv from Associated Mennonite Biblical Seminary.

Contributors

MUBARAK AWAD
Taught Finding Your Voice: Understanding Nonviolent Action for Today's Complex World, 2013 CSOP

Mubarak Awad is the founder of the National Youth Advocate Program (www.nyap.org) in various locations in the United States, which provides alternative foster care and counselling to "at risk" youth and their families. He is also the founder of the Palestinian Center for the Study of Nonviolence in Jerusalem, Palestine, and was deported by the Israeli Supreme Court in 1988 after being jailed for organizing activities involving non-violent civil disobedience. Mubarak has since formed Nonviolence International, which promotes peace education and non-violent action in dealing with political and social issues and works with various movements and organizations across the globe. He has also been an adjunct professor at the American University in Washington, DC USA since 1989 at the School of International Studies, focusing on promoting dialogue and transforming post-conflict societies and teaching graduate courses on methods and theory of non-violence. Mubarak was born in Jerusalem, Palestine, and currently resides in Gaithersburg MD, USA.

STUART CLARK
Taught Speaking Out... and Being Heard—Citizen Advocacy, 2012 CSOP

Stuart Clark has recently retired as the Senior Policy Advisor to the Canadian Foodgrains Bank, a food aid consortium of Canadian church-based emergency and development organizations (http://foodgrainsbank.ca/). Stuart worked at the Foodgrains Bank from 1998 to 2012 and was responsible for establishing the organization's work on public policy as it affects hunger in developing countries. He was the founding chair of the Trans-Atlantic Food Assistance Dialogue, a coalition of the major North American and European food aid programming NGOs collaborating on advocacy for the reform of the Food Aid Convention. He was also the founding chair of the Canadian Food Security Policy Group. He continues to work as a consultant to the Foodgrains Bank on public policy and food issues communication.

Stuart is trained as an engineer and has worked for thirty years in Bangladesh, Nepal, Vietnam, Ethiopia, and Canada on food-related issues (food processing, agricultural development, food aid, agricultural trade policy, human right to food, organic cereal production, etc.). Stu holds a bachelor's degree from the University of Alberta (Chem. Eng.), a master's degree from Queens University (Chem. Eng.), and a diploma of International Social Development from the Coady Institute, St. Francis Xavier University.

DAVID DYCK

Taught Frameworks & Foundations of Conflict Transformation, 2009 CSOP; Interpersonal Mediation in Your Community: Frameworks, Skills & Presence, 2011 CSOP

David Dyck is a seasoned conflict-resolution practitioner, having worked in the field for twenty-four years in a variety of settings as a mediator, trainer, facilitator, academic instructor, and workplace consultant. Since 2003, David has been an owner and partner of Facilitated Solutions, a Manitoba-based conflict-resolution firm (http://www.fscanada.org/). In this capacity, he assists organizations of all types to prevent, manage, and resolve conflict. David has presented training seminars across Canada as well as in the United States and Europe on conflict resolution, mediation, group facilitation, and restorative justice. David previously served as the lead trainer for the Nova Scotia Restorative Justice Program (1999–2002) and was the founding Program Coordinator of Circles of Support & Accountability Winnipeg (1999).

In addition to numerous professional courses, David holds both a bachelor's and master's degree in conflict-resolution studies. He has also found the practice of mindfulness to be an important resource in his personal life and in his approach with clients. David lives in downtown Winnipeg with his wife, Tammy, and their two young sons, Addison and Bennett.

MARTIN H. ENTZ

Taught Our Contested Food System: Cultivating a Just Peace, 2010 CSOP

Martin Entz is a professor of "natural systems agriculture" in the University of Manitoba's faculty of agricultural and food sciences (http://umanitoba.ca/afs/). Martin has spent twenty years developing food production systems based on nature's own template. Projects include no-tillage (conservation) farming, organic farming, integration of animals and crops for small-holder production, and development of perennial grains. Martin heads the Glenlea study—Canada's oldest organic cropping plots. Martin's international work includes a "pesticides reduction" project in cooperation with universities in Central America. Martin enjoys rural extension and interaction with farmers. Martin and his family operate a small farm near Libau, Manitoba.

HARRY J. HUEBNER
Taught Mennonite Approaches to Peace and Justice, 2010 CSOP

Harry J. Huebner is Emeritus Professor of Philosophy and Theology at Canadian Mennonite University (www.cmu.ca). He is also the Director of Interfaith Initiatives at CMU. He is a long-time teacher at CMU in the areas of Christian ethics, theology, philosophy, and peace theology. He has edited and co-edited several books and most recently is the author of *Echoes of the Word: Theological Ethics as Rhetorical Practice* (2005) and *An Introduction to Christian Ethics: History, Movements, People* (2012). From 1981 to 1983 he and his family lived in Jerusalem, where he worked with MCC in West Bank and Israel, adding to the voices of peaceful resolution to conflict. He is an active participant in Mennonite-Catholic Dialogue, and for the past six years he has been involved in theological dialogue with Muslim clerics from Qom, Iran. The latter dialogue has led him to teach several short courses on Christian ethics in the International Institute for Islamic Studies in Qom. He has also lectured at the University of Qom. Harry is married to Agnes, has three married children, and seven grandchildren.

OUYPORN KHUANKAEW
Taught Women and Peacebuilding, 2012 CSOP

Ouyporn Khuankaew is a Buddhist, feminist, peace trainer who has been working with activists in South and Southeast Asia since 1995. She incorporates Buddhist practice, feminism, and non-violence in all of her work. In 2002, Ouyporn co-founded International Women's Partnership for Peace and Justice (IWP) which runs its own centre and works with activists in Burma, India, Sri Lanka, and Thailand (womenforpeaceandjustice.org). IWP training uses anti-oppression feminism, non-violent action, and spirituality as a foundation for activists and activism. The training topics include Buddhist peacebuilding, non-violent action, counselling for trauma survivors, leadership for social change, gender and sexuality, feminism and Buddhism for change, and meditation retreat for activists. She leads an annual international meditation retreat for people exploring Buddhist spirituality as a path to sustain their life and activism. She has a master's degree in informal education.

GEORGE LAKEY
Taught Nonviolent Action Strategies for Social Change, 2011 CSOP

George Lakey was the Eugene M. Lang Visiting Professor for Issues in Social Change at Swarthmore College from 2006 to 2009 and continues to teach peace studies there. In 2010 he was named Peace Educator of the Year by the Peace and Justice Studies Association. He also directs Swarthmore's Global Nonviolent Action Database project (nvdatabase.swarthmore.edu). His eighth book, published by Jossey-Bass in 2010, is *Facilitating Group Learning: Strategies for Success with Diverse Adult Learners.* His first book, called "the handbook of the civil rights movement," was *A Manual for Direct Action.* His first arrest was in the 1960s for a civil rights sit-in; in 2013 he was arrested in a protest against mountain-top removal coal mining in Appalachia. He has led over 1,500 social change workshops on five continents, for a wide variety of groups including homeless people, prisoners, Russian lesbians and gays, Sri Lankan monks, Burmese guerrilla soldiers, striking steel workers, South African activists, Canadian academics, and leaders of Indigenous peoples brought together by the United Nations Institute for Training and Research in Geneva.

IVO MARKOVIĆ
Taught Faith, Music and Inter-Ethnic Reconciliation, 2012 CSOP

Ivo Marković is a Bosnian Franciscan, a musician, and a professor of pastoral theology at Sarajevo University (www.unsa.ba). He is a peace activist who moves easily and intentionally across the boundaries that divide people. Ivo began his work as a peace activist during the 1991–1995 war in the Balkans. Even as his father and other family members were killed in the war, Ivo worked for peace in his own village and throughout the region. Shortly after the war, Ivo founded the Inter-Religious Service "Face to Face" to encourage dialogue and reconciliation among the religious groups within Bosnia. One of the most successful initiatives of Face to Face is the interreligious choir, Pontanima, composed of people from the national and religious communities in Sarajevo. Instead of fighting each other, the choir chose to sing together the symphony of Abrahamic religions. In 1998, Ivo was awarded Tanenbaum's prestigious Peacemaker in Action Award for this work.

MAXINE MATILPI
Taught Human Rights and Indigenous Legal Traditions, 2013 CSOP; Taught Arts Approaches to Community-Based Peacebuilding, 2014 CSOP

Maxine Matilpi, LLM, is a member of the Kwakiutl First Nation and also has roots with the Ma'amtigila people. A former practising lawyer, she now teaches Women's Studies and First Nations Studies at Vancouver Island University (www.viu.ca) and serves as an Elder-in-Residence at North Island College in Campbell River. Her research interests are Indigenous and feminist legal pedagogies. She lives on Denman Island, where she practises both Nia and laughter yoga, and models in wearable art shows.

STAN MCKAY
Taught Covenants of Peace and Justice, 2011 CSOP

Rev. Stan McKay is an Aboriginal educator and was Canada's first Aboriginal Moderator of the United Church of Canada (UCC), Canada's largest Protestant denomination. He sought reconciliation and understanding both within and outside the UCC, and between Aboriginal and non-Aboriginal peoples. Stan comes from Fisher River, Manitoba, a Cree First Nation community. He is the former Director of the Dr. Jessie Saulteaux Centre. He received a career National Aboriginal Achievement Award in 1997.

SOPHIA MURPHY
Taught Speaking Out… and Being Heard—Citizen Advocacy, 2012 CSOP

Sophia Murphy is a writer, public speaker, advocate and lecturer who works on food security, agriculture, trade and international development (http://www.fondationtrudeau.ca/en/community/sophia-murphy). She is widely published and has worked for many civil society organizations. She worked for the UN Non-Governmental Liaison Service in Geneva for two years, and for over fifteen years she has worked with the Institute for Agriculture and Trade Policy in Minneapolis, where she continues to serve as an adviser on trade work. Sophia has consulted with a wide range of NGOs and has worked with many coalitions of NGOs and social movements. Sophia serves on the board of ActionAid USA. She is a one of the fifteen members of the UN High Level Panel of Experts to the UN Committee on World Food Security. Sophia has a BA degree in Politics, Philosophy and Economics from Oxford University and a MSc (with distinction) in Social Policy and Planning in Developing Countries from the London School of Economics. In September 2013, Sophia began a PhD program at the Institute for Resources, Environment and Sustainability at the University of British Columbia. She is supported in that work by a Vanier scholarship from the Government of Canada and a scholarship from the Trudeau Foundation. She lives in Squamish, BC, with her husband and their two children.

PIET MEIRING
Taught Truthtelling and Peace: An Insider's Perspective on South Africa's Truth and Reconciliation Commission, 2009 CSOP

Piet Meiring is an emeritus professor of theology at the University of Pretoria (www.up.ac.za). He is an ordained minister of the Dutch Reformed Church in South Africa. His field of study is Science of Missions and Science of Religion. In 1996 he was appointed by President Mandela to serve on the South African Truth and Reconciliation Commission (TRC), where he was primarily involved in reparation and rehabilitation issues, as well as co-coordinating the TRC Faith Community Hearings. When the TRC closed its doors, Piet Meiring was invited to a number of countries, including Rwanda, Zimbabwe, Indonesia, Israel/Palestine, Northern Ireland, the USA, and Canada, to advise on issues of reconciliation and healing. He visited Winnipeg to teach at the CMU (CSOP) in 2009 and, as special guest of the Canadian TRC, to speak at the First National Event in 2010.

KAY PRANIS
Taught Peacemaking Circles: Philosophy and Applications, 2011 CSOP

Kay Pranis teaches and writes about the dialogue process known as "peacemaking circles" (http://www.livingjusticepress.org). Kay learned about peacemaking circles in her work in restorative justice in the mid-'90s Her initial teachers in the circle work were Barry Stuart, a judge in Yukon, Canada ; and Mark Wedge and Harold Gatensby, First Nations people of Yukon. Since that initial exposure to the use of peacemaking circles in the justice system, Kay has been involved in developing the use of peacemaking circles in schools, social services, churches, families, museums, universities, municipal planning, and workplaces. Kay works primarily as an independent trainer in the peacemaking circle process. Kay has authored or co-authored several books about circles, most recently, *Circle Forward: Building a Restorative School Community*;

Kay has a particular interest in the use of circles to support social justice efforts addressing racial, economic, class, and gender inequities. That interest includes the use of peacemaking circles to understand and respond to historical harms to groups of people. The peacemaking circle process has been a source of energy, inspiration, and continuous learning for Kay for the past fifteen years.

KAREN RIDD
Taught Peace Skills Practice, 2010 CSOP and 2012 CSOP; Train the Trainer: Working for Conflict Transformation, 2013 CSOP

Karen Ridd is a dynamic educator, facilitator, and speaker with experience throughout North America and overseas, including El Salvador, Guatemala, Colombia, Thailand, and Cambodia. Karen is presently a sessional instructor in the Conflict Resolution Studies department of the University of Winnipeg (www.mscollege.ca), an associate of Training for Change in Philadelphia, as well as an associate trainer for Resolution Skills Centre. Karen holds a Bachelor of Arts (1984), a Master of Arts in Peace and Justice (2009), and a Diploma in Mediation Skills and has been working and studying in the field of conflict resolution since 1986. Karen began her affiliation with Mediation Services in 1995, when she became the training coordinator, responsible for carrying out and developing trainings, as well as overseeing the program as a whole. Karen presently lives in rural Manitoba and is the delighted mother of Ben and Daniel. She has received numerous honours for her work, including the 1992 Government of Canada 125th Anniversary of Canadian Confederation Governor-General's Award, the 1990 Canada YM/YWCA Peace Medal, and the 1989 Manitoba International Human Rights Achievement Award.

Index

A

B

C

D

E

F

CPSIA information can be obtained
at www.ICGtesting.com
Printed in the USA
LVHW082347180121
676848LV00015B/1402

9 780920 718261